The World of a Wainwright Bagger

Chris Stanbury

© Chris Stanbury 2010

All Rights Reserved. No part of this publication may be reproduced, stored in a retrieval system, or transmitted in any form or by any means – electronic, mechanical, photocopying, recording, or otherwise – without prior written permission from the publisher

Published by Sigma Leisure – an imprint of
Sigma Press, Stobart House, Pontyclerc, Penybanc Road
Ammanford, Carmarthenshire SA18 3HP

British Library Cataloguing in Publication Data

A CIP record for this book is available from the British Library

ISBN: 978-1-85058-854-2

Typesetting and Design by: Sigma Press, Ammanford, Carms

Photographs: © Chris Stanbury and Stan Hawrylak

Cover photograph: The celebrated view from Wastwater (Stan Hawrylak)

Printed by: Cromwell Press Group, Trowbridge, Wiltshire

Disclaimer: The information in this book is given in good faith and is believed to be correct at the time of publication. Care should always be taken when walking in hill country. Where appropriate, attention has been drawn to matters of safety. The author and publisher cannot take responsibility for any accidents or injury incurred whilst following these walks. Only you can judge your own fitness, competence and experience.

Dedicated to my wonderful wife Jenny, whose understanding and tolerance of my walking whims has enabled me to complete this journey

Contents

Foreword

Now everyone knows my view of Wainwright bagging. Train spotting with altitude. Rather a waste of 214 summits if you're going to dash from one to the other, ticking them off as fast as possible and rarely raising your eyes from your boot ends.

So why, I hear you grumble, has he agreed to say nice things on the back of Chris Stanbury's book?

Simple. Chris takes time to pause, to take in the view and to think about the meaning of life as he slowly works his way round the Lake District. The Wainwright bagging is a means to an end rather than a superficial ritual. Chris is a personable companion. Enjoy the long walk in his company.

Eric Robson

Introduction

There are 214 fells lovingly and meticulously described by Alfred Wainwright in his seven Pictorial Guides to the high places of the Lake District. Scafell is the second highest of these fells and one of only four mountains in England to attain the magical 3000 feet contour. So why was this wonderful high showpiece of Lakeland left until number 210 in my round of Wainwright's fells?

The answer is that it was in part due to an error of judgement and partly by an intentional design. My two long standing walking companions had climbed mighty Scafell for the first time in 1993. That same day, I made the decision to go solo and seek solitude in the wild and remote Northern Fells behind Keswick. I reasoned that I would soon get my chance to climb Scafell and on that particular day being alone seemed more important than even the lure of Scafell. That was perhaps an error of judgement on my part and for several years afterwards I had the nagging intention to make good the error and reach the summit of Scafell. But for a variety of reasons, including an aborted attempt due to dreadful weather in August of all months, it remained elusive. As the shape of my completion of the Wainwright fells began to emerge, I realised that within the scheme of this personal ambition it felt right that Scafell should be left until almost the last of the 214 fells. Not the final summit perhaps, but somewhere within the last ten. An error of judgement had led through the passage of time to a wonderful intention. It now seemed fitting to have left one of the highest mountains till near the end and for there to still be one spectacular panorama in Lakeland that I had yet to feast my eyes upon.

Then on a perfect sunny day in April 2007, with just a few small puffy white clouds in an azure blue sky, the call of Scafell could be resisted no longer. So it became number 210. In cold bare fact just another tick on a list of fells, but in vivid glorious reality with memories that will forever linger. For in the doing Scafell had become one of the key moments in an 18 year long celebration of the Lakeland fells, culminating in my completing the 214 Wainwright summits in 2007, the centenary of Alfred Wainwright's birth. Scafell was one of many pieces in the jigsaw of achieving that personal ambition, albeit a larger and more worthy piece than others.

Since the death of Alfred Wainwright in 1991 the climbing of all the Lakeland Fells has become increasingly referred to by fellwalkers as 'bagging the Wainwrights'. I like to think that this is as much driven by a kind of collective homage to a man who has become a legend in Lakeland history, as it is driven by the desire of some baggers to just create another tick list. But what exactly is bagging the Wainwrights all about? For me it has involved a constant mixture of and balance between the freedom and the ambition of the fells. Freedom and ambition may seem like strange bedfellows, but in the personal world of this Wainwright Bagger they have always been companions. The freedom to decide which particular Wainwright fell I would climb on any given day, sometimes on the spur or whim of the moment. Freedom also to decide not to climb a new Wainwright at all on a particular day, but instead to bask on an old favourite such as Skiddaw or Great Gable. So in truth my completion of the 214 fells happened in part by accident and in part by design.

Then there has been the ambition. A simple ambition, which thousands had completed before me and that no-one else, except perhaps a few walking friends, would probably give two hoots about. Yet too often in this world where celebrity and money rule, ambition is perceived as the achievement of status or the acquiring of money. It is something to shout about and have acknowledged by the masses. Yet surely ambition also has a truer and richer meaning that can reach profound levels in the fells; ambition in the personal and spiritual sense; in a cleansing and purifying sense; which is all the richer for not being linked with the acquiring of money or celebrity.

In this book, I hope to offer an insight into the world of a Wainwright bagger. In doing this I may inspire those who have not done any of The Wainwrights, or those who have only done a few, to perhaps fulfil their own personal ambitions in the hills. I hope also to inspire those who have done most of the fells, but lost inspiration for some reason along the way, to make the truly worthwhile effort of doing them all. However, I would not presume to offer any sort of agenda for completing the 214 Wainwright fells. The only rule is that there are no rules. Some people complete The Wainwrights in a few days and others like me take years or even a lifetime to do so. I have made a few suggestions, such as leaving a few of the classic fells till near the end of the round, but the freedom to choose your own route to complete The Wainwrights is, I feel, as vital as the ambition of completing them all.

This book is not a guide book. You won't find any 'cross over the stile and take a left turn' descriptions in this book (well the odd one maybe). Guide books have been produced far better than I ever could do one, particularly by a certain Alfred Wainwright. Instead this book is a series of essays designed to give a flavour of the enjoyment (well mostly enjoyment) that can be found in completing Wainwright's 214 fells and to reveal something of the temperament and character of a Wainwright bagger.

It has not been my intention to chronicle religiously every single Wainwright fell. A significant number of the 214 fells are not mentioned or barely get a mention. The criteria for me were based on my own personal experiences and which fells formed a significant piece in my personal jigsaw. So for example High Street, although undeniably a great Lakeland mountain, is absent because it has yet to provide me with a truly memorable experience worth recounting on the occasions I have climbed it, while Skiddaw has an entire chapter devoted to it. I can accept that Holme Fell, in the Southern Fells, may have provided the highlight of someone else's walking career. But for me the only time I have climbed it was a dull, cold and windy day in March, and although it did have a fine close up view of Wetherlam, there is not a lot else that inspired me about it that day. That is probably more down to me and the weather than the fell itself and I hope one day to make a better friend of Holme Fell.

I have at all times been conscious of trying to relate the story of a glorious and inspiring journey. So I quickly realised that a precise chronological description of every route up every Wainwright would make for a rather unattractive story. So although this book does begin with the start of my love of the Lake District and ends with the completion of my round of The Wainwrights and the final few fells, the large chunk in the middle, while roughly in date order, was more dictated by the desire to group my experiences into logical chapters and themes. If I have missed out your personal favourite fell, I apologise. For every experience on a fell that I have included in this book, there has been another experience, on another fell, that did not make it into the book.

In addition, this book makes occasional mention of another walking passion of mine, the mountains of Scotland. The Scottish Highlands have provided an important contrast in my journey towards completion of The Wainwrights. In describing a few of my Scottish experiences I hope to also give a flavour of another great walking challenge, Scotland's 284 Munros (mountains over 3000 feet) and how that challenge differs from the challenge of the Wainwrights.

Like snowflakes no two journeys through The Wainwrights will be alike and the personal highs and lows and favourite fells will differ from one person to another. I hope, however, in relating my personal account, to give a flavour of the wonderful lifetime event and experience that completing all The Wainwrights has been for me and can be for anyone determined enough to undertake and commit to it.

Chris Stanbury
February 2010

How a Love Affair Began

How does a love of the hills begin? It could perhaps be a key moment of revelation, such as Alfred Wainwright experienced when he climbed his first Lakeland hill, Orrest Head. For some it might be a climb of a great mountain, such as Scafell Pike, on a holiday when young that got stored in the mind and gradually over years became a true love of the high places. Others lucky enough to have been born in the shadow of the hills may have that love innate inside them.

For me it was not just one moment but several moments. It may seem odd in the telling but I can trace it all back to a walk to a cricket pitch in the Kent village of Langton Green! My elder brother Peter and I used to meet up each week on Sunday afternoon. For many years we used to play the card game Bridge with the rest of the family, but eventually and after many long arguments over scoring, bidding and such things, the Bridge days ended. So to occupy the time one Sunday afternoon, Peter and I decided to go for a walk. I was nineteen years old and until then walking had always been something that I did merely to get to somewhere more interesting, like a party for example. It was a means to an end. I had no concept of walking for the sake of it; for the love of it. But I did perhaps have a love of countryside, born from many years of family holidays to France and also a love of maps, from guiding my Dad in the car, not always successfully, around the French countryside.

The walk to the cricket pitch only took ten minutes and so in order to fully occupy a Sunday afternoon we soon decided to lengthen the walks, first to an hour, then two hours until eventually every Sunday was spent on a four or five hour exploration of the Kent and Sussex countryside. I loved these walks and look back on them fondly. I still live in Kent and still do these long low level walks when I can. But something was missing. I found that on the walks the best places seemed to be the places that had views, and these tended to be naturally the highest places. There was one such place near Groombridge in Kent that I dubbed unimaginatively 'The Hill', because it had no name on the map. Many an hour was spent there in peaceful contemplation, but the desire to walk needed a different fuel to become a love; it needed a direction and a purpose and, oddly enough, it was a television programme that lit the touch paper.

A programme about the Cumbria Way appeared on television. As I by now had a keenness for walking, I watched the programme eagerly. It documented a 70 mile journey through the heart of the Lake District, starting in Ulverston and ending in Carlisle. Now up till the moment I watched that programme, my knowledge of the Lake District had been zero. In fact it had probably been worse than zero, because it was limited to stereotypical images of Kendal Mint Cake, lots of sheep and Wordsworth's Daffodils poem. Now for the first time I saw that this was a wonderful landscape of high places and proper mountains, not just the slight folds in the earth that call themselves hills in South East England. Until I saw the programme about the Cumbria Way, I had lived in ignorance that there were proper mountains in England. Indeed I still encounter people, who when I tell them I am going to the mountains, say to me 'there are no mountains in England, just hills'. I have frequently imagined that if they were made to climb Helvellyn via Striding Edge they might change this view.

The following Sunday, when I met up with Peter, the first words that I uttered to him were 'Let's do a long distance walk, let's do the Cumbria Way'. He had also seen the programme and there ensued one of those lovely moments in life where two people have the same common idea, and the excitement of the idea becomes greater by being shared. As yet, however, we had no real concept of what 'doing the Cumbria Way' actually meant.

I must confess there was a considerable naivety behind our drive to do the Cumbria Way. It is however a naivety that I look back on with some fondness. I am not a great fan of fashion statements on the hills or having to have the latest expensive gear (more on this later), but our approach to gear for the Cumbria Way was, to put it kindly, rather lacking in consideration for what lay ahead. Our walking boots were as cheap and nasty as they come and I was soon to realise that this would equate to walking comfort that resembled placing one's feet into a man trap every morning. We had no waterproof trousers and our cheap waterproof jackets gave only a token resemblance to being waterproof. As for maps, we had no concept of the need to buy proper detailed large scale walker's maps and thought we could make do with a general Lake District Touring Map that had few paths or mountain landmarks on it. There was a reckless simplicity to our planning, which would gradually, though not entirely, be ironed out by experience.

On a Saturday in April 1989, we found ourselves in Ulverston, having taken a tiny two carriage train from Lancaster. I remember it being one of those typical hills weather days. The rain was coming down constantly but not in large raindrops, more in a kind of fine mist that, despite being fine, seemed to be every bit as wet as the proper stuff. Our cut price waterproofs were soon found wanting.

However being adventurous in spirit if not in experience, and with an afternoon to spare before we started the Cumbria Way route proper the next day, we decided to do a short walk. And a curious hill with a rather phallic shaped monument on top of it seemed the perfect place to start.

Hoad Hill was to prove one of two key moments that sealed my love of the Lake District. At 133 metres (or about 400 feet in old money), Hoad Hill is not a high hill. Indeed several hills in my native Kent were higher. Yet the moment I set foot on it, I realised that this was a different type of hill to those I was used to in Kent. It was rough, steep and bracken covered. Although just outside of the Lake District National Park itself, it was to be my first proper hill and the first encounter with the rocky outcrops that so distinguish the south Lakeland foothills and are found scattered wantonly on fells and in fields. Although within spitting distance of the town of Ulverston and approached by a tarmac lane from the town, it seemed as if I had entered into another world, a place on the perimeter of a new and glorious landscape. I can only imagine that Wainwright felt something of this sense of transition, as he climbed from the bustle and tarmac of Windermere up onto the rocky height of Orrest Head.

I mention that Hoad Hill was one of two key moments that sealed my love of Lakeland. Had there been a view that day in 1989, it may have been the key moment, but the view was obscured due to the mizzly rain and mist. So the love that began that first time on Hoad Hill was in retrospect, the love of doing a proper hill and the love of the enclosing glowering atmosphere that rain and mist produce.

You never forget your first hill and I have never forgotten Hoad Hill. I have climbed it dozens of times, by every route possible (and despite its small size I have numbered at least five routes up). I recall that half way up the main concreted path there is a sad inscription in a path slab that reads 'Peter died here', and I have often remarked to my own brother Peter that he might go the same way if he didn't quit smoking! The view from the top on a clear day is stunning and can be highly recommended for its fine prospect into Lakeland. There are very few hills of this low height that have such a commanding view, from the sweep of Morecambe Bay to the South, to the Howgills and Limestone Country in the East and of course North into the heart of the Lake District. From here the Coniston Range dominates, with its glorious sweep up onto the sharply pointed Dow Crag, down to Goats Hause and up again to the rounded massif of Coniston Old Man itself. There is also a distant prospect of the highest mountain in the

Hoad Hill, where it all began

Lake District, Scafell Pike. It has become something of a tradition of mine to climb Hoad Hill on the first day of any week long break in the Lake District. As a prelude to the hills, it is a place that looks into the National Park, but is not quite within it. Once you have been climbing the hills for a few years, as well as a desire for new hills, nostalgia for past hills creeps in, and a walk up Hoad Hill is for me about as nostalgic as it gets. You will perhaps meet the odd person up there, mostly dog walkers from Ulverston, but wait a few minutes and you are likely to have the place to yourself. It is not what I would call popular.

So to the monument that sits atop the hill. Well you may think that amongst other things it resembles a lighthouse, but surely you would dismiss such a thought? For what good would a lighthouse be on a hill that is several flat miles away from the sea? But it was in fact erected to act as a sea mark and was modelled on the famous Eddystone Lighthouse, although it never had a functioning light. Hoad Hill was chosen because although it is a few miles inland its monument would be easily seen from the sea.

The next day we started our 70 mile walk through the Lake District. The Cumbria Way is normally walked over five days, with an average of about 14 miles per day. It could probably be done in two or three days by a fit and determined walker, but this is not a journey to be rushed, it is one to be savoured. As a novice walker in 1989, it proved to be an ideal introduction to the hills and also an apprenticeship for the very different rigours involved walking on Lakeland paths, as opposed to the level smooth chalkland paths I was used to.

This book is not the place to describe the Cumbria Way in great detail, but I would like to give a few reminiscences from the walk to illustrate how over the course of five days in April 1989 a love blossomed; a love that would steadily, at first by accident and then by design, lead to the world of Wainwright and the 214 fells described in his guides.

The Gill in Ulverston is the traditional starting point for the Cumbria Way. After a confined start amongst trees, the landscape opened out and we reached Higher Lath farm, where we rested on some lush grass and I had the second key moment in my burgeoning passion for the Lake District. On Hoad Hill it had been about the delights of ascending and the essence of a hill that was cocooned in mist and had no view. Here at Higher Lath I saw my first prospect of and into Lakeland. In the foreground was the jumble of delightful foothills that make up the Woodland and Blawith Fells, and behind those minions was the Coniston range, still with an icing of late winter snow on the highest tops, in the good old days when April was both early spring and late winter rolled into one. If Hoad Hill had literally wetted the appetite, then this new and splendid view called me into it.

The first day of the Cumbria Way from Ulverston to Coniston will always hold strongest and fondest in my mind. Admittedly the second day from Coniston to Dungeon Ghyll in Langdale and the third day from Dungeon Ghyll to Keswick contain the grander mountain scenery that epitomises the heart of Lakeland. However for me the first day represents a gradual and ever increasing excitement, as over the course of a whole day of walking the fells behind Coniston get closer and closer. Each little rise in the folds of landscape during the first day's walk brings a new and closer prospect of this wonderful range of fells. At the close of the day, as you walk by the shores of Coniston Water and into Coniston village, the mountains that were distant and mysterious at the start of the day tower imposingly around you. By the end of that sunny spring day in April 1989, I knew that there really were mountains in England and I was hooked, although the 'man trap' walking boots had left me with dreadful blisters.

The following two days as we gradually worked our way from Coniston to Keswick were equally wonderful. It was the type of weather that the hills were made for, fresh and bright for most of the time, but with the occasional snow shower. These wintry flurries were not only a delight to be cocooned within, but once they had passed they revealed snow capped views of a tremendous clarity. Tarn Hows was visited for the first time, a famous and popular haunt, and it was curious how after the first mile or so of blister induced gingerness each day my feet got used to it all and I forgot the mild but continuous pain.

As we progressed I began to familiarise myself with the Lakeland terminology of 'fell' for a mountain or hill, and the concept of 'tarns' for lakes and 'becks' for streams. To the seasoned walker this may sound obvious, but having grown up in the South of England this was all new to me. In this basic education, I suppose I began to take pleasure in the study of the Lake District landscape; the names of streams and boulders; the hidden natural and man made history of the place; the concept of a land that is almost wholly shaped by man's activities.

The Cumbria Way does not visit any of Wainwright's 214 summits but it does have its own high point at Stake Pass, which at 1576 feet is actually higher than quite a few of Wainwright's Fells. In fact the section of walking between Langdale and Borrowdale is probably the toughest section and in terms of rock scenery the wildest section of the whole walk. During the course of nearly 20 years of hill walking I have noticed that one gradually develops fitness for this type of rough walking. Nowadays, even though at the age of 39 I am not perhaps in the very flush of youth, the walk up Stake Pass and down into the Langstrath valley would be quite easy and I have learnt through years of walking over rough stone, scree and boulder to enjoy and immerse myself in the pure physical effort involved. However in April 1989 I was a wiry figure, barely an adult and nothing in the South East of England had prepared me for the zigzag seemingly endless climb up to Stake Pass, and the long stony path down Langstrath. My concept of the word path changed that day. Nowadays I am grateful for any scrap of path I find, especially in the Scottish hills, where paths such as that down Langstrath are a luxury. However even though by the time we reached Keswick my blisters had developed blisters, I nonetheless realised that I had loved my first true walk on the wild side.

Day Four is to me on reflection the most romantic, for that day my enduring love of The Northern Fells and Skiddaw began. The night before, as we had stumbled into Keswick in near darkness, I had barely noticed the shapely outline of Skiddaw. But on a glorious fourth morning, I appreciated for the first time Skiddaw's majestic feminine grace and just as a love affair with Lakeland in general had begun a few days before, so started my first passion for a single mountain.

That day we wandered through Skiddaw Forest (not a real forest but a vast area of heather clad hills and moorland), which was also later to become a favourite haunt. The landscape had altered from the previous three days, not as dramatic or grand, but perhaps wilder and certainly lonelier. That was the first time that I experienced utter silence in the hills and, once experienced, it would call to me when I was far away. By the time you enter Caldbeck at the end of day four, Lakeland is behind you.

Caldbeck itself is a charming small town, notable for the grave of John Peel, the famous huntsman. I think my brother remarked that at this stage, after about 55 miles of tough walking, we were about ready to join John Peel in the cemetery. By comparison with the previous four days, the scenery of Day Five from Caldbeck to Carlisle, although pleasant enough, is lacking in any dramatic thrill. Throughout that last day it was the goal of completing the long distance walk that kept us going, along with frequent longing glances back to the ever diminishing mountains of Lakeland.

And so in the achievement of the Cumbria Way both freedom and ambition had been sated and satisfied. I had fostered a love of high places and mountains, of becks and tarns, of silence and solitude. However I had yet to climb any of Wainwright's 214 fells.

Skiddaw Forest

The First Wainwright

If I had thought that I was in love with the Lake District when I was on the five day journey of the Cumbria Way, I knew I was in love when I returned to my home in Kent. The crags and rocks, becks and tarns and the sound of silence all called to me from afar. Unfortunately at this point in my life, I worked as a clerk for a pensions firm, earning less than £6,000 a year, so I had to wait and save hard for six months before my next opportunity came to venture to the hills.

Soon after the Cumbria Way, my brother and I finally invested in some proper maps of the Lake District and over the coming months planned our next excursion to the hills. It may sound odd to anyone who has walked the hills for years, or whose first experience of the Lake District was climbing Scafell Pike or Helvellyn, but at this stage we still thought of the high places as places where ordinary walkers did not go, the reserve of hard men who probably had beards; of people with jangly climbing things. We did not know that every fell in the Lake District could be reached by any walker of average capability. Wainwright was to teach us that.

Our second journey to the hills was planned as another low level walk through the Lake District. But this time we planned to do some of the best bits of the Cumbria Way, adding new places to visit and designing a walk that was very much our own creation, or at least seemed so. Here was born another of the pleasures of the hill walker's world, which has lasted to this day and will always be with me, the pleasure of getting the map out and planning. Sometimes the plan may be a fantastical one that never actually comes to pass; sometimes the plan may only be enacted years afterwards; sometimes it is a plan for the very next day in the hills.

In September 1989 we were back in the Lake District and the plan became a reality. This time the walk went from Ulverston to Penrith, via Keswick and was a seven day walk of over 100 miles. This long distance walk however had one major difference that was not part of any pre-conceived plan. It was an accident rather than an intentional design. The difference this time was that I climbed my first Wainwright. Now the reason it was an accident is two fold. Firstly it was because at this stage I still had no concept of who Wainwright was. The second reason lies in the hill itself, High Tove.

High Tove stands, or rather squats, at 515 metres (or 1665 feet). I truly believe that all hills have some worth. However High Tove is one of those hills that makes even the most ardent Wainwright bagger want to paraphrase George Orwell's Animal Farm by concluding, having climbed it, that some hills are more worthy than others. It lacks shape and form and is really no more than a swelling on the wild central spine of Lakeland, a bit of a pudding. And like any good pudding it is also capable of absorbing lots and lots of liquid, which manifests itself in rather boggy surroundings (although by no means the worst bogs in Lakeland).

In fact so unpronounced is the summit of High Tove, that it is the only summit in Lakeland that also serves as a pass, being the natural route of least resistance between lake Thirlmere and the charming hamlet of Watendlath. And this is the second reason why our first Wainwright fell was climbed by accident. Our plan the day we did High Tove was merely to walk from Grasmere to Keswick via Watendlath. Yet in doing this we also unwittingly climbed a fell.

In a way I am glad that High Tove was the first, for although the fell itself is not the grandest, the approach is rather lovely. I recall a hot day that September as we climbed up from the old road that hugs the western shore of Thirlmere. This is a quiet pleasant road for walkers, unlike the busy A591 on the eastern shore which is not to be recommended for walking. A good path climbs up from the lake, although this path does not owe its creation to High Tove but to Watendlath. The path skirts some pine trees and hugs a forest fence, over which can be heard and occasionally seen a rushing, tumbling beck. The path climbs among rocks and boulders and beneath small craggy outcrops. By now we were getting to realise that Lakeland walks were made of stern stuff and we were also beginning to understand that the effort was nearly always worth the reward. Eventually, as with many such walks in Lakeland, the enclosure of the trees and the confined rock scenery came to an end and we entered another type of walking world; one of open gently inclined spaces, heather, bog and the sound of the curlew. Here existed the wild places that I was beginning to love.

After a further gradual climb and some squelchy mild bog, we found ourselves at the rather large cairn that marks the summit of High Tove and also the summit of the pass to Watendlath. A cairn and a high point seemed a good place to stop and so we did. I think my brother, looking at the map, announced that the place was called High Tove, but it was not until a year or so later that I realised that I had in fact climbed my first Wainwright fell. If ever there was an act that was less born of bagging, this was probably it. The top was appreciated purely because it was a good and natural place too stop.

High Tove lies at roughly the mid point of the wild central spine of Lakeland which runs from Keswick in the north to Grasmere and Langdale in the south. In particular the stretch between Bleaberry Fell and High Raise is a prime location for the lover of solitude and wild places. For those who enjoy wild, hard walking, with a plethora of bog to negotiate, the central spine is king. This is not a place however for the faint hearted and a good sense of whereabouts is required even in good weather, as the area is bleak and largely featureless. In poor weather good navigational skills are needed. Featureless ground can often prove trickier to navigate than craggy complex terrain, as I was to find out later in my walking career.

As I said, I consider that every hill has worth, and High Tove's worth is its wildness and silence. Yes the odd person or group of people may pass by, but they are all bound for Watendlath and won't disturb for long. I have a fondness for summits that don't have celebrity, the lesser lights of the hills. There would be little solitude to be had if everything in Lakeland looked like or had the features of Great Gable or Helvellyn. And so that day we drank in the solitude, ignorant of our achievement and as we descended the well designed path into Watendlath thought only of High Tove as one enjoyable part of many that day.

It was not to be long though before the high places and summits began to form part of our plans, rather than just being incidental to them. The two excursions to the Lakes that we had in 1990 proved to be something of a watershed between low levels walks and high level rambling. By now we had become used to planning low level routes through the Lake District and for our third long distance walk in May 1990 we planned the longest of all. In total this walk would cover some 150 miles in seven days. Again we started in Ulverston, but this time we decided to finish the linear walking in Keswick and give ourselves a couple of 'spare' days to do as we pleased at the end. But May 1990 ended up being a long distance low level walk that kept getting side tracked by the temptation of the high places. By now we considered ourselves to have some experience of low level rambling and had begun to develop a basic knowledge of the Lake District. Hills such as The Old Man of Coniston, The Langdale Pikes and Skiddaw, were now things that we knew and recognised and because they had an air of the familiar about them, they became a little less fearsome. It seemed that if we could use the rough and stony paths of Lakeland to get up to over 1500 feet, then why could we not go that little bit higher?

So it was that our usual first day walk from Ulverston to Coniston, which by now was sticking less and less to the prescribed Cumbria Way route, came to include what we considered to be our first true Lakeland summit, Beacon Fell, which lies in the pocket sized area of wild country to the east of Coniston Water (bear in mind that we had not considered High Tove to be anything other than a pass).

Twice we had flirted with Beacon Fell, as we took the Cumbria Way path around the hollow that encloses the lovely Beacon Tarn. Now we found ourselves sitting beside the tarn once more, on a lovely May day and the urge to climb the fell became a reality. I am lucky that my times by Beacon Tarn and on Beacon Fell have generally been blessed with good weather and in over a dozen visits I cannot recall any rain, or strong winds. This is a place that deserves a visit in good weather as both the fell and the tarn are prime places to do nothing more than aimless relaxing. They are places where walking agendas can easily fall apart in quiet contemplation. Any good walking agenda should have room to be changed or even abandoned if we are to be truly free in the hills.

I consider the area of small heather and bracken covered fells which includes Beacon Fell to be a mini wilderness. Wilderness is an odd word, a word that means many different things to many different people. If we

Beacon Tarn, a mini wilderness

think of wilderness in the sense of the Australian outback or Antarctica then there are no remotely comparable wilderness areas in the British Isles. Even in the wildest reaches of Scotland, such as Letterewe or the Cairngorms, the nearest road is no more than 10 miles away. In the Lake District there is nowhere more than four or five miles from a road and everywhere the land is steeped in man's influence. And yet standing on Ben Macdui in the Cairngorms, or crossing the remote reaches of Upper Eskdale in the Lake District it is hard not to categorise these places as wilderness. This is because to me there is another definition to wilderness, a definition that on this crowded island becomes more relevant with the passage of time. For me wilderness is as much about how the landscape makes a person feel and react on the inside as about its true wilderness characteristics on the outside. Yes it does require certain wild external factors in the landscape around you, but it is also a state of mind. Does it matter if a place is three miles from a road or a person, or if it is 1000 miles from a road or a person? If I am alone and if my environment removes me from civilization, am I not blessed with at least the impression of wilderness?

That is why for me the tarn and the fell, which both owe their name to an ancient beacon, are a mini wilderness. There are places by the tarn where you can escape people and spend half an hour or more reclining on some heathery perch, with only the gentle lapping of the water, the occasional plop of a fish coming up for air and the ever present treble twittering of the curlew.

The top of the fell itself is another wonderful place to contemplate this mini wilderness. I have seldom found many people up there, although I would be lying if I said that it cannot be popular on some sunny days. Here though space is king and the view from the top seems much higher than its 800 odd feet would suggest. Perhaps the two most remarkable aspects are the bird's eye, full length view of Coniston Water and the close up view of the ramparts of Dow Crag and Coniston Old Man. Obviously more distant views can be had from higher hills and mountains, but are there any views in Lakeland that are more perfectly designed? On a clear day looking southwards you should be able to make out the monument on Hoad Hill. You can also, if you really wish and if the clarity is very good, spot Blackpool Tower and Heysham Power Station. But perhaps spotting such man made things would spoil the illusion of a mini wilderness.

Beacon Fell was climbed by design, but what we did not know was that we had once again ventured onto a hill described by Alfred Wainwright, this time one of his Outlying Fells. I can see perhaps why Wainwright added Beacon Fell as part of his appendix volume. The fell has a lower altitude than any of the fells in the seven main guide books and lies just outside the main mountainous area of the Lake District. Nonetheless there is also another part of me that feels that this fell, along with quite a few others in the Outlying Fells, actually has more merit as a fell that some of the 214 true Wainwrights. Climb Beacon Fell and then climb the heathery blob of Ling Fell near Bassenthwaite Lake and see which you feel has more merit as a hill.

Our diversions from low level walking continued the next day. The day's plan was a walk from Coniston to the village of Boot in Eskdale, via the Walna Scar Road and pass and then up over Hardknott road pass. Although this was in itself quite a long low level walk it was one that for reasons of thrill and excitement at the high places we decided, on the whim of the moment, to extend. The walk out of Coniston and up to the start of the Walna Scar road takes in one of the steepest sections of tarmac road that I know of, but eventually the gradient levels off at a small car park and the cars are left behind as the walk proper begins. The Walna Scar Road is in fact more of a rough track than a road and in places the path is quite stony. It is however a joy to tread as it climbs fairly gradually to Cove Bridge. All around is a place, seemingly of wild moorland, but where man's influence is rife, both in the form of ancient cairns and stone circles and in the more recent form of the quarries and mine workings. It is in some ways a reminder that the image of Lakeland as a wild pristine place is far from the truth. In fairly recent memory many places in the hills thrived with mining industry. Lakeland should be preserved, but it would be wrong to forget its industrial heritage.

Cove Bridge is one of my favourite non-summit places in the Lake District. Here the presence of human endeavour exists in the form of a beautifully crafted stone bridge which arches over the sparkling clear waters of Torver Beck. The bridge makes a perfect photo subject, with the mountain wall of Brown Pike, Buck Pike and Dow Crag lurking behind. If the weather is hot and you arrive at Cove Bridge in a sweat, this is a perfect place to indulge in one of my favourite mountain pastimes, head ducking. Now I am not sure whether Wainwright ever indulged in head ducking, but I don't think he would entirely have disapproved. Basically I have always found that it is one thing to genteelly sprinkle some beck water over your face to cool yourself, but nothing cools the body quite like a good head ducking in a beck or rocky pool. The further you can get your head under the better. However choose your spot well, as ideally you will need some solid flat rocks close at hand to place both hands on before you duck. Also be aware that although the weather can be quite nice for head ducking at 1000 feet, wet hair can leave one feeling decidedly chilly once up at 2000 feet. Of course one should also be careful to choose a spot that is not too deep, steep or slippery. Those things aside head ducking, if a little bizarre, is a wonderful way to cool down. As long as we respect the landscape and don't spoil or damage it, why should it not be a place to indulge in such innocent, childlike pleasures? Too much of life is spent being stuffy and conventional and in doing what others perceive to be the normal thing. As long as it does not offend or annoy, I think there is ample room for a little eccentricity in the hills.

Leaving behind Cove Bridge the path now steepens as it hauls its way to the 2000 feet high pass of Walna Scar. At the pass a fine view opens out to the North and West. I remember being thrilled by this view the first time I saw it and indeed on all subsequent occasions. It was the first time I had seen Harter Fell in Eskdale at close quarters, with its forestry skirt of alternate light and dark green pine trees. More dominant than even that were the views of Scafell and Scafell Pike from this impressive side, fully justifying their status as the highest mountains in England.

The Walna Scar pass was supposed to be our high point, before we gradually descended into the Duddon valley. But today an eagerness to climb further and see the view from even higher overcame us. Many times over the previous year we had looked at Brown Pike, Buck Pike and Dow Crag from a distance, but now the first of these three tops was within striking distance. Being May, daylight hours were long, and so we broke free from our planned route, climbed the steep pull on to Brown Pike and in doing so reached our highest point to date.

Now Brown Pike is another of those places that makes you wonder why it is not one of the 214 Wainwright fells. In a sense that day our ignorance of The Wainwrights made Brown Pike seem all the worthier. Its cairn is neatly perched just a few yards away from a fearful plunge down to the tiny Blind Tarn (aptly named as this is about the only place you can see it from). The yawning chasm that exists between Brown Pike and Coniston Old Man has left me feeling a slight vertigo at times. I can see why Wainwright did not give Brown Pike a separate chapter in his guide books, it is after all merely the terminus of the ridge of which Dow Crag is the parent, but then Bakestall in the Northern Fells seems to me to be merely the terminus of the parent fell Skiddaw and it merits a separate chapter in Wainwright's guides. However, I should not harp on about such things too much because the arbitrary nature of The Wainwrights is also one of the things I have most loved about them. There is no height definition to a Wainwright as there is to say a Scottish Munro. Munros by definition have to reach 3000 feet and usually involve 3000 feet's worth of effort. Wainwrights can be anything from a 15 minute stroll like Little Mell Fell, to a long day's outing such as Scafell from Eskdale. And unlike Munros, where the list seems to keep having mountains added to it and subtracted from it, you know that once you have done the 214 Wainwrights there will never be any more additions to the list, even if peculiar bagging folk like me do think that Brown Pike deserves promotion!

On Brown Pike I experienced my first high mountain view (it stands at around 2,200 feet). In some ways the view is similar to that from the slightly lower Walna Scar pass, but the extra height, coupled with the plunging crags, lends it a proper high mountain feel. Our excursion that day continued on to Buck Pike as for the first time we experienced the delights of high ridge walking. We had thought up till this point that progress on the high mountains would be slow and dangerous. Now we found out that, at least in some places, progress could be just as pleasant and smooth as at valley level. On this type of ridge walking we could continually glance at the Scafells, at Harter Fell, at the expanse of moorland and low lying hills leading out to Morecambe Bay and even again to Hoad Hill and its monument. This was surely a walker's heaven.

We had languished on Brown Pike for over an hour, soaking in the view and by the time we reached Buck Pike we knew that we had to head back to Walna Scar and complete our walk. We still had many miles ahead of us over Honister Pass and down to the village of Boot. So unbeknown to us we stopped our first ridge walk just shy of the Wainwright of Dow Crag. Still it gave us an excuse to come back another day, if such an excuse were needed. Once I had visited Cove Bridge and Brown Pike, I knew that they would always be favourite and often visited places.

The heat of the sun baked us as we crawled over Honister Pass, but at least this was one bit of road walking where the cars were almost forced to go at our pace. Eventually we arrived tired and hungry at the hamlet of Boot. That night we had a room in the local inn. It has always amazed me how quickly the body recovers from a long walk once the comforts of a bath and a hot meal have been indulged in. We soon found ourselves down at the bar, having a few cheeky pints and playing pool. I recall, in my youthful naivety, challenging several extremely large burly locals to several frames of pool. I found myself on a lucky winning streak. I am sure these hulking guys half wondered whether to continue enduring my lucky streak or whether to do something more enjoyable, like trying to squeeze my head into one of the pool table pockets.

The next day's walk still remains the longest walk I have ever done and also one of the most ridiculous in terms of its planning. The walk, 25 odd miles from Boot in Eskdale to Ennerdale Bridge, via Wastwater and the Black Sail Pass, was in itself a decent enough idea. It was however the planned route of getting from point A to point B and the lack of our basic ability to plan the shortest route between these points, that still today leaves me shaking my head. From precisely behind the pub we were staying at in the village of Boot, a good path runs over moorland to Burnmoor Tarn and ends up smack bang at Wasdale Head, a distance of perhaps some four and a half miles. I am sure we must have noticed this route on the map, but instead of taking it we chose instead to take a minor road route that meandered through Eskdale Green, Santon Bridge and Nether Wasdale, before finally following the entire length of Wastwater to reach Wasdale Head. The length of this route to Wasdale Head was more than double the length of the Burnmoor Tarn route and it was entirely on tarmac! What were we thinking of? Considering when we finally got to Wasdale Head we still had to climb over the Black Sail Pass and then walk the entire length of Ennerdale Forest and Ennerdale Water and considering the day was hot from start to finish, our route was one of positively masochistic levels of naivety and poor planning.

The only reason I can give for our blindly ignoring the obvious route and instead sticking to the roads, is that we were still at this stage a little in awe of the wild places and regarded the safety of the minor roads as a comfort blanket to be held onto at all costs, rather than cross a wild tract of unknown terrain. Perhaps we were also a little scared by the thought of taking a route called The Burnmoor Corpse Road, as the path between Boot and Wasdale Head is known. Perhaps we did not realise that the corpses in question were merely conveyed between Wasdale Head and Boot for burial and that it was unlikely therefore that we would actually encounter anything grisly on this route. There was however one small upside to our plan. It enabled us to walk along and admire the entire length of Wastwater.

Now over the years I have discovered that each of the lakes in the Lake District has its own peculiar character. The pointless but fun question is often raised as to which is the finest of the Lakes. To me it's a bit like having some precious stones laid out before you and trying to work out whether diamond is finer than, or ruby is finer than, emerald. There is little doubt however that Wastwater is the most dramatic of the Lakes, reeking as it does of primeval forces and the chaos of nature in the raw. My first sight of the screes that plunge down into England's deepest lake left a lasting imprint. It is the type of in your face drama that makes a man feel small and ever so slightly terrified. It is worth considering that the part of the screes that can be seen above the water line are not the whole story, as the screes continue on down to the deep bed of the lake. A large pear drop shaped boulder at the foot of the visible screes testifies to the constant shift and gradual erosion taking place here. Such change cannot be measured in a person's lifespan; it is a thing of thousands and hundreds of thousands of years.

If we had not walked down the length of Wastwater that day, we would also have missed out on the classic view down the lake to Great Gable and the enormous muscular shoulder of Scafell. Great Gable, just a name on a map before, was now an image ingrained into my subconscious. Over the years it would become one of my favourite mountains.

If the planning of a circuitous road walk to get us between Boot and Wasdale Head smacked of early naivety, then perhaps we made amends with the next section of the walk over Black Sail Pass and down to Ennerdale Water. This stretch is proper walker's terrain and crosses some wild country. Names such as Pillar and Kirk Fell now became realities to the left and right of our path. The final stretch of the walk from the Black Sail hut to Ennerdale Bridge, although flat and on good forest tracks, was long and arduous at the end of the day. Ennerdale Water was seen for the first time, one of the quieter lakes whose charms are those of peaceful, lonely beauty, although Anglers Crag and Bowness Knott do add more than a hint of drama to the lake.

I must confess that walking into Ennerdale Bridge at nearly 9 o'clock at night it was my brother who had more energy left in him. For my part I was so exhausted by the end of that day, that I felt as if my soul had departed from my body and left an inarticulate zombie behind. By opting not to take the shorter Corpse Road route I had ended up feeling like one of the departed myself.

If the previous two days of walking left lasting imprints of wonderful lakes and mountains in the mind, the next day was something of a damp squib in more ways than one. The choice of Floutern Pass, to cross from Ennerdale to Buttermere, was admittedly a good route choice on paper, but here I was to learn that the maps don't always tell you everything, as this is one of the boggiest places I have encountered. That day I twice sank down to my thigh in rich peaty bog. Floutern Tarn, which looked an inviting spot on the map, turned out to be a dreary stretch of water, although the overcast weather that day probably did not do it justice. Even so I can't ever imagine it competing for a prize with the likes of Sty Head Tarn or Grizedale Tarn, unless it was a prize for solitude, for it has bags of that.

Thankfully an old friend of mine had arranged to meet us at the Fish Hotel in Buttermere for lunch before giving us a lift to Keswick, although on reflection I am not sure the staff at the hotel appreciated the bog ridden entity that graced their establishment that day. Peat bog smells foul!

The last few days of that holiday were based in Keswick and during our stay in this wonderfully situated town we again broke new ground, for not only did we climb another Wainwright, but we also for the first time breasted the magical 3000 feet contour.

In Praise of Skiddaw

Of all the mountains in the Lake District, I have perhaps the strongest affinity with Skiddaw. This mountain has had its detractors over the years; some who would claim that it is no mountain, but merely a very large hill; others who associate it with the Main Line or Tourist Route and ignore its finer qualities; other Lycra clad types, with ropes and jangly accessories, who point to its lack of crags and scary places. There are many though who love this benign mountain and indeed Wainwright was fulsome in his praise of it, devoting 28 pages of guide book to it (almost as many as for any other mountain).

Personally I consider Skiddaw to be one of the most beautifully structured mountains in England, perhaps even in Britain. Yes, it does not have the sharp ridges of Hellvellyn, or the dramatic crags and buttresses of Scafell and Scafell Pike. But can these other highest mountains boast the elegant outline of Skiddaw? Do they present a face that is as instantly recognisable as Skiddaw from Keswick? Helvellyn, although a wonderful mountain, shows a somewhat characterless face towards Thirlmere and from the Ullswater side its famous edges and cliffs cannot really be seen. Scafell is a massive sight from Wasdale, but does it have the beauty of Skiddaw? Even Scafell Pike does not present such a symmetrical profile and from a distance can often be hard to identify. But there is no mistaking Skiddaw.

Skiddaw's appeal is a feminine one. To me it is a great mother mountain, embracing in its graceful curves its many children including Carl Side, Dodd and the baby of the litter Latrigg. Its close high neighbour Blencathra, while equally as fine a mountain, has a more masculine character, with its sheer front, and the crags and ridges that radiate from its summit. Blencathra and Skiddaw are therefore like sister and brother.

Skiddaw has a number of different faces, apart from its picture postcard Keswick aspect. Its Northern aspect is perhaps the least familiar, but Skiddaw still appears enormously lofty from the North, with great grassy flanks, topped off with the distinctive summit cone of grey slate. When viewed from Skiddaw Forest to the west, Skiddaw loses some of its impression of height, as Skiddaw Forest itself is over 1000 feet above sea level. Here the summit ridge above Sale How and Hare Crag resembles a great whaleback, even having the same blue grey colouring as a whale.

The classic Skiddaw profile from Walla Crag

Skiddaw still looks very high, but lacks some of the sheer hugeness of its other aspects.

On the other hand Skiddaw perhaps looks disproportionately enormous and at its most massive from the Bassenthwaite Lake side to the East. Travelling down the A66 by Bassenthwaite Lake, the mountain soars up in an impressive three tiered structure, with Dodd Wood and fell being the lower tier, Ullock Pike, Long Side and Carl Side ramping up the height and forming the second tier and finally behind them the third tier of Skiddaw's summit ridge itself, seemingly up with the Gods. From here Skiddaw is like some enormous fortification, with an inner keep and outer ramparts.

The final aspect from the Southern Keswick side sees Skiddaw at its most graceful. I have often thought that from this angle Skiddaw takes on something of the classic mountain shape, only with the rough edges of the classic mountain shape somewhat smoothed down to leave an inviting, welcoming and friendly mountain. The view from Ashness Bridge is one of the most photographed in the district and that is in part due to the wonderful subject of this southern face of Skiddaw.

It is perhaps the benign quality of Skiddaw that is to me its most appealing characteristic. That is not to say that any ascent of Skiddaw, even via the Main Line, should be undertaken lightly and without due care. I am sure that people have died on Skiddaw, although you would have to be pretty stupid or reckless to do so. However, as long as due mountain care is taken, Skiddaw from Keswick or the tourist car park and up the main line is one of those mountains that can be enjoyed in safety in most weathers. Whereas in high winds and rain one might baulk at an ascent of Scafell Pike or Helvellyn, I have done Skiddaw several times in hideous weather. I have been on Skiddaw in mist more times than not and again either with the help of the Main Line or with some basic navigation managed to safely get myself back down. Snow might be a problem on some of the narrow ridges and near some of the high crags of other mountains, but on Skiddaw, while again some care is needed and proper winter layering should be worn against the cold, a fantastic time can be had playing around in the snow.

Again I would stress that Skiddaw, like any other 3000 foot mountain, should not be underestimated. The friend can easily bite back and the summit ridge can be positively Arctic and is exposed to all the elements. But if you are the sort that wants to pit yourself against the elements, test your navigation and just enjoy wild weather, then Skiddaw on a poor weather day is a relatively secure place to do so. Indeed in bad weather it is a good training ground for the kind of conditions an inexperienced, but committed hill walker, can inevitably expect to encounter in his walking career. Better to experience mist, wind, hail and snow up here and gain some confidence through straightforward route finding and navigation, than to find oneself on Scafell Pike in bad conditions, mistakenly heading for the rough boulder fields of Broad Crag and Ill Crag, or even worse on the wild Cairngorm plateau in Scotland. Even on Skiddaw it is best though to know your limit and know when to turn back if need be. I have experienced a couple of times, in severe wind and rain mostly, where carrying on up Skiddaw has seemed at best highly unpleasant and at worst dangerous. So Skiddaw is a good place to find your own personal limit of weather conditions, but be careful to recognise when to leave the summit for another day and let the elements triumph. No-one should ever feel a lack of bravado if they turn back. Bravado can be as great a hazard as the weather or any crag or plunging drop. The bravado mentality can be most prevalent in large groups of walkers. The maxim that if you are in a group you should always pace yourself at the slowest member's pace and stamina is a very correct one.

And if you find that cramps your desire to pit yourself against nature in the raw then go alone!

Having perhaps slightly got on my soap box and pontificated a little it is time for a confession. In May 1990 my brother and I set off from Keswick to climb Skiddaw and although he reached the summit, I did not! It was not a particularly great day for weather, a bit drizzly, with a cap of grey cloud on Skiddaw's summit, but on reflection and with the hindsight of many far worse days, it was perfectly and easily doable. But as we got to the end of the pine forestation and just before the car park at the top of Gale Road, a heavy shower and the massive flank of Skiddaw rising before me into the mist caused me to have second thoughts about carrying on. Now I am not one of those walkers that write only about being macho and appear to have nerves of steel and never to make any navigational errors. I have always adopted a slightly cautious approach to mountains, and even though my personal boundaries have increased with time and experience, I still tend to err on the side of caution. However that day in 1990, my caution was unfounded. That day my brother, who wanted to go on, was not doing so for bravado and he did not try and drag me with him. He had correctly judged the conditions and his own limits and thought it perfectly safe. There are times when physical limitations halt us on the hills and other times when our own mental limitations get the better of us. Standing beneath Skiddaw the mental hurdle of climbing a 3000 feet mountain for the first time, of going into a realm where I had never been before and on one of the highest of England's mountains, got the better of me.

About three quarters of an hour after Peter had headed on up Skiddaw and I had headed back, I found myself shopping in Keswick for nothing in particular, as I tried to distract my mind from the fact that I had probably turned my back on a great mountain experience. And then as I emerged from one of the many outdoor clothing shops in Keswick the worst fate for anyone who has turned back from a summit happened, the sun came out and Skiddaw's summit cleared. Any justification I might have had in turning back now seemed feeble. The grey and black thoughts of concern that I had had for my brother's safety alone on the mountain were replaced by greener hued thoughts of envy and jealousy. I kicked myself back to the bed and breakfast. However, such is brotherly love that after another half hour or so, I found myself wandering down from my room and looking up at the bulk of Skiddaw that so dominates the street ends of Bed and Breakfast land in Keswick. My thoughts now were that Peter had probably arrived on the summit. There was still a little envy, but I also now longed to hear his story.

Peter made the summit of Skiddaw that day and what he told me of the summit and its fantastic view made me resolve that if the next day was one of fair weather, I would also reach the summit of Skiddaw. I am lucky that my brother has never been in the least bit concerned about climbing the same mountain on consecutive days and baulks at the very thought of bagging hills. He has made an art form out of climbing his favourite fell Lords Seat and probably holds an unofficial record for the most ascents of that fell. So Peter was more than happy to do Skiddaw again the next day.

The next day the weather was fine with some high puffy clouds and a slight breeze, but plenty of sunshine and little prospect of any impending change from fair conditions. I soon realised that the tourist route up Skiddaw was in fact a bit of a slog in its early stages. The first part of the climb, from just past the Hawell Monument to the shepherds of Lonscale, has had some recent work to upgrade the path, which is now a broad gravely track. Someone climbing Skiddaw today for the first time might think that this gravel track is a bit of an eyesore, or an unsightly scar on the flanks of Jenkin Hill. However let me assure you that it used to be a lot worse. The new gravel path is so fine and smooth to walk upon that it encourages people to do just that and thereby lessens the erosion to either side of the path. Prior to the recent work on the path the mainline route was some 20 feet wide in places, and was an ugly scar. Ascending Skiddaw by this route was a toilsome trudge up eroded peat and unstable stone. A myriad of diversion paths had been formed by those who wanted firmer walking and this had gradually widened the existing path. Now there is just one well made gravel path about five feet wide, and the scar of the numerous old paths and ruts are gradually healing. The new gravel path may not be aesthetically appealing, but on a route of this popularity it is the best solution and a credit to those that toiled to construct it.

However, back in 1990, we had to contend with the steep rutted peaty scar until it levelled out on approaching the top of Jenkin Hill. From here the route up the mainline becomes one of those wonderful high level promenades that are a walker's heaven. Now above 2000 feet, the views expand and especially prominent, as you stroll along this level bit of ridge, are the views towards Coledale and mighty Eel Crag, the soft outlines of the Newlands round, the southern aspect towards the highest mountains of Scafell Pike, Bow Fell and Great End and perhaps above all the aerial views of Derwent Water that begin to appear.

Eventually at a gate (oh dear, I did say I wouldn't mention gates) the bulk of Skiddaw Little Man starts to obscure the view South and West, as the high level promenade continues. Instead there are extensive and wild views over the peaceful landscape of Skiddaw Forest, a place that has qualities of light, shade and colour that change and shift according to the moods of the weather.

Then after a second gate (last mention of gates I promise) the slate dominated final pull up onto the whaleback of Skiddaw commences. This always seems longer than it is and the first time I did it I began to realise at about this point what climbing 3000 feet actually meant. Those who cheat slightly by climbing from the Gale Road car park perhaps fail to appreciate the true height of Skiddaw when climbed from Keswick. I have always preferred to climb Skiddaw from Keswick, unless including it as part of a more lengthy expedition in the Northern Fells.

The whaleback summit of Skiddaw teases, the highest point being right at the Northern end of the ridge. A final dip and rise leads to the true summit, where there are several large shelters (on most days you will welcome one), a triangulation pillar and a squat round view indicator. And what a magnificent view it is, although in truth it is less a view of nearby surrounding mountains and more one of distance and depth. On a clear day, the distance leads you across the vast northern plains and farmsteads of Cumbria to the Solway Firth and beyond to Criffel and the Southern Uplands of Scotland. The depth leads the eye down to Bassenthwaite Lake, 3000 feet below and viewed as if from a plane. The view from Skiddaw is maybe not the most beautiful in Lakeland, but it is perhaps the most expansive and has the greatest feeling of height and space. How you judge it will probably depend on whether you prefer your view to be of vast distances or you prefer to have a myriad of peaks closely arrayed around you.

From the summit the return down the mainline can be done in an hour or less by a walker of even average fitness (the luxury of the improved path has made the return even quicker than it used to be). However it is worth making a detour from the mainline by an obvious path that leads up onto Skiddaw Little Man. Wainwright in his Northern Fells guide chapter on Skiddaw Little Man posed the question as to whether this was the finest view in the Lake District. And whatever your opinion regarding whether this view is the finest, there is certainly no finer place to appreciate the Vale of Keswick and Derwent Water from on high. Derwent Water, which appears to be a massive body of water when by its shore, seems rather small from the lofty vantage point of Skiddaw Little Man.

Arrayed around Derwent Water are a panoply of beautiful mountains too numerous to name. The overall impression is one of serene engaging mountain outlines, shapes that will become familiar friends to any fellwalker, such as the graceful Newlands Round, Castle Crag and Kings How (which together form the famous Jaws of Borrowdale) and the high ridges of Coledale.

In April 2007, the year I completed The Wainwrights, I found myself on the summit of Skiddaw Little Man, on the last day of a long week of mountain walking. Even though I had stood there ten times before and even though I had seen my fill of mountain views that week, this special view still had the ability to take my breath away. That day I spent a full half an hour absorbing every graceful curve of lake and mountain beneath me, feeling for a moment like a king surveying his natural kingdom; not in a powerful way but with a sense of awe, love and reverence. On a map Skiddaw Little Man is no more than a subsidiary bump on Skiddaw. However when you are there it becomes a wholly separate and glorious entity, with its own character and own unforgettable memories.

Having perhaps sung the praises of the main line route up Skiddaw, it is worth stating that this is merely the starting point for an exploration of the fascinating mountain that Skiddaw is. One of Skiddaw's greatest attributes is that it has many ways of ascending and descending and as the main line tends to attract most of the walkers, the other routes up Skiddaw are to be recommended to the lover of a more solitary, remote experience. Anyone who aspires, as I do, to climb as many of Britain's wonderful hills and mountains as possible, will soon realise that a lifetime is too short to do justice to all mountains and a great many wonderful places can only be visited once. This is why I have for a long time had certain favourite mountains that I have made it my business to gain a deeper love for than can be gained just by climbing the hill on one occasion, by one route and seeing the view on one particular day. Skiddaw is one mountain I want to crawl over and gain a comprehensive knowledge of.

For variety and perhaps a taste of the drama that some think Skiddaw lacks, a climb from Bassenthwaite via Ullock Pike is recommended. Ullock Pike has a graceful appearance and on closer acquaintance is an interesting gradually tapering climb. The view of Bassenthwaite Lake from the summit is classic and the ridge from Ullock Pike to Long Side has a slight feeling of exposure and drops on both sides, which is perhaps lacking on Skiddaw generally. The final haul from Carl Side onto Skiddaw is one of those climbs that break in the fledgling hill walker. This final

Skiddaw's massive summit ridge from Long Side

flank of Skiddaw both looks and is massive, with a very short section of mild scree to negotiate. Scree is one of those often encountered masochisms that the hills throw at us, but it is worth remembering as you trudge up scree, that it can work in reverse in descent and provide a very quick way down.

I can remember a long haul onto Beinn Eighe, in Scotland's magnificent Torridon area. It had taken me and my companion several hours to climb to the main summit of Ruadh-stac Mor, via the wild and impressive Coire Mhic Fhearchair. Although I knew that descents are usually quicker than ascents, I still expected it to take some hours to get back from the far flung summit to the car. However, as we headed back along the ridge from the summit, we saw what appeared to be a scree shoot that led off onto the vast grey flanks of the mountain and made a beeline for the general area of the car park. Now this was the daddy of all scree and I can only compare descending it to a ride down an escalator, with the only way of slowing the ride being to dig ones heels into the scree. That day we descended from a height of over 3000 feet to valley level in 25 minutes.

Looking back at the scree I shook my head with a vague sense of disbelief at what we had just descended. So although scree can be a curse, it can also sometimes be a blessing!

The great eastern flank of Skiddaw that drops over Hare Crag and Sale How can also be recommended for a lover of solitude and rolling heather landscapes. Sale How is one of Lakeland's inglorious puddings but it is a fine place to wallow in loneliness and silence. It is less than a mile from the main route up Skiddaw, but might as well be a thousand miles away. This is another example of Lake District wilderness in small dimensions being more a state of mind than a factual reality. The route down over Sale How to the rather desolate grey Skiddaw House is also a fine way of varying the return route, having climbed Skiddaw by the popular main line. Once at Skiddaw House, the Cumbria Way makes an easy though spectacular course beneath the crags of Lonscale Fell and above the plunge of the Glenderaterra Beck. This route will eventually lead you back to either the Gale Road car park or Keswick.

A connoisseur's route onto Skiddaw can be had by climbing the south-west arête of Skiddaw Little Man. Those with a love of drama and exposure will also enjoy this route, which makes a beeline for the cairn on Skiddaw Little Man on a narrowing ridge that although very steep, somehow never quite competes with Sharp Edge or Halls Fell on Blencathra. It is a fine hard climb nonetheless and gains in loneliness over the more popular ridges of Blencathra. In fact, this is a place best appreciated alone.

There are many other ways onto Skiddaw. My best walking friend, who shares my deep love for Skiddaw (more about him later), has even climbed it via the seemingly sheer front face, which is virtually pathless and has an almost cast iron guarantee of solitude (I'm going there as soon as I can). I will leave the other ways for your own personal perusal and exploration.

No paean for Skiddaw would be complete without a mention of Keswick, the town beneath it. Over the years I have become very fond of Keswick. It seems to me the perfect base for walking in the Lakeland hills and is my favourite Lakeland town. That's not to say that I have any dislike for Ambleside or Windermere, but for me they just don't quite offer what Keswick does. From Ambleside you can step out of your accommodation and do the wonderful Fairfield Horseshoe, but not a great deal else is immediately to hand in the way of high mountains. Windermere has its beautiful lake, but the town is really on the edge of the true mountainous area of the Lake District (although Orrest Head is of course a fine view point). The thing about Keswick is that there are so many walks and hills that can be done without even having to use a car or public transport. As well as the whole Northern Fells range, the Coledale Round can easily be reached, the Newlands Round is but a short walk away via the lakeside path, as are Walla Crag and the remote fells of the Central spine. I have passed many nights out in Keswick (I won't go into too much detail), and generally found the town and its people to be friendly and welcoming. Keswick also has a vast selection of places to stay, from homely comfortable bed and breakfasts, to self-catering houses and grand hotels.

When thinking of Skiddaw I must also give mention to the man who used to run the corner shop in the midst of Keswick's Bed and Breakfast land around Eskin Street and Southey Street. He was a great character and always used to have a cheery word to say to everyone who entered his little shop. He also had a good memory for less frequent visitors, as he always remembered Peter and I, despite the gaps of months between our visits. However one thing did slightly let him down. He was not the

A snow plastered Skiddaw Trig Point

greatest of weather forecasters. If you were climbing Skiddaw, which we often were, he might say 'eh lads it's clearing on Jenkin Hill, you should get a fine view today'. That would be the signal for driving rain and wind to accompany our ascent. If on the other hand he said 'climbing Skiddaw are you? You won't see owt from up there today', that would mean that a peerless view out to Solway and Criffel would be had. Eventually we learnt that if we always relied on the weather to be the exact opposite of what he said it was going to be, then his forecasts had some value. In seriousness though, he was a character and it was a shame when his little shop closed and his trade became absorbed into the ever-growing supermarket conglomerate. Many times, in many places, I have watched my food being hurled disdainfully down the checkout, by some straight faced supermarket checkout worker who does not say a word and I have reflected on the charms of the man in the corner shop.

Skiddaw had now become only my second of Wainwright's fells after already having done many miles of walking in Lakeland. Soon that was to change as a new influence entered my life and heralded a wonderful period of discovery in the high places.

Two Old Men and a Young One

On the first of September 1990, my 21st birthday, a very dear friend of mine gave me a present, which although not highly valuable in a monetary sense, was perhaps the most valuable present in an inspirational way that anyone had ever given me before or has since. The present was the book *Wainwright on the Lakeland Mountain Passes*, and was my first introduction to a man whose work and devotion to the hills was to become a driving force behind my own burgeoning love of the Lake District. Here, in one volume, was a book that roamed over the whole Lake District and introduced my mind to places that instantly became names I longed to visit.

In those days we did not visit the Lake District in winter (although this was soon to change) and winter was a period of discontented, but stupidly self-imposed exile from the hills. However, the winter of 1990/1991 was still a winter of content. For during this winter both I and a new found walking companion called Stan poured over Wainwright's picture filled volumes such as *Fellwalking with Wainwright*. I keenly awaited the subsequent *Wainwright's Favourite Lakeland Mountains* and finally *The Valleys of Lakeland*, published after Wainwright's death. Also at about this time the series of television programmes with Alfred Wainwright and Eric Robson walking the landscapes of Lakeland, Scotland and Yorkshire were repeated. For the first time, as well as reading about the hills and seeing pictures of them, I could see marvellously atmospheric programmes, with glorious views of them.

There was something about this old man and the deep earthy voice and character of his companion that was both relaxing and at the same time inspiring. In combination they seemed as perfect to hill walking videos as Morecambe and Wise were to comedy. There was nothing showy or flashy about their presentation. It was a simple love of the wild places that shone through. Such was the intimate atmosphere generated by the programmes that watching them made me feel like I was a silent companion on the walks.

It may perhaps seem strange that Alfred Wainwright, a man of 80 years old, should appeal so much to a couple of men barely out of their teens, but he became to us, as to many others, the great father of fellwalking. His well chosen words became catchphrases for us. He seemed to have found the key to a philosophy about the hills that we were only just beginning to touch upon. It is sometimes said that deeply religious people radiate an aura of spirituality. Well to us Wainwright radiated a love and understanding of the high and wild places, as if by spending so much of his life in them, he had somehow unlocked their secret.

At this stage I was still not aware of a specific desire to climb all 214 Wainwright Fells and had never heard of or encountered a Wainwright bagger. Indeed, I am sure Wainwright bagging as such has only come to the fore as a pastime in the last dozen or so years. However, I was nonetheless inspired to make plans for Helvellyn, Pillar, Blencathra, Bowfell and many other great mountains and ridges. But first I had to right a wrong. One old man, Wainwright, had entered our lives and filled them with excitement and now another old man left a lasting impression on me.

In September 1990 we climbed the Old Man of Coniston for the first time. We had now become three, due to the introduction to the group of my best friend Stan. Over the previous three trips to the Lake District my brother Peter and I had learned that although we occasionally had the odd brother's argument, we by and large loved the hills in the same way. The problem now was that although Stan was my best friend, a best friend does not always make a best companion on the hills. You need to have an innate seed within you that if given the chance will love the wild places and is just waiting to be born. Another friend of mine used to profess, when I told him of my trips to the hills, that he 'hated the countryside', a view that was entirely alien to me. Nonetheless in all other areas of friendship this hater of the countryside and I were close. This illustrates why a good friend does not necessarily make a good walking companion, and it is best to choose and consider wisely who you go walking with. To fail to do so can at best dilute the hills experience and at worst completely spoil it.

Peter and I took something of a gamble with Stan. He had never walked up a hill in his life and his entire preparation for an arduous week of walking in the Lake District was a five mile flat walk in our home territory of the South-East. Fortunately, as will be seen, our fears were unfounded, and for Stan September 1990 was to prove the start of his own devout love of the Lakeland Fells that would see us 'bag' many of the Wainwright Fells together and would culminate with Stan and I completing the 214 fells on the same day in 2007, the centenary year of Wainwright's birth. However on Stan's first trip in September 1990, there was to be one moment where I did doubt the wisdom of bringing this best mate, a moment for which on reflection he was entirely blameless.

The Coniston Range from Beacon Fell

Whereas Peter and I had had over a year of gradual acclimatisation to rough mountain walking, Stan had just one day as we walked from Ulverston to Coniston, before tackling the hills head on with a walk up the Old Man of Coniston. It did not seem to unduly bother him however, as he had always had that kind of wiry, athletic frame that naturally takes to the rigours of hill walking. Indeed some of the distances he can cover put a more sizeable lump of a person like me to shame.

Stan had little choice in the matter when it came to the Old Man of Coniston. The agenda was driven by Peter and I and our desire to get onto Dow Crag and the Old Man, having previously left them due to time constraints. The reward was worth waiting for. Dow Crag, with its 1000 foot cliffs plunging down into Goats Water, is not only magnificent to look at from below, but also must be one of Lakeland's airiest places to be on. For the summit sits right on the edge of the drop and is accessed by a short but easy clamber over rocks. I remember sitting on that airy perch for the first time, in a stiff wind, and leaning my upper body forwards to peer over into the 1000 feet of abyss below, where the wind was whipping up spray and white horses on Goats Water. This is one of Lakeland's most exposed summits and it was one of the first mildly exposed places I had visited in the hills. However I have enjoyed a sense of thrill here, rather than a sense of dread. It is one of those rare places where a mere walker can feel like an eagle on a high and impregnable eerie. Here you can relax in relative safety but with a sense that peril is but a clumsy manoeuvre away. I think the lack of a sense of dread comes from the fact that the drop is only on one side and the other side of Dow Crag falls away in merely grassy slopes to the Duddon Valley. If the summit of Dow Crag was as steep on both sides as it is above Goats Water, then it would be a truly heart racing place and would merit a place among Britain's most exposed summits. Nonetheless the summit is not for those with no appetite for a big drop. If being suspended at the top of the Big Wheel at a fair frightens you then the utmost summit of Dow Crag is best avoided.

As we headed for Goats Hause, which forms the low point between Dow Crag and the Old Man, the mist began to descend. For all of us this was the first time we had been in mist up above 2000 feet. We found ourselves enjoying the pleasure of being immersed and enfolded into the mountain's weather. This mist though was a brief fleeting thing that day and approaching the summit we had one of those never to be forgotten mountain moments, a clearance. At the summit of the Old Man of Coniston, the dark clouds still lurked only a couple of hundred feet above our heads, but this was enough to reveal the extensive panorama. As with Skiddaw the view from the Old Man of Coniston is one of distance, as the foothills of South Lakeland stretch out beneath you towards the sea. Hoad Hill can be spied again and even Blackpool Tower. The Old Man also has immediate depth to its view and its triangulation pillar stands on the edge of another of the big plunging drops that are a feature of a number of the Coniston fells. I have experienced the Old Man in sunshine and rain, and have even been forced to retreat from it by strong winds, but that day the weather conspired to make a special scene.

While a high mountain view, on a fine cloudless day, is a wonderful thing, conditions some might call bad weather can add a whole new dimension to a view. That day although the dark clouds hung above us, intense sunlight could be seen underneath the clouds and into the distance, the clarity was supreme and the half-shadowed, half-lit nature of the weather, lent the view a peculiar ever shifting, ever changing, two tone quality. After thirty minutes or so on the summit the clouds, which had temporarily lifted their skirts for us, dropped them down again and the rain began. We headed immediately down for Low Water, Coppermines Valley and the village of Coniston. However we did not mind the rain one bit, for our minds were filled with the heady memories of our finest wild walking experience to date.

The mood changed the following day as we went back to low level walking between Coniston and Grasmere. Stan, who had seemed pretty keen and up for it the previous two days, cut a silent almost ghostly presence that day. If we spoke to him he gave either a grunt or a short curt response. All had appeared so promising as I had shared the previous two days of hard walking with my best mate. It seemed as if a new and lifelong chapter of shared experiences in the hills was about to be added to our friendship. Now it seemed to me as if Stan had lost his enthusiasm. The truth was somewhat different and on reflection now I feel a bit guilty for doubting him. Yes, Stan was lacking in enthusiasm and yes, he was tired. But it was not due to the fells or the walking, which he had already decided he loved, but due to incessantly loud snoring from Peter, in the twin room they had shared the previous night. A wrecked night's sleep is probably the worst preparation for a long walk but the damage to Stan's spirits was short lived. When we returned from that holiday in September 1990, our friendship developed a new shared interest as we poured over maps, videos and guidebooks to plan for the next break.

In September 1991, we both purchased our first of *Wainwright's Pictorial Guides*. It may seem strange that it had taken us a year from finding out about Wainwright to buying his guides, but there was a reason for this. Whereas the recent books such as *Fellwalking with Wainwright* were available in our home town of Tunbridge Wells in the South-East, the *Pictorial Guides* were not to be found anywhere locally and it was only a chance encounter with them in a Keswick bookshop that led me to buy them. In those days they were still published by the *Westmorland Gazette* and the first two guides which I purchased, which were *The Southern Fells* and *The Northern Fells*, still sit on my bookshelves with a slightly different cover to the newer ones. Later the rest of the *Pictorial Guides*, along with the guide to the *Outlying Fells*, appeared in bookshops in Tunbridge Wells and were immediately purchased by us.

And yet even though I now had all the *Pictorial Guides* and had soon read them cover to cover, and even though I now had so many places and peaks I wanted to visit, I still had no specific plan or desire to complete all 214 of Wainwright's fells. Yes, I had doubled my tally to four

Wainwrights, but the sheer volume of hills I had not done was too massive to contemplate yet as a whole entity.

For now it was about the high places and the ridges and over the next year or two these would be the focus and would yield not only dozens of those new hills that a bagger often labels as 'ticks', but more importantly dozens of enduring life enhancing memories.

On High Mountains and Ridges

When I am old and can hopefully look back upon 50 odd years of hill walking, I think that my glorious days of discovery of the high places of Lakeland in the early 1990's, will stand out nostalgically as an especially memorable and joyous time. While a love of the Lake District encompasses valleys, rivers, tarns and lakes, there is no doubt in my mind that the most thrilling, exciting and wonderful places are the high fells and ridges above 2000 feet.

It is in these places that the worries and stresses of life can be escaped. From a remote mountain vantage one can survey humanity and existence and in doing so gain a sense of perspective on the fleeting problems and worries that occupy us for much of our day to day lives. The fact that the mountains don't really give a damn about you or your issues and will be there for millions of years after your memory is long forgotten, far from being a terrifying thought, is actually one that can alleviate a person's troubles through that very sense that the span of a human life is an insignificant thing. I have often found, in the high, remote and wild places, seemingly enormous personal issues can be reviewed from an unbiased and detached stance and as a result nagging problems often seem, or even become, of lesser importance. There is nothing like the high places for cleansing the mind.

However the summit of Scafell Pike is not perhaps the ideal place to get away from humanity and sooth troubles. England's highest point attracts many thousands of visitors each year. However on the perfect warm May day in 1991 that we chose to climb Scafell Pike, our thoughts were not of solitude or remoteness, but simply of the excitement of the anticipation of having our fifteen seconds of being the highest people in England.

I can of course see the appeal of climbing to the highest point in the land, even for someone who has never climbed a mountain before and will never climb one afterwards. Unfortunately because of this appeal Scafell Pike has become a magnet not only for genuine lovers of the hills, but also for people whose only objective is to go back and tell all and sundry that they have been to the highest place in the land. Again I have nothing against that as such, but all too often such people come very ill prepared for the task at hand. Some of the problem lies in the fact that the popularity of the fell, and the troop of people heading up and down it most days, leads people to believe that fell walking is an altogether easier and less risky pastime than it actually is. After all people as young as five have climbed Scafell Pike so surely anyone can just park at the bottom, romp up and have their time at the top of England and romp back down again? There's a good path, so surely there is no need to check out the route beforehand or take a map? It's a glorious day so surely you don't need to keep one eye on the weather? Unfortunately, all too often lack of preparation and consideration of distance, weather and gear lead to very nasty and sometimes fatal experiences.

The day I first climbed Scafell Pike there were people doing it in trainers and at the end of the walk I can recall a notable instance of people

Scafell Pike and Scafell from above Lingmell Gill

underestimating the mountain. We reached the car park at Wasdale Head knackered from our exertions. It was about 6 pm and cloud had now rolled in on the high fells. The signs were that poor weather was coming in and that some heavy rain would soon arrive. At this moment, a couple with a young boy of about seven years old approached us and said,

"Which mountain is Scafell Pike?"

We thought they were just interested in identifying the mountain from below rather than actually climbing it, so we pointed them in the right direction. Their next question however got us somewhat concerned.

"Looks like we can get up and back in a couple of hours. What do you reckon?"

Understanding that they wanted to climb the mountain, I informed them that it would probably take at least three hours to even reach the summit, let alone get back from it and that the weather looked like it was turning nasty and it was quite late to be setting off. I normally would not be so frank but I felt I had to be considering that this couple did not even know which mountain was Scafell Pike, had no idea how long it would take to climb and had a young child with them. They seemed to take some notice of what I had said and I watched them debate the issue for a minute or two, as we took off our walking gear and got ready to leave. It seemed that the mother was a little concerned about the venture, but the child had the blind enthusiasm of youth and the dad seemed too pig-headed to agree with the mother's concerns and so bring sense to the proceedings. So they headed off, regardless of my advice. I don't know what happened to them and had they not had a child with them I would not have cared too much. I did check the local news the next day and no-one seemed to have died or been rescued on Scafell Pike. I can only imagine the mother's sense won the day and they turned back, once the light began to fade and the rain began lashing down.

I wish this was the only time that this type of person had approached me in the hills, but it has been a fairly common occurrence in my near 20 years of hill walking. Several times I have had people come up to me on a summit and ask me which hill or mountain they have just climbed. How anyone can set off to climb a mountain without even knowing what they are climbing is beyond me.

Every year in July thousands of walkers descend on Wasdale Head to climb Scafell Pike as part of the Three Peaks Challenge. This challenge involves climbing the three highest mountains in each of mainland Britain's countries, Ben Nevis in Scotland, Snowdon in Wales and Scafell Pike in England and all within a 24 hour period. People are understandably attracted to the personal challenge of doing this and also to the added incentive of raising money for various charities. Unfortunately many people are underprepared for the rigours of not just one challenging climb, but three, without much rest in between each climb. The schedule usually also dictates that Scafell Pike, being the furthest of the three peaks from a main road, is climbed at night, something an experienced walker would need skill for, let alone a novice. Too often well meaning people, looking to do their bit for charity, will get a kind of blindness to their own exhaustion and the prevailing weather conditions. When tired, decision making tends to be less focused and concentration withers. Add to the tiredness the determination to achieve one's aim that often accompanies such undertakings and it can be a recipe for mountain disaster. Inexperienced walkers don't realise that even in July the high places can be frightening in the wrong conditions and the Mountain Rescue Service will testify to the number of call outs they receive from this annual event with people lost in high winds and driving rain, or just ill equipped for the challenge and exhausted by it.

Don't get me wrong, I am all for charity and there is no reason why a fit person with the right planning and a little experience should not be able to complete the Three Peaks Challenge. However I also feel that even aside from the safety issues of such an event there are other environmental considerations. Trying to complete such an exercise in 24 hours leaves very little time for the usual social niceties, and all too often people in their hurry use the mountain as a toilet, which is both unsightly and unwanted in the hills. If people need to do such a thing, perhaps they should bring a bag and a pooper scooper and take their mess back with them!

Perhaps also on a more controversial note, I would question whether the hills are even the place for such mass charity events. The environments of Ben Nevis, Snowdon and Scafell Pike are some of the most precious in these islands. These are national treasures, in the same way that Buckingham Palace or Leeds Castle is. There are many thousands of ways to raise money for charity without risking the delicate environment of our upland places. Many of these ways, such as the London to Brighton cycle challenge, The Great North Run, or The London Marathon are equally physically challenging for those wanting such a thing, but none of these spoil our precious natural environment to such an extent. Or better still money could be raised in many non mass challenges, such as completing the Coast to Coast route solo, or with a companion or two. Surely however, there must be a point when the well meaning and obvious benefits of raising money for a charity are outweighed by the damage and destruction caused by thousands of people using the hills in such a way.

Having said all of this about adequate preparation, I guess when you read of my own first account of Scafell Pike below, the words pot, kettle and black may spring to mind. Like on many other walks previously I had my usual gear with me, waterproofs, adequate food and drink, sun lotion and my trusty walking boots. As we ascended from Wasdale via The Corridor Route, the proportions of England's highest mountain excited and slightly unnerved us. I can still recall over 15 years later craning my neck from the early part of the path at valley level to look up over the ramparts of Lingmell towards the seemingly inaccessible summit of Scafell Pike. This was obviously going to be a big tough walk, an altogether more physical challenge that my only other 3000 foot climb, the gentle main line up Skiddaw. The same sense of a true mountain environment continued along the rocky shelf of The Corridor Route. Then at Lingmell Col we branched left onto the final pull up to the summit of England. We neglected the short detour to Lingmell, not being in true bagging mode at this stage in our walking careers.

There were perhaps 200 people crowding around the massive summit platform. We had to vie with some Spanish tourists for our fifteen seconds of being the highest people in England, before descending down the stone steps from the summit platform and allowing someone else to have their turn. While such crowds on summits are something of a personal hate of mine, being a lover of solitude, I don't moan too much about such things, as there are a great many places in the Lake District where solitude can be found when wanted.

That day the thrill was not however in being alone, or out on some limb of wilderness, it was simply the thrill of being at the highest place in England and the sense of a gradual progression of ever higher hills in the Lake District that had started with lowly Hoad Hill and had ended here. The thrill was perhaps tempered by a slight edge of sadness that there was never going to be anything higher to climb in England, but in another sense, had I known it, this was only to be the end of the first chapter of many in the hills and there was and still is so much more to explore.

Scafell Pike is indisputably the highest point in England, but it is not my personal favourite Lakeland viewpoint. Yes, it is a vast panorama and yes, it is amazing to find oneself looking seemingly a long way down on something that is nearly 3000 feet high like Great Gable, but I often feel that the view from the utmost summit lacks depth, being set in the middle of quite a broad plateau of a summit. I prefer the views from Skiddaw, Scafell and Helvellyn to the one from Scafell Pike, although others may beg to differ with me and are entitled to their opinion. How you judge a view depends on a number of deeply personal reactions to that view from within your own subconscious. Your reaction to what you see is as much about what's within you as what is on the outside.

My enjoyment of the view from England's highpoint was also tempered that day by a couple of rather unusual and embarrassing occurrences. Firstly the place where I chose to sit and look at the view was on a rock that proved to have a rather sharp point on it. As I sat down I heard a tell tale tearing noise that signified the rock point ripping through my trousers. The second problem was my boots. These were those same blister traps that I had worn on the Cumbria Way walk two years earlier. Over the course of two years of wrangling with my feet, the boots had eventually been tamed and they had either gradually moulded themselves into the shape of my feet, or my feet had gradually moulded themselves into the shape of my boots. Even though they were purely functional inanimate objects, I had become fond of these boots and they had been my constant companion on some of the best days of my life. The worn lines and grooves of those boots were testimony to many fine days in the hills. So when, just before the Scafell Pike holiday, I noticed that the soles of my beloved boots were wearing thin, I thought the only solution was to save these inanimate friends and get the boots resoled. A fine idea perhaps but instead of taking them to a reputable boot repair shop, I chose a budget price shoe repair kiosk. And that day, at the highest point of the highest mountain in England that decision came back on me with vengeance. I can confirm that the summit of Scafell Pike is definitely not the place for the soles of one's boots to start coming off, but that is what a glance at my boots now confirmed was happening. So there I was with a hole in my trousers and the soles of my boots coming off, in the company of about 200 people. It was time to go.

The trouble was that our choice of route down was not ideal for a wearer of boots with flapping soles and split trousers. We came down via Mickledore and the screes and by sods law about 150 of the 200 people on the summit had the same idea! As this horde followed us and much to the amusement of my two walking comrades, the soles on my boots came ever further off, till the boots resembled flip flops and the hole in my trousers became ever wider till it had the proportions of a kangaroo's pouch, a sight that must have in equal measure amused and horrified the 150 people behind me.

Fortunately the soles of the boots and the trousers just about lasted till I got back to the car. Had the soles come off, an embarrassing and humorous incident could have become a more serious one. All of which goes to show that preparation both before climbing a mountain and on the mountain itself is key. In fact although I have said that there are no rules to this hill bagging lark, I would add one codicil to that, be prepared.

In my own stubbornness through not getting an important item like my boots properly mended, or even discarded for a new pair, I could have encountered serious consequences. Luckily my under preparation just resulted in a good laugh for my mates and a probable point of discussion over a pint in the pub for about 200 other walkers.

Little was I to know, that day I climbed the highest mountain in England and it became only my 8th Wainwright summit that I was to 'bag' over 200 more Wainwrights before setting foot on the near neighbour and second highest mountain of Scafell. My hills CV, if you like, would have a glaring omission in it for over 15 years.

The same could not be said of the summits of the Coniston Round, which were by now becoming favourites of mine. The breaks of the early 1990's nearly always seemed to begin with a stay in Coniston followed by some variation of the various mountains that make up the Coniston round. Having previously made our way down from the Old Man of Coniston in rain, via the beautiful high mountain tarn of Low Water, we had better weather for our next assault on the round along the wonderful high ridge to Brim Fell and then, via Levers Hause, on to one of my favourite places, Swirl How.

Shakespeare famously wrote 'What's in a name? That which we call a rose by any other name would smell as sweet.' Far be it from me to question the words of The Bard but when it comes to hills, rather than roses, I have often found that mountains with interesting names tend to also have interesting summits. Helvellyn has something brooding and vaguely Satanic about its name, and the mountain itself with its superb scary ridges and cliffs, lives up to that name. The name of Sour Howes on the other hand does not particularly inspire one to go and climb it and a closer acquaintance confirms that the fell lives up to the image conjured up by its name. Swirl How provokes images of fingers of mist swirling around a high peak perched on the edge of a big drop, and closer acquaintance with this wonderful fell does not disappoint.

As you may have gathered by now, I am always a great fan of mountains whose summits are situated on the edge of a big plunge. To me places like that convey a true mountain atmosphere and also tend to give a greater sense of depth to a view. In this regard Swirl How is a classic with the cairn perched abruptly above a downfall of crags leading towards Little Langdale. Although the view does include a vast stretch of the foothills of South Lakeland, it is the view into the heart of the high mountains of Lakeland that makes this a classic. Particularly shapely in appearance from here are the Langdale Pikes, Bowfell and in the distance

Skiddaw. On one particular winter's day of note I remember taking the short route onto Swirl How from the Three Shire Stone at Wrynose Pass. It was one of those beautiful winter days where the sky is a pure deep blue and the wind is calm enough for the cold not to bite too hard on one's face. Stan and I set off as the first rays of this perfect morning reached the flanks of the mountainside. As we ascended over Little Carrs and Great Carrs (another Wainwright), Little Langdale way down below us was shrouded in a layer of mist. It was as if under that layer humanity slept and we were privileged to be on our own up high before the world woke up. From Swirl How the low rising sun lit up Seat Sandal and the Helvellyn range in hues of gold and orange and we could see that the layer of mist extended in a vast panorama that stretched across South Lakeland and rose and fell in little undulations as it encountered the smaller fells around the lakes of Coniston and Windermere. It was one of those summit moments that one thousand fold returns any amount of effort expended to get there; one of those moments where the past and the future, the movement of time and schedule that so dominate our modern lives, are forgotten and for a few moments there is only the now. Such moments are best experienced alone or in this case with a friend whose sense of joy is equal to your own. We felt the kings of the mountain on that February dawn.

By this time I was beginning to realise that in Stan I had another companion like my brother Peter, who I could share the hills with and who appreciated them and all they stood for in the same profound way that Peter and I did. Throughout the last nearly 20 years of walking, it has been a constant source of joy that I have had not just one walking companion, but two with whom I could share the wonders of the hills. The only thing I have against Stan, and it is not at all Stan's fault, is that he tends to be fitter and faster than me on the hills. I have always had a great amount of stamina in my broad shoulders and tree trunk like legs and this has served me well on long mountain days. However, I do sometimes wish that my legs could carry me a little faster and I do tend to find that Stan has this ability to leap his way down hills, like a hare, when I am floundering gingerly trying not to break an ankle about half a mile behind.

Having said this stamina is a good attribute to have when it comes to tackling some of Lakeland's big and famous rounds. The early 1990's were also for me and my walking companions about experiencing these great rounds for the first time. Names such as The Coledale Round, Newlands Round and Mosedale Round had suggested themselves to us as we poured over Wainwright's books and videos in the winter of 1990/1991. The great thing for any walker about rounds such as these is that you expend most of your energy early on, getting up above say 2000 feet, and from there onwards have a high level horseshoe shaped promenade, where glorious views are soaked up for hours on end with only a little ascending or descending. For baggers there is an extra plus as these rounds include usually at least half a dozen of Wainwright's fells for the same effort that can be expended on other days just bagging one fell.

The Coledale Round is justifiably popular. Some people will prefer to tackle Grizedale Pike first, but I have always found that this is a nice peak to end the day with, as after some initial steepness and looseness its descent is gradual and grassy. It's a personal preference but Causey Pike has usually been my first summit when I have done the Coledale Round. Strictly speaking I have always understood that The Coledale Round proper would comprise Causey Pike, Scar Crags, Sail, Eel Crag (or Crag Hill as the Ordnance Survey Maps refer to it) and finally Grizedale Pike, as these summits form the natural high horseshoe around Coledale Beck. However, there are also several other Wainwright fells, such as Wandope, Hopegill Head and of course the massive Grasmoor, that can be added onto your own version of the Coledale Round. In fact over the years I think I have done about five or six different versions of a Coledale Round and of course one of the joys of fellwalking is devising your own routes and moving away from the traditional rounds. You can make your own Coledale Round as easy or tough as you wish to. On a day when I was feeling particularly full of energy I once did about ten Wainwright fells in one day here, but generally I tend to like taking my time on the ridges of Coledale and there are so many different routes on this range that if you neglect say the slightly out on a limb Whiteside one day, it can always be an excuse, if one were needed, to come back to this delectable range again.

The mountains of Coledale and Newlands are for me about graceful shapes and symmetry. These shapes after a few years of fell walking become familiar and loved outlines and one of the most appealing shapes is that of Causey Pike. Causey Pike is one of those summits that generate a great deal of affection in walkers, even though it is not especially high or fantastically craggy or dramatic. Its summit knobble is just simply a wonderful place to be and its familiar serpentine spine is pointed out by many who never even climb the fell.

The first time I climbed Causey Pike it was by the time honoured and direct route to Sleet Hause and from that flat depression up steeply on to the summit. This route has its merits, being the shortest linear approach to the summit of Causey Pike. In making its beeline it quite deliberately avoids Rowling End and instead heads up the enclosed flanks of the fell. And why not some may say? Causey Pike after all is the Wainwright fell and therefore the objective. Rowling End is just the blunt end of the fell and not baggers' territory. For too many years I thought the same way, as in my mind I always headed for the summit I wanted to tick off. However as the years have slipped by and I have matured in my attitude to walking, I have begun to realise that part of the joy of doing the Wainwrights is doing the slightly unusual things, the routes that are not the usual popular ones that on a Sunday will find hundreds of people trooping lemming like up them. So having climbed Causey Pike several times I decided to finally break away from the lemming inside me and instead branched off the usual Causey Pike path and headed for a steeper, narrower path that leads up onto Rowling End. And as with many other times when I have chosen to forsake the hordes, I found here a new delight. For the path up onto Rowling End is one of those narrow, shelf-like paths, which hugs the edge of a steep drop without there ever being any real sense of danger. On such paths height seems to be gained much quicker and the effort seems less as you become immersed in the pleasure of your immediate surroundings.

The route up onto Rowling End is simply a joy to tread. Towards the top the path levels off a little and there are some nice flat, grassy seats to be found to flop onto and contemplate the view down towards the village of Stair and the Newlands Valley, or lie back and contemplate the sky with the heather behind for a pillow. Rowling End is not so much climbed for its summit, for the summit is neither a tick towards a list, nor is it a particularly well defined place, being merely a pile of stones at the butt end of a high flat promenade. No, the delight of Rowling End is to be had in the joy of the climb and the path and in watching the hordes ascend the time honoured route up Causey Pike, from a situation of comparative seclusion. More and more as my Wainwright tally has increased, I have found it is not always necessarily the case that the summit is the high point of a walk . There is equal joy to be had in the act of climbing, finding peace and solitude on unfrequented sinewy paths and in beautiful intimate places. I have learnt to spend less time hurrying to the summit, as if it were the sole objective, and more time enjoying the walk as a whole, and making immersion in the whole walk the objective.

But of course there are Wainwrights to be had aplenty on the Coledale Round and if you want to attain them it is best not to hang around on Rowling End for too long! From the broad heather and grass top of

Rowling End at approximately 1400 feet, Causey Pike rears up rather impressively and the remaining 600 feet of ascent looks hard work. However, the climb onto Causey Pike is yet another delight and never feels like effort or slog, due to the beauty of the winding path and the ever increasing sense of height. Thinking of that climb, I am reminded of the contrasts that can be had in different days on the same hill. When I first climbed Causey Pike as part of a complete Coledale Round in 1992, it was a warm September day. Stan and Peter were with me and we took the usual route up the hill accompanied by a number of other walkers. On the top of Causey Pike it was warm, the sky was blue and T-shirts were worn as we soaked in the wonderful view for half an hour.

By contrast, during a recent trip up Causey Pike in October 2006, the weather was cold. Although I started the climb in the afternoon, there was still a frost on the shaded parts of the path up Rowling End. The sun was out but it provided little warmth or comfort and all around were threatening looking shower clouds. A strong breeze accompanied and chilled me, although out of the breeze I still managed to find some

Catbells from Rowling End in Autumn Colours

delightful spots to recline and soak in the late autumn warmth, as if in an echo of summer. I met no-one on Rowling End, but did meet about five walkers coming down Causey Pike as I began my ascent up it. By this time there were showers over Skiddaw and Helvellyn, and judging by the white fingers of precipitation that came from the black clouds, they were showers of hail and snow. And yet in the Vale of Keswick the sun still shone and a full rainbow could be seen spanning across the low lying fields of the Vale. As I ascended further the snow shower gradually moved towards and then over the great pyramidal hunks of Hindscarth and Robinson, directly opposite me and perhaps only a mile or so away as the crow flies. From a high and sheltered niche near the top of Causey Pike, I donned my waterproofs and watched the eerie white fingers of snow drape themselves around first Hindscarth and then Robinson, until the fells succumbed to their grasp and disappeared from sight. And yet apart from the odd spot of sleety snow, my vantage point was dry and the sun still shone over the Vale of Keswick. Five minutes later the snow shower had rolled on towards Buttermere and the peaks of The High Stile range, and Causey Pike and I had both escaped its clutches. However on the actual summit of Causey Pike the wind picked up. The view was still remarkable, with the ridges of Newlands, the Central spine and the Helvellyn Range laid out before me in side profiled symmetry and ever increasing order of height. But these were not the conditions for stopping. I took my gloves off to take a photo, quickly put them back on before my fingers froze and left glad to have avoided hypothermia.

So which was the finer of these two contrasting ascents of Causey Pike? The first ascent was about the summit and the summit was duly enjoyed to the full on a glorious warm day. On the later ascent the brief stop on the summit made it just a minor occurrence on a day that had been dominated by solitude, the wonderful path up Rowling End and the sublime vagaries of the weather. The only answer I can give is that each of these 214 Wainwrights can be a different thing on a different day and neither day was better than the other, just different. Doing the Wainwrights in a strictly factual sense is about touching 214 cairns or trig points or piles of stones or whatever else is there, but it is also about so much more.

Before moving on from Causey Pike, it is worth mentioning the one other interesting feature of the fell. Not only is Causey Pike a great viewpoint, but its summit sits upon a rocky knobble that requires a little bit of scrambling. It is true that this extremely brief excursion into the realm of hauling oneself up rock can be circumvented, but it is probably the least scary of all the scrambly bits of Lakeland, and anyone who baulks at it should really think twice before tackling any of Lakeland's more celebrated scary places. All it really amounts to is a short cleft of rock, perhaps eight feet high, with good handholds. One quick push and stretch and you are on Causey Pike summit. I've always enjoyed doing this little rocky step and it has made the summit sweeter. The knobble is also the first and most prominent of the series of undulations on Causey Pike that Wainwright compared to a serpent's undulating back. It is a feature that enables Causey Pike to be one of those fells that is readily identified and keeps popping up in views from other fells. In conclusion, Causey Pike although only 2000 feet has much to be proud about.

From Causey Pike, a wonderful high level ridge walk continues over Scar Crags and Sail (both Wainwright summits), before ascending, via a steep but satisfying ridge onto the first of the Coledale giants Eel Crag. For me the Coledale Fells contain four of the finest of Lakeland's high mountains: Eel Crag, Grasmoor, Hopegill Head and Grizedale Pike. These four great fells radiate from the high central apex of Coledale Hause and

The heart of the Coledale Road

having made the climb to the Hause they all can easily be climbed in one go and without too much effort expended. The view from each of these four is very fine, yet although all are in close proximity, each view is entirely different and therefore each fell uniquely characteristic.

Let's begin with Eel Crag, which from the A66 coming out of Keswick seems the central and highest point of the Coledale Group, although Grasmoor behind it is in fact just higher. Eel Crag is only some 700 feet higher than Causey Pike but that difference between 2000 feet and above 2500 feet makes all the difference in terms of all round views. Were it not for the bulk of Grasmoor just overtopping it and obscuring a few degrees of the view, Eel Crag might lay claim to be the finest view in Lakeland. Even so it is still one of Lakeland's finest summits. It is a view both of distance and depth. It shares with Skiddaw the great sweeping arc of the coastal plains of Cumbria, leading out to the Solway Firth and lending it a positively awesome sense of height. But this is also a view of and into mountains, particularly to the east and south, as ridge upon ridge and fold upon fold of mountains spread into the distance. All of Lakeland's highest mountains are in view and a great time can be had identifying something like 75 of the Wainwright fells in view, either with the help of *Wainwright's North Western Fells* guidebook or, if you have been doing this bagging thing for a few years and want to see how much you have learnt, without the guidebook. A survey column or triangulation pillar marks the highest point and a walk a few yards east reveals another of those wonderful drops that make a viewpoint, as the mountain plunges down into the depths of Coledale in tumbling crags. However Eel Crag is another of those crag and tail type mountains that are typical of Lakeland, so although the crags drop fiercely down to Coledale Beck, the route down to the gap between Eel Crag and Grasmoor is of an easy rounded gradient and predominantly grassy.

There is then a stiff pull up onto Grasmoor, the highest point of the Coledale Group, but it is well worth the effort. As you walk along a shelf like path dramatic views of Buttermere and Crummock Water come into sight. When the sun is shining these twin lakes, separated by a narrow channel of land, sparkle like diamonds far below. The view from Grasmoor summit is equally as extensive as that from Eel Crag. Westwards it is unobstructed and probably even finer than Eel Crag. On a clear day you will easily see the Isle of Man, which often seems to hover, as if suspended in mid air, on the Irish Sea. Wainwright seemed to be a bit at odds with Isle of Man spotters, but personally I have always enjoyed picking it out. Along with Southern Scotland's sentinel Criffel, sight of the

Isle of Man is generally a benchmark for good clarity. If you can see Ireland or Wales, well that's another matter and ever rarer! For a true sense of height, wander a few yards away from Grasmoor's summit in a westerly direction to a lower cairn, where Loweswater comes dramatically into view.

Heading back to the hub of Coledale Hause and over Sand Hill you soon arrive at Hopegill Head. To me, if Eel Crag and Grasmoor are muscular and masculine in form and appearance, then Hopegill Head and Grizedale Pike are more graceful and feminine in form and outline. Hopegill Head, like Swirl How in the Coniston Fells, is a place where the summit is perched on the edge of a drop, and its beauty for me lies in this small summit and the view down the wild Hope Gill, which makes a perfect photo frame with Cockermouth and the northern plains as a backdrop. You can't really escape any other walkers on the small summit of Hopegill Head, so it is a summit best experienced alone.

There is no need to return to Coledale Hause to climb the final great fell of the group, Grizedale Pike. There is a delightful airy path that skirts the edge of Hobcarton Crag, with views plunging down to Whinlatter Forest (whose man made acres you will either love or hate, but I personally have grown to rather like). Whereas the summits of Grasmoor and Eel Crag were wide and broad, Grizedale Pike, like Hopegill Head, has a small dainty summit. I usually find myself here late in the day, as I prefer to end an excursion of Coledale here. As the shadows lengthen and the hills turn rich colours of gold and orange and the hordes head away from the fells, Grizedale Pike is a wonderful place to sit and to admire the Vale of Keswick and the massive architecture of Skiddaw. From the summit of Grizedale Pike the path makes a fairly direct beeline down to Braithwaite and the amenities of civilization that you have for a few hours revelled in removing yourself from, now call to your tired body and aching limbs. Many are the delights of Coledale and endless days can be had devising different routes and revisiting different summits in different weathers and at different times of day. The Coledale group is so much more than just a collection of summits occupying a relatively small area on a map.

Sitting next to the Coledale Round, and equally if not more celebrated, is the Newlands Round. Yet for reasons which will become apparent, I have never quite got to grips with Newlands as I have with Coledale. Yes I have done all the summits of the round and more than just the once! But whereas the weather has conspired in my favour on Coledale's peaks, it has in the main conspired against me with Newlands. This is why I have always maintained that it is one thing to do a summit but it is another thing to really experience a summit. An extreme and very unfortunate example would be to imagine for a moment a Wainwright bagger who had fallen foul of the weather Gods. Cursed like Job, the Gods had conspired to ensure that each and every summit this poor walker visited was in cloud or misted over. Yet this bagger had persisted with all the spirit of Job, until he had conquered all 214 Wainwright summits. So in the technical sense he would therefore have completed his round of Wainwrights even though he had not seen the view from any summit. This is why I again say that my philosophy about the 214 summits has increasingly become far more about the whole experience and that includes the view. So yes I have just completed my round of Wainwrights, but I must now go back and visit all those hills where I have not yet seen a clear view, or else I will somehow feel that I have not done them justice. I am sad enough (sad in the derogatory, modern sense of the word) to actually keep a database of the Wainwrights and one column in that database is for whether I have seen a clear view or not. I shall not rest till I have seen a clear view from all the 214 summits and I make no apologies for that.

All of which brings me back to the Newlands Round and tales of bad luck. Unlike the Coledale fells, which have yielded their views to me on a number of occasions, Newlands has been reticent to reveal the best of itself to me. Yes I have seen the views from some of the fells around the Newlands valley, but in several excursions I have been generally cursed with bad luck. The first time I did the Newlands Round was in May 1992 on a short break and accompanied solely by my brother Peter. I have traditionally found early to mid May to be one of the most delightful times of year to walk on the fells. Temperatures tend to be on the pleasant side of warm and the odd shower clears the views. However this particular break was timed for the Spring Bank Holiday at the end of May and for once in this country a Bank Holiday coincided with a heat wave. I have generally found that comfortable temperatures for walking are somewhat different to comfortable temperatures for sitting on a beach and sun bathing. For me a ground temperature of between 16 and 20 degrees Celsius is about ideal for walking. Lower than that and cool clothing tends to be needed on the tops. Warmer than that and walking becomes a sweaty uncomfortable business. The day we did the Newlands Round it reached 26 degrees Celsius at ground level, which if you were sitting in your garden or down at the beach would not seem especially hot. However when one is struggling up Scope End and Hindscarth, with water supplies rapidly diminishing and the sun beating continuously down, thoughts of Lawrence of Arabia, deserts and oases come to mind. In addition, and as bad as the heat that day, although not as physically discomforting, was the haze that accompanied it.

Of all the most pointless types of weather for a lover of fell walking, I consider heat haze is a very strong contender. Strong winds can be irritating and force you off the fell, but they can also be exhilarating. Rain and mist can obscure a view and be uncomfortable for a while, but once you are soaked it can be quite enjoyable, and if you are lucky the mist may clear or the rain may abate. Heat haze has no redeeming qualities. For a lover of view bagging like me it is the enemy. The heat haze that day as we struggled and sweated up to Dale Head, the highest of the Newlands' fells, was so extreme and thick that it was more like a summer fog. But it was a fog without redemption. There was little chance of rising above the fog and experiencing an inversion with the clouds down below us, as might have happened in the chill of autumn or winter. This haze was a complete view killer. I had read eagerly about Dale Head, with its large cairn perched on the edge of an abyss and views plunging down to Newlands Beck with Skiddaw framed in the distance. The reality that hazy day on the summit, was that the cairn itself was about the only aspect of the view that we could see clearly. We could just about make out the hazy looking bottom of the Newlands Valley below us, a classic glaciated U-shaped valley, but not done any justice that hazy day. Skiddaw, a mere half dozen miles away, had all but vanished and was just a vague suggestion of an outline. On my only other trip to Dale Head, low cloud hung over the fell and I again saw no view! So Dale Head has probably been my most unlucky Wainwright, and seeing a perfect view from that fell is one of my highest priorities in the hills now I have completed the 214. I have twice been there in name, but I have yet to experience the true spirit of the place. Often when I have returned to a fell or mountain after having seen no view previously, I have found that the summit has saved something special for me. Perhaps Dale Head has a golden day in the future just waiting for me and perhaps the recollections of haze and cloud will one day be forgotten and replaced with an indelible experience. Such are the glorious uncertainties of hill rambling, but would any of us really have it any other way?

Views sustain the mind, but after we left Dale Head for the return leg of the Newlands Round, it was more the body that needed sustaining. Dale Head tarn was perhaps the highlight of an otherwise forgettable day, although I expect the other walkers who witnessed me bathing in the tarn, with nothing but Speedo swimming trunks on, probably tried to expunge that part of the day from their minds. It was shortly after we left Dale Head tarn, that I ran out of drink. No problem, I thought, as I filled my water bottle from the upper reaches of Newlands Beck. The trouble is that the upper reaches of Newlands Beck do not quite have the flowing qualities of the mature beck, especially after several days of dry weather. A cursory glance at the beck water I had just scooped up into my bottle revealed a nice thriving eco-system of insect larvae and other bugs. At this point I felt a kinship with some Ancient Mariner style character stranded at sea, with water around in profusion, but all undrinkable. The miles over High Spy and Maiden Moor still evoke memories of haze and dehydration. I cursed those safety tips I had read in countless guide books about always having adequate food and water for your walk. What was I supposed to do, I grumpily thought, carry a water tank on my back? On Maiden Moor, Peter, ever the elder brother, revealed that he had in a slightly annoying but undeniably sensible way, kept and rationed a carton of orange juice in his rucksack. You never forget someone sharing such items with you on the fells, just as you never forget it if they don't. That day Peter shared the orange juice with me and we remained brothers!

But although Newlands has been slow to reveal itself to me, I still have a love of these fells. Newlands, like Coledale, is a collection of beautiful shapes, which pop up in views from other adjacent fells and over the years become friends. Catbells and Scope End are low but striking in appearance. The great wedges of Hindscarth and Robinson always remind me of a couple of Egypt's pyramids. Newlands' fells are not foreboding or aggressive; they are simply beautiful and majestic. They are fells which imprint themselves on the subconscious and can be recalled at will in the mind's eye.

Scary Places

I will be the first to admit that rocky places with big drops on either side are not my natural environment. That is not to say that I don't have a head for heights, or that I don't enjoy scrambling. However, I tend to approach such things, especially first time, with an equal mixture of excitement and dread, that tends to swing more towards excitement if the scary place turns out to be easier or more enjoyable than expected and tends to swing more towards dread if what I have read about the scary place turns out to be a gross under-exaggeration of the truth.

Fortunately Alfred Wainwright wrote books for walkers and not rock climbing types. Wainwright himself admitted that his legs were too long to be good for climbing. Luckily for us fell walkers the scary places of Lakeland are described in great detail in Wainwright's guidebooks. They are also described from a walker's perspective. If Wainwright says that a crag or rake is for climbers only, a humble walker can rest assured that he won't want to go there. Likewise if Wainwright says that a ridge or arête is within the capabilities of most walkers with a head for heights, then you can generally expect that most walkers can do it.

Wainwright's guides provide the sort of reassurance and level of detail that will comfort a walker unfamiliar with the realms of mild scrambling. However when it comes to Scotland's scary places such reassurance and detail is sometimes impossible to find in a land that is so much vaster than the Lake District and has so many scary places on its many hundreds of mountains. As well as completing the Wainwrights, I have also climbed over 50 of Scotland's Munros (mountains over 3000 feet) and have encountered my fair share of scary places in the Highlands. And I have learnt one thing, the guidebooks tend to slightly under-emphasise the fear factor for a walker of average scrambling capabilities and head for heights like me. In a Scottish guidebook a passage might read 'contour down the rough slopes of Ben Whatever, which involves some mild scrambling'. When you are actually doing Ben Whatever you feel that what should have been written is 'take the terrifying and brown underpants inducing set of rocky ledges, without a path, and with several moments where you feel that your life may be about to end, until eventually you reach the safety of ground level, shaking and incontinent'. In all seriousness Scotland's mountain guidebooks are written by some of the people I most revere in the walking world and these people are hardened and used to Scottish experiences. Just as Scotland is a higher, vaster, craggier place than Lakeland, so its mountains routes are generally longer, wilder and at times scarier.

Wainwright wrote his guidebooks from the perspective of an intimate knowledge of Lakeland's hills, although he was also highly knowledgeable about Scotland having climbed many mountains and photographed all 277 (at that time) Munro's (there are now 284, but that's another matter). Scotland's guidebook writers are merely writing from the perspective of a place where there are literally dozens of Striding Edges and Shamrock Traverses, and a lot much much worse. It is worth bearing in mind that the word scrambling basically means anything that requires the use of hands as well as feet. This by definition encompasses a whole world of experience, from the simplest short scramble, like the little rocky knobble on the summit of Causey Pike, to a more serious undertaking such as Sharp Edge, to where scrambling merges with very simple and basic rock climbing on something like Jack's Rake. The lines between scrambling and rock climbing are blurred and quite difficult to understand, but at its most diluted I would say that scrambling ends and rock climbing begins anywhere where a person would feel more comfortable with a rope and other climbing gear. I have not yet ventured into the climbers realm, although if I want to complete my other hills ambition and climb all the 284 Scottish Munros, I will have to enter the world of the rock climber to complete most of the Black Cuillin Munros on Skye. Nonetheless climbing will very much be a reluctant means to an end for me. If I do the Cuillin Ridge it will be in the company of hardened climbing types on a guided course.

All of this is a prelude for my own personal account and description of some of the scary places of Lakeland and a few by comparison in Scotland. If you are like me, someone who falls midway between the extreme poles of 'turns to a jelly when confronted with any sort of drop' and 'hangs from rock faces using nothing but fingers and chalk', I hope my honest descriptions will prove valuable. If your legs do turn to jelly at the thought of steep drops and rocky places, turn to the next chapter as this chapter is no place for you. If on the other hand you are someone who hangs from the sheer face of Scafell Crag for fun, then you may indulge in a laugh at the expense of my own efforts.

It is worth bearing in mind, before you set off to climb something like Striding Edge or Sharp Edge for the first time, that countless thousands of people have gone before you, including children and octogenarians. There is nothing here that cannot be done with a little spirit and most of these places I have called scary are, if you have a little head for heights and are sensible, extremely rewarding and satisfying. They afford the mere walker a sense of the mountaineer's world. In doing them a great sense of achievement and ambition fulfilled can be had. When I say achievement and ambition, I again mean that type of personal achievement and ambition that cares not for fame or fortune and is the purer for it. For no-one will applaud your achievement if you run down Keswick's main street shouting that you have just done Sharp Edge.

Striding Edge was my first scary Lakeland place and I had read and fantasised about it for months before actually setting out to do it. The aerial view of Striding Edge, from the final push up to Helvellyn, has appeared on countless postcards and in many guidebooks. It looks intimidating when viewed from above but then a lot of mountain features looks worse from a little distance than when close up and under foot. Admittedly in winter conditions, with snow or ice on the edge, it is a dangerous mountaineering proposition. However, in calm fair weather conditions, it lives up to expectations in terms of excitement, but does not evoke too many feelings of dread. It is an exhilarating and enjoyable scary place, rather than one that leaves you shaking, unless you shake at the slightest incline or mention of rocky places, in which case you will have already moved on to the next chapter. I have often found that approaching such places for the first time, it is very easy to get psyched out from carrying on. The key is not to let the mind play games with you before hand but to wait till you get to the scary place and have it in front of you and you will either find that in intimate acquaintance it suits you and you enjoy it, or that it is not for you and you want to turn back.

Striding Edge and Helvellyn were names that evoked a harsh and unforgiving mountain before I climbed them and as I approached High Spying How, which is the place where normal easy fell walking gives way to something a little more exciting and tricky, I admit I was more nervous than excited. However, once actually embarked upon the edge, I realised that it was actually rather enjoyable. For the most part the edge is fairly level but quite narrow. It requires a little gumption to keep to the crest, but the drops are not entirely immediate and in calm non-wintry conditions it feels quite safe while still being exposed enough to be exciting and exhilarating. In fact I have seen people struggling on minor ledge paths away from the actual crest of the edge and appearing in much more difficulty than they would have been if they had just followed the crest. Only at the end of Striding Edge is there a bit of an obstacle to progress in the form of a knobble of rock, about 12 feet high. It's quite

Kevin on Striding Edge

easy to get up this obstacle, but once on top the 12 foot rock chimney to get down the other side looks a little daunting. Take heart though in the fact that it is easier to negotiate than it looks and there are good handholds all the way down. Having said this, and again adopting my confessional policy of honesty about such things, the first time I did Striding Edge, my mind and nerves got the better of me and I bypassed this rocky knobble. Instead I took a rough and rather loose ledge path that runs around the base of the knobble. Having since gone over the knobble, I can testify that the bypass path is every bit as awkward as keeping to the crest of the ridge and does not have any of the sense of exhilaration to be had from sticking to the crest.

Having tackled this obstacle and effectively completed Striding Edge, there still remains the final steep and scrambly clamber up onto the flat plateau of Helvellyn's summit. I have always found this airy scramble to be more exhilarating than frightening. However I did once see a couple of walker's so in fear of this final clamber that they ended up trying to contour around the flanks of Helvellyn's face. Had they not been shouted at by about 20 walkers and urged to come back to the main path, their course would have led them straight to the fearful plunge of cliffs on the face of the mountain, from where the only foreseeable route for a non-climber would be a fall straight down into Red Tarn beneath!

For those who do not suffer too much from vertigo, the final pull onto Helvellyn is one of the most thrilling places a walker can experience in the Lake District. Directly beneath you is the classic picture postcard view of Striding Edge, looking more terrifying in profile and now you can see the drops on both sides. You can feel a certain pride at having conquered the edge and a sense of awe and wonder at the edge beneath you. The first time I did Striding Edge, I was so keen to get to the top of the third highest mountain in England that I rather rushed this final haul. Subsequently however I have taken to stopping on this amazing steep face to appreciate the feeling of height and space, which are matched by only a few places that a walker can attain in Lakeland. If you close your eyes here for a moment and then open them suddenly, this sense of space and drop is almost overwhelming.

Helvellyn has a view that befits one of the highest places in England and it is one of my personal favourites. I have often found that being high does not necessarily always guarantee a sense of height, but here on Helvellyn's summit there is little doubting how high you are. It seems as if every peak and bump in Lakeland is arrayed around you. Scafell and Scafell Pike, the only mountains higher in the Lake District, are sufficiently distant so as not to obscure what is effectively a 360 degree panorama. I am an emotional man and big views like this often bring tears to my eyes. These are not tears of sadness but of joy and of wonder. I challenge even the stony hearted not to be impressed by the view from Helvellyn. A wander to the edge of the summit cliffs, taking care of course, reveals an amazing double tiered effect of sheer height, as first Red Tarn appears way beneath you at the bottom of the cliffs, and further out and much further down sits beautiful Ullswater. Here 3000 feet seems somehow more to the mind.

I was glad the first time I did Helvellyn to have done Striding Edge in ascent, before descending down Swirral Edge, as I think the walk is finer this way round. The highlights come at the start of the day when you are freshest and Striding Edge is also more exciting and longer than Swirral Edge. Indeed the first time I did Helvellyn, Striding Edge met and exceeded my expectations, whereas Swirral Edge, which I had also heard nasty things about, was a bit of a let down, seeming short and quite easy by comparison. Swirral Edge should not present any difficulties in good weather and you will find it easier than Striding Edge. However under ice or snow, or in high wind or poor visibility, Swirral Edge comes into its own as a fearful place. Accidents are quite frequent here and if you fall off Swirral Edge the next stop is Red Tarn several hundred feet below. Accidents can also happen towards the end of a days walking, when the mind starts to tire and wander, so take care on Swirral Edge.

The final reward of a classic day in the fells is the summit of Catstycam, not only another Wainwright summit for the list, but also a very fine view point, enhanced by a small summit on the edge of a precipitous downfall of crags. The view of Ullswater from here is dominant and perhaps even finer than that from Helvellyn. There is also another bonus for leaving this summit as your last highlight of the day, instead of bagging it first. For if you reach the summit of Catstycam after about 4 or 5 o'clock in the afternoon you may well have the summit to yourself. It is the kind of summit best appreciated in solitude or with kindred spirits. There is too little space on Catstycam to accommodate hordes!

The walk back to Glenridding can be varied by taking in yet another Wainwright in the form of Birkhouse Moor, which is yet another fine viewpoint for Ullswater, although an unexciting summit otherwise. It was not until May 2005 that I finally bagged Birkhouse Moor, having thought previously that I had already done it. I was later hauled up by Wainwright's guidebooks which told me that on previous climbs of

Helvellyn via Striding Edge, in my excitement to do the edge, I had missed the top of Birkhouse Moor altogether. There were a few more mopping up exercises at the end of my Wainwright round, but at least I figured with Birkhouse Moor that it gave me another excuse, if one were needed, to climb Helvellyn. So completes one of the finest circular mountain walks to one of the finest mountains.

Having done Striding Edge and Swirral Edge my appetite for all things edge like in the Lake District and for scary places in general was well and truly whetted. If I can do Striding Edge, I thought, what's to stop me doing Sharp Edge on Blencathra. So in September 1991, Stan and I set out to do just that. Peter however decided against Sharp Edge and instead opted to climb Blencathra via the rounded Blease Fell. As we stood by Scales Tarn and pondered the little ant-like figures of people crawling along the razorback of Sharp Edge, thoughts of the comfort of Blease Fell and Peter climbing it without a care in the world kept occurring to me. In truth at that point, I was more nervous than Stan, who has an irritating habit of appearing fearless and calm in scary places, when I am experiencing something akin to a near death experience. Scales Tarn is a beautiful stretch of water lying in a classic glaciated hollow beneath Tarn Crags and the summit ridge of Blencathra. But as I sat by its peaceful waters my eyes were fixated on the ants heading along Sharp Edge. I had something of the all consuming feeling and nervous focus to be had before an appointment with the dentist or before an exam. From Scales Tarn, Sharp Edge has an almost two dimensional profile and this means that the people going along it really do look they are going along a knife edge arête. In reality this is not quite the case.

The good thing about Sharp Edge, for anyone like me who does such things, but does them with due trepidation, is that it is much shorter than Striding Edge. However on the downside there is more of a sense of exposure and imminent drops. I exhibit a tell tale sign when the excitement and exhilaration of something enjoyable like Striding Edge is replaced by the nervous anticipation of something a little more tricky like Sharp Edge. I tend to go very quiet. And as we started along Sharp Edge I went very quiet. This was not helped by two things. Firstly Stan kept reminding me that I was being very quiet and secondly the sun was directly ahead of us as we walked along Sharp Edge, its glare making it difficult to see the next stage of the edge. In my mind, with the way ahead blinded by the sun, the dangers of the unknown increased. With hindsight, I can now testify that my mind was ruling to some extent over the reality of what lay beneath my feet. For apart from a slightly awkward exposed shuffle along a slab polished by numerous nervous clenched behinds, the ground beneath you is no more difficult than Striding Edge. In fact towards the end of the edge, I found myself actually starting to enjoy it and engaged in something more than just monosyllabic conversation with Stan. I found the final scramble up Foule Crag a delight, although it is a steep scramble requiring frequent use of the hands. By this time Peter's figure had popped up on the summit ridge above us and it was not long before we joined him.

From the top of Foule Crag it is a surprisingly flat promenade along the summit ridge of Blencathra to the highest point Hallsfell top. This is a wonderful ridge, which after the nervous exertions and use of hands on Sharp Edge you can stroll across with hands in pockets. This is effectively part of the Saddleback that gives Blencathra its alternative, but less romantic and more prosaic name. The views are now expansive, especially out eastwards, where the vast flat plateau of the M6 corridor eventually rises up to the level ridges of the Pennines. The summit of Blencathra is perhaps surprisingly only marked with a little pile of slates but that does not matter. Other summits have larger and bolder cairns, trig points and other furniture, yet lack the drama and majesty of the summit of Blencathra. Here the sense of height is paramount, as the eye trends down the full span of the mountain to the A66 below. The constant stream of tiny vehicles heading along the dual carriageway, although not ideal in any view, nonetheless give a certain perspective to how high the summit is above the landscape below. Fine views are had over the little watery jewel of Tewit Tarn and south to Thirlmere. The central spine of Lakeland is well arrayed, as are the Newlands and Coledale fells. There is also a fairly good side on view of most of Derwent Water, although the views from Skiddaw Little Man of that lake are superior. Behind you to the North is the heather clad loneliness of the Northern Fells and behind that on a clear day Solway, Criffel and the Galloway hills. But perhaps most striking of all in the view from the summit of Blencathra is the narrow rocky ridge that makes a beeline for the highest point of the fell and curves impressively down beneath you to the valley floor. This ridge is Hall's Fell or Narrow Edge.

It is not without good reason that Wainwright describes Hall's Fell as the finest ascent route to any mountain in the district. Yet for some reason I have always found that Sharp Edge is more popular, as people are drawn by the lure and reputation of that name. That is not to say that you are likely to be alone on Hall's Fell, but in my experience it certainly does not attract the crowds like Sharp Edge and is therefore more of a connoisseurs route. The initial part of Hall's Fell, from the kennels at Gategill (noise of dogs predominant here, but preferable to noise of cars), is a slog up bracken and heather, although the route is always quite obvious. It is only above the 2000 foot contour that the excitement really begins to mount and from here onwards to the summit of Blencathra is a delight. The ridge is quite narrow and rocky in places, although there is nearly always a bypass path below and although the crest has a sense of exposure and height, the sheer drops are not immediately at hand and I have always found the experience more enjoyable and exciting than terrifying. I have always stuck to the crest and there is no reason why an able walker with a bit of a head for heights should not do so. As with all such edges and ridges though, the proposition can be a lot more dangerous under snow, ice or in high winds.

Oddly enough it was on my first ascent of Hall's Fell, in May 1993, that I had my first encounter with a Wainwright bagger and in doing so the seeds of my own possible completion of the 214 summits were sown. Up till that time I had merely been doing as many new fells as I could, without any real sense of counting them or completing them all. I know now that my 50th Wainwright fell was Great Carrs but I had no idea it was my 50th when I did it. I had no real concept of being a bagger, or any real desire to do all the fells in the guidebooks. I imagined in the early days that there would be some fells that I would probably never have the inclination to visit.

Here on Hall's Fell I can pinpoint an exact moment in time when a change and a sense of focus came into my fell ramblings. On the crest of Hall's Fell, I met a man who bore more than a passing resemblance to Jimmy Saville. He must have been at least 70 years old and had untidy shoulder length hair. His hair should by all rights have been white at his age but it still retained echoes of the blondness that must have flourished in his youth. The man appeared to be a solo walker and had an air of wisdom and cragginess about him that spoke of a long time love of the hills, rather than a casual flirtation with them. We took to talking and shared some experiences of favourite fells, and then suddenly he popped the question.

"How many have you done?"

He was of course referring to the Wainwright fells. I gave an honest answer that I did not know my exact count, but I made a guesstimate of around 50. The old man replied that he had done 164 of them and reckoned that he would be able to complete them all in about another two years if his old legs would let him. With the keenness of youth I started to ask him about some of the fells I was keen to climb but had not yet done. He eulogised about Raven Crag and Fleetwith Pike, fells I had scarcely even considered. Eventually, as any polite fell walker should do, we both realised that we had said all we wanted to, and I made the excuse of needing a drink stop so that he could have his solitude back. I then noticed that he was in fact not alone but was walking up Hall's Fell with his wife, who instead of sticking to the crest was down below us on the bypass path and appeared not very happy or contented there either. The old man had told me that after he reached the summit of Blencathra he was heading back down via Sharp Edge, so goodness knows what his wife made of that, given that she seemed terrified by Hall's Fell. I am not sure whether being cajoled down an arête is grounds for divorce?

That evening ensconced in my bed and breakfast room in Keswick, for the first time I formally counted my Wainwright tally, with all the enthusiasm of a child counting sweets. With the new fells I had done that day (Bannerdale Crags and Bowscale Fell), I worked out that I had done 59. Then I thought of the old man of 70, nearing completion of his round of Wainwrights, and I thought of myself at age 23, and already a quite respectable 25 percent or so towards completion. For the first time the idea of completing every fell in Alfred Wainwright's seven guidebooks became a determined and realistic ambition. When I spoke to Stan at the breakfast table the following morning he also confessed with obvious enthusiasm that he would like to do them all. Peter on the other hand has steadfastly refused to become a bagger, although he still has a very respectable tally of about 100 Wainwrights to his name.

More on the controversial subject of bagging later (I've devoted a whole chapter to my thoughts about it) but for now some final words on Blencathra. Were it not for the grassy flank of the mountain stretching spaciously over Mungrisdale Common, this would surely be one of the finest and purest mountain forms in Britain. Even despite this, it is still a classic mountain with a wealth of exploration to be had on it. There are other fine routes up the mountain such as Doddick Fell, that I have yet to explore and a complete exploration and intimate knowledge of Blencathra is one of my own personal plans now that I have visited all Wainwright's 214 summits. It is no coincidence that Wainwright devoted more pages of guide book and more route descriptions to this mountain than any other of Lakeland's fells (36 pages in all). It is Blencathra and Sharp Edge that I look back to longingly whenever I leave the Lake District via the A66, heading east for the motorway. Its image is etched into my conscience. When I am not on the mountain its presence still lurks within me and will call me back for the rest of my walking days.

But the Lake District's thrilling or scary places are not just limited to the celebrated edges, although these understandably attract the majority of the crowds. There are other exciting places which are well away from the beaten track and the tourist paths. These places were designed as traverse routes for climbers to reach the great mountain crags. However although the paths were formed for climbers, nonetheless walkers with a little head for heights can also enjoy them and so enjoy being within the heart of the mountains, while others stand on top of them oblivious to their secrets. Perhaps the finest of all these traverses is the High Level route and Shamrock Traverse on Pillar. The reason for this path's existence is the famous Pillar Rock, a 500 foot wall of crag, jutting out from the main body of Pillar and the domain of climbers alone. However by taking the High Level traverse, you can experience close up views of Pillar Rock, from a relatively safe vantage point, while those who have trudged up the normal route to Pillar's summit, will see nothing of the famous Pillar Rock.

The wall of Pillar

The normal approach up Pillar from Wasdale Head starts pleasantly enough, but typically of many big fell walks the early stages are where the leg work is done and the main rewards come later. There are fine views to be had to the vast and rather oppressive wall of the head of Mosedale, while the sight of the sheer scree opposite coming down from Dore Head leaves you wondering how this could possibly be a descent route from Yewbarrow. Dore Head is steep on acquaintance but perspective makes it look vertical as you ascend to Black Sail Pass. At Black Sail Pass the views begin to open out and the subsidiary summit of Looking Stead is a fine place to appraise Ennerdale and the High Stile ridge opposite.

On leaving Looking Stead probably about 90 percent of walkers continue to push on up the final 800 stony feet to the summit of Pillar. If you are bound for the traverse route though, you will be glad that you are in a 10 percent minority heading away from the crowds by taking a minor path shortly after Looking Stead, which heads across the mountain rather than up it. This is a place for the hills connoisseur, the lover of solitude and immersion within a mountain, rather than for the person who only cares about attaining and touching the summit itself. People may stare after you as you leave the treadmill, and wonder where on earth you can be heading. Why would anyone head round the side of the fell, when the top is just a few hundred feet up a broad path? I am thankful for such people. Indeed on the three times that I have done this traverse, if I have met another person apart from Stan who was walking with me, I can't recall doing so.

Almost immediately after you leave the main path, you start to get a sense of true mountain exploration, the kind of feelings that the early pioneers of the fells must have had in spades. The High Level traverse is more rough that dangerous, with the path occasional fading as rashes of boulders impede progress. However it's not that easy to get lost, as the path pretty much hugs to the only natural line of resistance across the fellside. Above you are sheer cliffs and pinnacles of naked rock and below you steep ground leads inexorably down to the head of Ennerdale. When I first did the Shamrock Traverse with Stan in September 1992, although the way ahead along the traverse was clear and sunlight shone down in the Ennerdale valley, a mist lurked over the crags and pinnacles that towered above, creating an awesome and eerie feel. Those of wilder fancy (myself included) could imagine this to be a realm of giants and dragons, like something out of Tolkien's fiction. This is one of many examples I have had in my walking years of weather conspiring to add an extra dramatic element to a walk.

Eventually you will arrive at Robinson's Cairn, surely one of the finest stopping places in the Lake District. From here you can sit and look at the massive buttress of Pillar Rock, contemplate the plunge down into Ennerdale, and look ahead with a little apprehension to your next section of path along The Shamrock Traverse. Take heart though, for in my view this is not as bad as it looks. After an initial nasty climb up scree you find yourself on the traverse proper and this is definitely the one real danger point of the walk. It is only short but the rocky ledge seems to slightly slope towards the imminent drops, and you tend to feel like it is best to hug the opposite wall of rock, rather than risk going too close to the edge. I have also found this ledge quite slippery in wet weather. At the end of the traverse there is a stretcher box, which hopefully neither you nor your companions will need. To the left is the scramble up onto Pillar's summit, the way for walkers to take, and to the right lies Pisgah and High Man of Pillar Rock, which is climber's territory. On our second visit to this spot, accompanied by my girlfriend Jenny, who was later to become my long suffering wife, a sense of manly macho bravado got the better of me and Stan and we decided to clamber up onto Pisgah, a knobble of rock preceding the main mass of Pillar Rock. Jenny sensibly stayed at the stretcher box, no doubt wondering about this reckless imbecile that she had just got engaged to and whether it would be a good or bad thing if the fool perished on Pisgah. I have to confess that this period in our early twenties was the height of myself and Stan's competitive bravado years and as we got into our late twenties and early thirties we began to cherish our mortality a little more. In truth though clambering onto Pisgah involves little more than a head for heights and an easy scramble.

The top of Pisgah is a fantastic place, a scramblers privilege and I have to confess to some embarrassing clenched fist photos of me being taken. However any ideas of going any further were soon arrested, as we crawled to look at the vertical drop down from Pisgah and onto High Man. At this stage any real thoughts of becoming a climber evaporated. I have no desire to go onto High Man. On Pisgah I found my personal limit.

From the stretcher box at the base of Pisgah the final climb up onto Pillar is exhilarating. The path is steep, without being dangerous and the view down into Ennerdale as you gain height is tremendous. I cannot think of many places in Lakeland that a walker can get to, which have a greater sense of height and drop than this. A pure and simple Wainwright bagger could tick off Pillar without ever seeing its great hidden secrets. However the Shamrock Traverse is as fine a thing as any Lakeland summit. But go alone or perhaps with one or two companions at most, as this is not a place in my view for parties and hordes. It is a sanctuary.

Finally we emerged onto the flat summit area of Pillar and a welcome trig point, large cairn and shelter greeted us. On this first climb of Pillar, we drank in some brief but classic views down to Ennerdale Water and the great sweep of the Cumbrian coastline, before the mist, which had been flirting with the summit the whole day, and had given us drama on the traverse, rolled in completely and denied us a lengthy study of the view. The rain began shortly afterwards, in large pelting drops which seemed to have a tinge of iciness in them. So on that first climb of Pillar we headed straight back down from the summit and into Wasdale.

However there were plenty of excuses, if excuses were needed, for coming back to Pillar. Apart from the joys of doing the Shamrock Traverse again and seeing a clear all round view from Pillar there was also the desire to complete the famous Mosedale Round, of which Pillar is the high point, but which also covers an additional four Wainwrights and includes a couple more dramatic and quite exposed places. Once you have left Pillar and bagged the stony and flat summit of Scoat Fell, it is but a short walk to Steeple, one of the Lake District's finest and smallest summits. Geographically Steeple is not really a separate mountain, being merely a protrusion coming off Scoat Fell, but it is nonetheless a very worthy protrusion. For the lovers of thrilling walking the ridge between Scoat Fell and Steeple, although short, is very sweet. It is not in the same league of scariness as Sharp Edge or Striding Edge, but it is delectable nonetheless.

In Wainwright's Favourite Lakeland Mountains book he describes the view from Steeple as 'an awesome scene gripped by a deathly stillness'. Wainwright obviously never climbed Steeple on an August Bank Holiday weekend like I did. There was no hint of deathly stillness as I shared the summit with about 50 hot and sweaty walkers, including a rather annoying party of about eight young men. If I could bestow a personal award entitled 'most annoying tossers I have met on the fells', this group might well scoop the honours (although there is some other stiff competition, which I will mention later).

After a few years of walking on the fells you develop almost a sixth sense as you approach a summit for which walkers you might want to associate with, if you have to, and which you definitely want to avoid. Crowds on some of the fells are inevitable and the freedom of the fells is intrinsic in a walker's right to roam. However, if I have ever indulged in silly antics or personal rituals of joy on the fells, it has almost exclusively been on fells where I have been alone and no-one else is there to care, or when I have just been with my fellow walking companions who know me well enough and usually join in. When there are crowds, I generally like to be as unobtrusive as possible, unless someone obviously needs a hand or is in distress. These eight idiots however had other ideas. They seemed to have found it monumentally funny that the name Ennerdale, whose valley is viewed from Steeple's summit, sounded very similar to the name of a famous prime time English soap opera. That might be mildly and briefly amusing if they had simply shared it among themselves, but instead of so doing they made complete idiots of themselves and annoyed the hell out of everyone else, but saying the word 'Ennerdale' out loud and then chanting equally loudly the theme music from the soap opera whose name sounds like Ennerdale. And they did not just do this once for a laugh, but over and over again. Although I am a complete pacifist, after about the tenth rendition the sinful thought could not help entering my head that it might be a relief to everyone else on the summit, if their chanting could be abated by the administering of a subtle push or eight, sending them on a one way flying visit down to the valley they were so keenly chanting about! I have only been on the summit of Steeple once, but the desire to experience some of that 'deathly stillness' that Wainwright describes, is enough to make another trip in the near future, and this time perhaps at daybreak in the depths of autumn or winter, when no-one is about, save perhaps the odd discerning walker.

Having retraced your steps back to Scoat Fell, there is grand high level ridge walking to be had over Red Pike, with the enormous profiles of Scafell and Scafell Pike dominating the views ahead. This is one of two Red Pikes on the round of Wainwright's 214 fells. The other one towers over Buttermere. When you reach the col at Dore Head, unless you have an urgent need for a quick route off the mountains, resist taking the loose and nasty scree run down to Mosedale, for there is still one final and fantastic fell to be climbed on this wonderful round.

Both as a place to be on and as a place to look at from below, Yewbarrow ranks as one of the finest and shapeliest fells in the Lake District. Its steep flanks and narrow summit give it the appearance when viewed from below of an overturned boat hull, or the nave of a great cathedral. And standing at Dore Head the steep end facing you, called Stirrup Crag, is a scary place to contemplate, if not actually that scary when underfoot. It is technically a scramble over Stirrup Crag and onto the summit, but it is short and there are ledges and holds as you climb its cracks and grooves to eventually arrive on the grassy summit ridge of Yewbarrow. The summit is a lovely contemplative place, although I consider the finest views from Yewbarrow are not to be had from the summit itself, but on the descent towards Wastwater. As you head from the summit over the upturned hull of Yewbarrow, the birds eye view of Wastwater and the sense of altitude, exposure and steepness perched high above the lake, make this one of the most exciting and thrilling prospects in the district. The descent down to the Wasdale Road is steep, but avoids the crags of Bell Rib and Drooping Crag via a loose stone ridden gully (not a nice place), which eventually transforms itself into a lush grassy path running by a wall (a divine place for one's feet at the end of a big round). So completes another of Lakeland's classic rounds and this one has the added bonus of more than its fair share of scary places. If the round includes the Shamrock Traverse at the beginning and Yewbarrow at the end, it is possibly the finest and most dramatic of all Lakeland's rounds.

Before concluding this chapter about scary places, I want to return briefly to Scotland. In my own experience it was quite natural having developed a love of Lakeland to want to progress further and climb some

Yewbarrow

of the mountains in Scotland and indeed I have been going there every year since May 1992. However I just want to emphasise again, for those also keen to embark on Scotland's mountains as a natural progression from the Lake District, that it is generally a more serious undertaking. As I have said there are many places far more scary and dangerous than even Sharp Edge that need to be traversed or climbed to reach the summit of all of Scotland's peaks. In the 50 odd Munros and twenty or so Corbetts (Scottish mountains between 2500 feet and 3000 feet) and Grahams (Scottish mountains between 2000 and 2500 feet) that I have done to date, I have encountered several scary moments. My first climb of Britain's highest mountain Ben Nevis was via the celebrated Carn Mor Dearg arête. This in photographs looks horrendous, but underfoot was actually no worse or more exposed than Striding Edge and less awkward than Sharp Edge (although it is not far short of 3000 feet high so needs respect and good conditions). However at other times in Scotland I have encountered scary obstacles where there was little mention of them in the guidebooks.

One time, coming down from the very airy summit of the Corbett of Beinn an Eoin in the marvellous Torridon landscape of North West Scotland, Stan and I came across a series of nasty rocky ledges, which had to be got down by various motions of arms and legs. I always make a habit of reading all the various guidebook route descriptions the night before any walk and they did not really mention this, probably because in terms of Scotland it was not that difficult or scary, even though it was quite scary to me. I remember taking my rucksack off on one of these ledges and losing hold of it. It was rather disconcerting watching the backpack bounce its way ever more rapidly down over the ledges and crags and wondering what would happen if I slipped and went the same way. Incredibly the backpack, as well as the camera and CD walkman within, were retrieved unscathed. Had I fallen I would not have been so lucky.

The landscape of Scotland's Torridon area is savage and chaotic, but also profoundly beautiful. Torridon is a place where the mountains assert themselves as individual characters. The term *inselberg,* or island mountain, is often used to describe the singular nature of these peaks, and perhaps the three most famous Torridon giants are Liathach, Ben Eighe and Ben Alligin. It was on the latter of these three that I encountered another of Scotland's slightly played down scary places. I had understood from reading about and speaking to people about Ben Alligin, that it was the easiest to climb of the three great Torridon peaks. Ben Eighe was generally reckoned to be the next most challenging, whereas Liathach was reckoned to be not only the most difficult of these three *inselbergs,* but also one of the most challenging of all the mountains on the Scottish Mainland.

So equipped with my experiences of Sharp Edge and Striding Edge, I thought that Ben Alligin and the well known Horns of Alligin, that are a feature of that mountain, would be relatively simple. Again though I came to realise that in Scotland, 'easy' or 'easiest' is a relative term. In fact all three of the famous Torridon triptych are awkward and hard climbs that rank alongside any of the famous walker's challenges in the Lake District. It is just that Ben Alligin is easier by comparison with the other two Torridon giants.

From below the Horns of Alligin don't look too bad. Three humps on a ridge with a steep ascent to get on to them. This is one of the rare occasions though where the reality underfoot was worse than the perception from a distance. In fact the steep haul up to the Horns of Alligin is difficult enough in itself, being one of the steepest clambers on to the back of a mountain that I have ever encountered. At times it felt like climbing a giant ladder. When I emerged at the top of the ladder and onto a brief flat area prior to the main business of the Horns of Alligin, I was suddenly faced with one of the humble hills walker's nastiest dilemmas. The Horns now looked slightly forbidding to this mere mortal, but on the other hand to bail out at this point would mean descending the nasty ladder path that I had just come up, which appealed even less as a thing to go down than it had to climb up. At this point those who hang off rock faces for fun may again have a laugh at my expense, but I will be honest and say that this was one of those points in my walking career when nerves overtook enjoyment. Even Stan, who had previously been on the Horns of Alligin, said that they seemed nastier second time round, and now that he had passed thirty years old and had some sense of his own mortality.

I decided to put my head down and get the Horns out of the way, trusting to the fact that if Stan could do them I could. However on top of the first Horn I was suddenly faced with what appeared to be a dozen feet of so of sheer rock face, which it seemed I would have to descend to get onto the second Horn. Nerves became fear at this point, and it did not help having an elderly couple at the bottom of the drop telling me how easy it was to get down. Thankfully this couple also saw the fear in my eyes and helpfully informed me that there was another way. This way was a bypass path, or a scared walker's comfort blanket. This was music to my ears. Thoughts of descending with my tail between my legs and a night spent cursing over a scary place that had conquered me, were now replaced by the possibility, nay likelihood, that I might actually reach the summit of the Munro. Having bypassed the first Horn, the second and third Horns were not a problem, with walking akin to Striding Edge. The narrow path along the third Horn must be one of the finest situations for a mere walker in the entire British Isles. The sense of being suspended above a vast wilderness of lochs, moorland and sea takes the breath away and for me brought emotions of joy and disbelief (and a sense of relief too). Now with the scary places behind us, it was just a long but pleasurable pull up the curving ridge onto Sgurr Mhor, the summit of Ben Alligin.

A little more on Scotland later, but for now my intention has been just to say a little by way of contrast, about some of Scotland's scary places. I have generally found that you learn more from your own experiences and mistakes than from guidebooks or other people's experiences. However that does not mean that guidebooks and gentle advice from others are not also useful allies. There is risk involved in venturing into any mountainous area and those that are averse to such risks will probably not need to be told to stay away. The key, however, is about how you manage and minimise that risk. For would any of us really enjoy this hill walking lark half as much if the element of risk was taken out? And in taking a calculated risk or two do we not learn about ourselves and develop hidden strengths?

In fairness though to Peter and Stan, I could not really conclude my chapter about scary places without mention of the one glaring absence in my scary places CV. On the day, in May 1993, when Peter and Stan drove to Wasdale Head to climb Scafell via Lords Rake and the West Wall Traverse, I had instead chosen to spend a day in my favourite Northern Fells. For the last 14 years, I have been constantly reminded, scolded and cajoled for having not climbed Scafell, and more particularly for having not climbed it via Lords Rake and the West Wall Traverse. I have watched the video that Peter and Stan made of their ascent so many times that I feel that I have actually been there. Despite the fact that I have climbed as many fells as Stan and about 100 more than Peter, I have never been allowed to forget that they are ever so slightly manlier than me by dint of having been on Lords Rake and the West Wall Traverse.

Thankfully I have now got these two beloved fellow walkers off my back in so far as climbing Scafell is concerned. It was, however, a real shame, or perhaps a relief, that by the time I finally came to climb Scafell in April 2007, a large perched boulder had made Lords Rake all but out of bounds. So I guess that until that boulder decides to crash its way down the mountainside of Scafell, I will have to put up with more years of ribbing about the one major scary place for walkers in Lakeland that I have not done. However in finishing, and by way of a counter punch to Peter at least, I seem to recall him waiting on the summit of Blencathra having climbed up via Blease Fell, while his brother toiled over Sharp Edge! But I'd better get on with another chapter before this gets personal.

Bagging in Winter

An imaginary hill bagger could set out to climb all 214 Wainwright fells exclusively on warm summer days and another imaginary hill bagger could set out to climb the 214 but only by climbing them in winter. If, having completed their respective rounds, these two hypothetical walkers met in a pub for a chat about their experiences, they might come away from their chat each feeling that they had not in fact completed the same fells. The views they described might seem the same in some details but different in others. One might describe a landscape of shades of green, brown and grey, rich in bracken and heather. The other would talk of a world that was brilliant white or steely silver, with stark black edged outlines. One might describe long lazy days soaking in the sun and relaxing for an hour in contemplation of life. The other would speak of winds so raw that they redden and burn the face, of spectacular, crystal

The author on a fresh snow plastered Sand Hill

clear, snow filled views, of hail, frost, ice and blizzards. Even the very ground they had walked upon might seem different as one described sticky bogs, lush grass and rocky paths and the other described virgin pathless snow, bogs so frozen that they crackle beneath your feet and blades of grass encased in icicles.

The fact is that although these two walkers would have done the same fells in name, their experiences would be wildly and radically different and this is why for me winter walking has been such an essential and contrasting part of my Wainwright round. In winter you experience wondrous sights that you just simply don't have at other times of the year. The same fell that has been climbed in the warmth of a June day can be totally different in February. I can also honestly say that of the top ten walking experiences I have had in the Lake District as many as half have been in winter conditions. I am not a great fan in any case of warm or hot weather walking. For me the period between about the end of May and the end of August is pretty much the closed season as far as fell walking is concerned. I have climbed in every month of the year but I have found myself more and more of late going to the hills either in autumn or winter, or maybe in the wonderful spring freshness of April. I would never want to confine my walking solely to winter. I would miss too much the delight of basking on a fell for an hour, with a light warm breeze and no-one around. However it cannot be denied that the fells become a different place under proper winter conditions. They are altogether more challenging and yet the rewards for undertaking the challenge are greater. The very fact that seeing the Lake District under a proper winter covering is these days so rare, makes it all the more special. Snow heightens each and every crag on a mountain and the higher fells can seem positively Alpine.

I hope in this chapter to convey something of the feel and euphoria of winter walking in the hills and perhaps inspire those who have not ventured out of the comparative comfort zone of temperate walking to do some winter expeditions. It will be tougher and you will need your wits about you, but the rewards more than compensate for the effort.

No commentary about the winter hills would be complete without a word about safety. Virtually every winter walk description I have read in any guide-book has begun by emphasising that in winter the fells become a totally different and potentially more serious undertaking. There are many factors that can potentially conspire against an unwary winter walker. Daylight hours are shorter and therefore the need to carefully plan the timings of your walk becomes greater. In summer the only difference between finishing a walk at seven o'clock in the evening and eight o'clock in the evening might be one less pint in the pub. In winter the difference between finishing a walk at 4 o'clock in the afternoon and 5 o'clock in the afternoon, could be the difference between having some daylight left to see the path ahead of you and stumbling around in the dark. An extremely poor or carefree attitude to timing could see a walker stumbling around in the high places after dark. This would be very dangerous or even life threatening if poor weather or even blizzard conditions set in. You will also need to take into account when planning the timing of your walk the fact that thick snow or thick ice will slow down the fast progress you may be used to in summer. I have often found that in winter you give yourself more options and more time to enjoy the beauty of the frozen fells if you take maximum advantage of the available daylight. In late spring, when the hours of daylight are long, I might often enjoy a hearty breakfast, do a bit of shopping and then start a walk at 10.30 in the morning. On the other hand I have frequently begun winter walks at six or seven in the morning, in the early dawn embers or even in total darkness.

On any fell walk at any time of year the prevailing weather should be considered, but in winter conditions it is even more vital to know the forecasted weather before setting out. In addition while weather forecasting is getting more and more accurate, it is still a good idea to keep an eye on the weather during the actual walk and assess what it is likely to be doing an hour later. In mountainous areas the weather does not always do what the forecast says it is going to do, so it is important to learn to read the approaching signs of bad weather, such as encroaching high level cloud, or the highest tops misting over. Whereas in summer a blue sky day will often only gradually give way to something nastier, I have started a winter walk in crisp sunny conditions only to find myself in a blizzard a couple of hours later. The weather can change quickly on the hills at any time of year, but in winter the need to look out for the signs of changing weather and bale out of the walk if need be, can literally be the difference between life and death. Weather patterns also tend to be more fickle in winter. Very rarely does winter provide day after day of settled weather such as summer often does.

Another thing that seems to be mentioned in every winter commentary and would be amiss of me not to mention here, is the need to have adequate winter walking gear. I have known myself wearing four or five layers of clothing and still feeling cold on the fells. It is always better in winter to feel relatively warm at ground level and just right on the high tops, than to feel just right at ground level and chilled to the marrow on the summits. No matter how fine the winter landscape arrayed before you from a fell top may be, you will find it hard to enjoy it if your whole body is convulsed with the cold. Make sure your boots are waterproof and invest in a pair of gaiters. I can tell you from my own bitter experience that snow has a way of creeping into boots that are not adequately protected and numb cold feet are not ideal when you have a long walk ahead of you. General wisdom also says that for any serious winter undertaking on the fells, when heavy snow or ice covers the ground, you should have a pair of crampons and an ice axe. The crampons fix to your boots and aid your grip on the snow and ice and the ice axe can be used to cut your way into steep snow slopes or to arrest your fall if you find yourself sliding uncontrollably off the fellside. Having said this I must confess that in my early days of winter walking, when my clerical salary would hardly stretch to a waterproof jacket, I did not purchase an ice axe or crampons and it is only recently that I have done so. That is my own folly and I may just have been lucky never to have had an accident on the high snow bound fells. An ice axe and crampons would be unnecessary on say a winter jaunt up Little Mell Fell. However I can only advise forking out a hundred quid or so for an ice axe and crampons if you are going to winter walk on high snow covered ridges or on steep and craggy fells. It may turn out to be the best hundred quid you ever spent!

Anyway enough of the advice stuff for now and on to another subject that should be close to the heart of any lover of Britain's wild places. The subject of climate change. There are many scientific theories and debates about climate change and global warming. Although I admit that I have absolutely no expertise in this field, I have definitely noticed changes in winter conditions during the 14 winters that I have been walking in the Lake District. Up to and including the year 2000 I had eight winter expeditions to the fells and on six of those eight trips there were proper winter conditions, with extensive snow cover on the fells. My early trips all had extensive snow cover. However in the last ten years I have only known extensive snow cover on three occasions. Indeed on two winter excursions there has been absolutely no snow and in 2007 Stan and I found ourselves sweating and toiling on Green Crag in Eskdale on a peculiarly warm February day.

Although this is perhaps not a very scientific method of judging climate change, I think that there has been a trend over the 14 winters I have been to the hills, away from proper winter conditions with a full snow covering and towards milder conditions with little or no snow, the last two winters being a colder exception to this general trend. This is a change not just noted by myself and fellow walkers. Scientists study the snow cover experienced each winter on our hills. It is reckoned that in as little as 15 years, Snowdon, the highest mountain in Wales, may be snow free all year round and the ski resorts of the Cairngorms in Scotland have been experiencing gradually less snow cover and shorter and shorter skiing seasons.

It would be a shame if our children, or our children's children, lived in a country where the season of winter was virtually devoid of snow, ice and frost. It would be a shame if future generations of walkers might not see the glories of Britain's hills in full winter's garb.

Changing the topic slightly again, I have often thought that in some ways the hills and fells of Britain are like a vast playground; a place where us adults can somehow reconnect with the simple pleasures and joys of our childhoods. When the hills present themselves robed in winter white, this feeling of child like anticipation is at its height. I can recall a number of times where I have woken up in the car, having had a few uncomfortable hours sleep, to a brilliant winter blue sky and the fells plastered in winter coats. At such moments the knowledge that a full and extensive winter walk lies ahead generates the type of thrill and excitement that I can remember experiencing on Christmas morning just prior to present opening. I can also recall walking through Keswick on a winter's evening after a hearty meal and heavy snow starting to fall in the streets. At that moment the excitement and prospect of a proper winter walk next day, is similar to the thoughts and feelings I used to have as a child on that most magical of nights, Christmas Eve. I often consider that just as humanity has in recent times moved further away from nature and towards an urban environment, so we have also lost touch with the simple pleasures in life. I am a great believer that every now and then we should reaffirm our natural roots and also let ourselves be filled with simple childlike pleasures.

My acquaintance with the winter fells came some years after The Cumbria Way gave me a love of hilly places in general. Indeed it was not until four years after my first trip to the Lake District that Stan and I undertook our first winter trip. While it was exciting to plan spring, summer and autumn walks during the self-imposed exile of our winters away from the hills, there was no doubt that the period from the end of October to the end of March was a long and dark time to be without our beloved fells.

I forget who first had the lateral thought of actually alleviating the winter gloom by going to the Lake District, but once the idea was mooted it very soon became a reality. Peter unfortunately has not accompanied Stan and I on our winter trips, preferring the warmth and relaxation of the warmer times of year, rather than being frozen half to death.

The winter trips have always been what I would describe as ad hoc trips. We have usually begun checking weather forecasts in detail straight after New Year, with a view to choosing that perfect period of weather after heavy snow has fallen and a ridge of high pressure has then set in. Sometimes we have had to wait until late February to get the right conditions. Sometimes proper winter conditions have not arrived despite waiting and we have gone anyway. With the advent of the internet we are now able to study detailed mountain forecasts and even look at websites showing pictures taken of the fells and how much snow cover there is, the day before we are due to go! Nothing gets the excitement flowing faster than seeing snowy Lake District landscapes posted on the internet the night before you are due to go there and climb. On the other hand nothing is more depressing than seeing snow plastered pictures on the internet when work and other commitments mean you cannot go.

Now having decided to go to the winter hills in February 1993 you would think that we would have done some planning, research and reading about winter hills and conditions. The truth, however, was that beyond the knowledge that we would need to wrap up warmer and keep our wits about us in terms of weather conditions, our approach was very much a naive one of 'let's suck it and see'. In retrospect I think we were quite lucky not to get into more trouble than we did on the winter hills in those early days and I think we also displayed a certain youthful enthusiasm and ignorance of danger. I would not of course recommend such an approach, but on the other hand having survived such an approach, I can look back on this innocent naivety and in a funny way cherish it. In the early days of the Lake District's popularity poor working class folk used to spend nights on the fells armed with nothing more than the hob nail boots and jackets they worked in. If they got cold they used to wrap themselves in newspaper. Again I would not advocate such a basic approach these days, but perhaps today there is a slight trend with all the gismos and gadgets and ultra protective clothing that are on the market to overprotect ourselves from some of the raw experience of the hills. Certain items of equipment are necessary or even essential, but it would also be easy to spend a few hundred pounds extra on the most expensive gear and end up being cocooned and cosseted, when all that is needed is to be comfortable.

Blissfully ignorant of any need to purchase crampons or an ice axe and with just a few extra jumpers for protection against the cold, it might have been advisable perhaps for our first winter walk to have been something fairly moderate and with an easy short escape route. Somewhere, perhaps like Catbells, Walla Crag or Lingmoor Fell. However, instead of our first winter fell walk being driven by the need to cater for our winter inexperience, the choice of walk was instead driven by my own personal need to claw back some Wainwright fells that Stan had already done and I had not. On a previous trip to the Lake District, Stan and Peter had done The Fairfield Horseshoe above Ambleside, another of Lakeland's classic rounds. While they did this I pottered around Rydal Water and Grasmere, nursing a badly twisted ankle on a short low level stroll. There are few things worse for a fell walker than the knowledge that your companions are enjoying panoramic views and bagging new peaks, while you are reduced to hobbling along cursing your luck. So I determined that at the next available opportunity I would get those ticks and complete the Fairfield Horseshoe. That next opportunity just happened to be on a foggy winter's day in February.

Now far from being an ideal choice for a first winter walk the Fairfield Horseshoe is in fact a serious winter fells expedition. The higher fells of Hart Crag and Dove Crag, as their names suggest, have fearful cliffs and where there are cliffs and snow there are cornices. A cornice for those not familiar with the term is where snow has formed and collected on the edge of a cliff or precipice. The problem with cornices is that when walking along a ridge they can appear to merely be the natural edge of that ridge. However if you happen to step on a corniced edge you will suddenly find that instead of treading on terra firma, you are in fact off the fell altogether and there is only the corniced snow between you and the void below. This corniced snow will rarely hold and people have died from mistakenly stepping onto cornices thinking they were just part of the ridge or route they were on. Such a mistake is more difficult to make in clear weather where you can see the ridge ahead of you and where it plunges away in cliffs. Lost in mist however, or even worse in a whiteout (when the white falling snow merges, in poor visibility, with the white snow plastered fell to cause disorientation) it is easy to accidentally find yourself on a cornice.

So upon reflection both possible cornices and the prevailing foggy conditions made the Fairfield Horseshoe a poor first winter walk choice.

Then there is the reputation of Fairfield itself. Although I am not quite sure where the 'fair' part of the name comes from, 'field' is certainly an apt term for the large flat and quite featureless summit plateau. It is not a place to stumble about lost in poor weather or visibility and although I do not wish to be morbid, Fairfield has claimed more than its share of hill walking fatalities.

Such thoughts however were far from our minds as we headed up from Ambleside, via Low Sweden Bridge and onto Low Pike. About half way up Low Pike at around the 1000 foot contour, we had our first experience of treading on Lakeland snow. At first it was poor quality patchy snow, which had melted in places to reveal bare grass. But with every hundred feet gained the snow cover gradually became deeper and more extensive. The climb up Low Pike follows a dry stone wall for its entire length and as we entered the thick mist this wall provided a useful navigational aid. These dry stone walls form an impressive feature of the Fairfield round. The walls plunge down to Rydal Beck and are some of the finest and most precipitous in the Lake District. From high on the ridge you can only admire the energy and labour that must have gone into buildings these walls. The steep slopes they are built upon are difficult enough ground to walk upon, without having to heave large stones up and then proceed to construct them into such fine walls.

On this first trip round the Fairfield Horseshoe, we were denied the views by the thick mist, but there was plenty to keep us interested and our attention focused. From the imaginatively named Low Pike we continued to follow the wall onto the equally imaginatively named High Pike. By this time our footfalls were making deep boot prints in the snow. This was not fresh soft powdery snow, but compacted sticky snow and a number of other sets of boot prints showed us that walkers had been here both today and on previous days. On some windier and nastier day the snow had drifted fiercely against the dry stone wall, but today it was merely good fun to test the depth of the drifted snow with our feet and laugh when one of us went down to our knees, or even thighs, in snow. At this point, with the wall beside us as a beeline escape route back to Ambleside if needed, it was all childlike joy and little danger as we tested the drifted snow and had snowball fights. The thing about winter fell walking though, is that safety and simple indulgence in child like snow play, can quickly be replaced by dangers to command all the attention of your adult wits. Perhaps it would have been the wiser option, on a first winter walk, for us to have headed back from High Pike, having had our safe fun in the snow and bagged a couple of Wainwrights as well. However we appraised the situation with our limited experience and as the wind was light, no snow was actually falling and the wall continued to be our guide, we proceeded above the 2500 foot contour on to Dove Crag and then to Hart Crag where, about 300 feet of ascent from the summit, the guiding wall ended.

On Hart Crag I recall a watery white sun desperately trying to punch a hole in the fog. Devoid of sun like intensity it more resembled a pale moon. Its appearance was fleeting, a thing of a few seconds, but it was enough to give us a little hope that the mist might be thinning or burning off, and buoyed with such hope, we continued.

Again at this point, with the wall that led all the way to Ambleside just a short distance below us, we could have made an easy descent. There is however no wall to guide you from Hart Crag to Fairfield and although there is a good path in normal conditions, the path had disappeared under the snow cover. All we had to guide us was the compass and the boot prints of others, which could only be relied upon if the wearer of the boots had in fact followed the correct route. The mist, which had threatened to part on Hart Crag, now thickened and darkened considerably. Its greys and whites merged with the greys and whites of the snow on the ridge around us and for a few minutes we stumbled around lost in a featureless environment. At such times you have to trust to the compass and we did, although it was a little frightening to be at over 2500 feet and reliant on our, at that stage, fairly limited knowledge of navigation. For a while we proceeded not entirely certain where we were going but trusting in the little red compass needle. In such conditions the mind needs to keep keenly focused and yet oddly enough can become rather confused and indecisive. This was one of those moments when fell walking goes from simple pleasure to potentially life threatening danger. In such moments all the usual joy and *élan* of hill walking evaporates and thoughts of making it safely off the mountain and whether you will ever see that pint in Ambleside come to the fore.

The ridge between Hart Crag and Fairfield is not the best of places to get lost in mist and winter conditions. The proximity of the massive cliffs of Deepdale and the ever present likelihood of cornices add to the seriousness of the place. Wainwright in his *Guide to the Eastern Fells* says of this place that 'it is important, in mist, not to stray from the path: danger lurks'. But with a bit of luck and some reasonable compass bearings we finally reached the summit plateau of Fairfield and were glad to find the summit shelter along with about four other walkers who could confirm to us that we were on top of Fairfield. It had only been a brief episode of getting mildly lost, but I have never forgotten that sinking feeling and rush of adrenalin that accompanies losing your way in winter conditions on the hills.

Once on Fairfield, enjoyment began to seep gradually back into proceedings, as we knew that it was just a simple due south compass bearing from Fairfield to the next Wainwright, Great Rigg. As our spirits lifted we experienced what I can say was probably my first great winter moment of thrill, a moment that was fleeting but added to the sense of awe. Fourteen years later I can still vividly recall this occurrence. After about five minutes on the summit the watery sun appeared again trying to poke a hole through the mist, but this time it actually succeeded. The wind had picked up a little on Fairfield's summit and suddenly and unexpectedly a hole was torn in the mist, through which we saw a momentary glimpse of St Sunday Crag looking majestic and positively Alpine in its winter clothing and with high clouds skirting and enveloping it. It lasted a few seconds before the thick mist returned and it was gone.

We waited and were granted a further two fleeting moments of view in the direction of St Sunday Crag. Each time the spectacle was thrilling and we looked at each other in wonder. As this shifting spectacle was happening and providing the sole snippets of views for the entire day, I recall a solitary walker approaching the cairn on Fairfield, touching the cairn and then in almost the same movement heading away from the summit. This type of walker mystifies me. The sole purpose seems to be walk to a pile of stones, touch said pile of stones, and then immediately head on. Perhaps he had seen it all before, but even now when I have seen so many natural wonders in the fells, I would never dream of parting from a summit while such a weather spectacle was going on. In fact you would have to drag me away from it!

Perhaps finer than the fell walking days, with infinite views from the start of the walk to its end, are the days when the hills are largely cloaked in poor weather but for a few minutes or perhaps even a few seconds reveal some spectacular dramatic scene. After the third appearance of St Sunday Crag we waited and waited till the cold began to creep into us, but Fairfield did not yield any more of its far reaching panorama to us that day. The mist had descended for good and accompanied us in thick folds over Great Rigg, Heron Pike and Nab Scar. On finishing our first winter walk, in spite of the moment of getting lost, we knew we were hooked by the winter fells. We had had a glimpse of the wonders of winter views, now we hankered after an extensive winter panorama. Over the year gap between our first winter trip in February 1993 and our next in

February 1994, we mugged up a little on winter hills and began to learn a little about such things as cornices and whiteouts.

Personally I have always considered that a fell is only half done if you have not seen the view from it. This is especially true when that view is from something as high and well known as Fairfield. Views are not by any means the sole reason for climbing fells but unless they are seen from the fells you will find it hard to get an overall picture and knowledge of the landscape around you. The knowledge gained from seeing views will eventually enable you to recognise one fell from another, even from a distance.

Our second Fairfield round in winter demonstrated admirably that the same walk can provide two wildly differing experiences. This time there was little to worry about on the weather front, as azure blue skies and light winds greeted us, promising utmost clarity of views. A check of the forecast indicated that this weather was going to hold throughout the day. It was the perfect winter walk forecast and a much safer day to be on the Fairfield round than our previous visit. I remember from the streets of Ambleside looking up towards a snow plastered horseshoe, with the snowline again at around 1000 feet and knowing that a magnificent winter outing beckoned. It was strange to recognise the same wall on the ascent up Low Pike and High Pike, but to also now see the wide ranging views. The view of Dovedale from Dove Crag is a particularly fine prospect of intimate sylvan beauty. On such winter days the sunlight dazzles almost blindingly off the pure whiteness of the snow and even though the air temperature is barely above freezing, I have often ended such days feeling slightly sunburnt!

On the same spot between Hart Crag and Fairfield, where we had got briefly but frighteningly lost before, we saw several large cornices. The boot prints of previous walkers showed clearly where the path was this time. Where the cornices had formed the snow was beautifully untouched by human mark, but dangerous and frightening in its beauty. We realised at this point the perils that had lurked around us when we were stumbling around in the mist the previous time.

Oddly enough on the flat summit of Fairfield, snow was strangely absent. Perhaps strong winds had blown the fresh snow off the highest point on a previous day. In the place of thick snow there was something we had not come across before and something that cried out for a good pair of crampons. Fairfield's summit was covered by a layer of impenetrable thick ice. We did not so much walk over the summit plateau as skate over it, trying to use the occasional patches where some grippy snow still remained as stepping stones to make progress. It was reasonably safe, as in the clear visibility we could easily see where the summit plateau ended and steered a half walking, half skating course, keeping well clear of the cliffs. Eventually we reached the summit of Fairfield and at last we saw the vast winter panorama that we had been denied before. From the summit a myriad of snow plastered peaks spread around us, with every high Lakeland summit in view. Particularly fine though were the views over the High Street Range and out to the winter white ridge of the Pennines. The wedge of St Sunday Crag loomed large and imposing, though not as impressive or seemingly high as on the fleeting views seen previously. A dominant feature were the nearby mountains of Dollywagon Pike and Nethermost Pike, whose cliffs stood out sharply emphasised by the snow and the sun. The dominant feature however was the profile of Striding Edge, in its winter's garb a place for only the most experienced walkers and climbers. The edge, when viewed from this angle, can often merge into the bulks of Raise and Catstycam, but that day the snow somehow delineated every ridge and fell as a separate entity. It was without doubt the finest view that I had seen at that time.

Although I have said that we made every effort that day to steer clear of cliffs and cornices, we could not resist going over to the cairn that marks the route over Cofa Pike and St Sunday Crag and taking a sneaky, vertigo inducing peek over the cliffs of Fairfield and down to Deepdale. The drop was awesome, but a cornice about three feet from where we stood warned us to go no further.

When I think of Deepdale and the dramatic cliffs of Fairfield, it serves to remind me that whereas some knowledge of a fell or mountain can be had from climbing to its summit, there are some fells whose true appreciation can only be had by an exploration of the valleys beneath it. Deepdale is a place of savage beauty, with the cliffs of Fairfield and the massive buttress of Greenhow End giving the impression more of Scotland's Glencoe, than of Lakeland. On a wild winter's day in 1999, the wind and the frequent showers had limited our fell bagging to a trip up lowly Hallin Fell, with its intimate view of Ullswater a grand reward out of proportion to its short climb. However on a windy winter's day even a low summit like Hallin Fell is not a place to linger. So Stan and I ended up with a half day in winter at our disposal and as we had always planned to one day look at Fairfield's grandest aspect we decided on a walk down Deepdale. I recall sitting on a rock beside Deepdale Beck and looking up at the series of snow filled gullies that emanated from the summit plateau of Fairfield. Our eyes saw a couple of black specks in one of the gullies, which appeared to be moving. A look through the binoculars, which I always carry in my rucksack, revealed a couple of ice climbers hacking their way up to the summit plateau. Not my idea of fun, especially on a day of high winds and frequent showers, which were no doubt blizzard like on the high tops. Watching these specks of humanity on the towering cliffs, I could now comprehend the true character of the mountain called Fairfield, a comprehension that could not be truly had from just standing on its flat summit plateau. It gave me a sense of how often we tramp along the high tops without a care in the world, but with danger and terror lurking only a few feet away.

On the return walk back down Deepdale, Stan decided that he wanted to explore the rocky environs of a little stream coming down from the flanks of St Sunday Crag. After ten years walking together we were used to each others whims and we have never been walking companions who like to be joined at the waist. It impinges too much on the sense of freedom. So Stan explored his stream and I carried on down Deepdale and in doing so unwittingly provided us both with our own unique and unforgettable experience.

About three minutes after I had left Stan, I noticed that one of the day's frequent showers was approaching me from the direction of the Far Eastern Fells. The white fingers suspended from the shower cloud told me that this was not a shower of rain, but held something potentially wintrier and therefore more exciting. I stood transfixed by the approaching weather, and as I was in the safety of a valley, I longed for the shower to enfold me. The shower moved perceptibly towards me, as first Angletarn Pikes disappeared under its spell and then the valley of Patterdale also faded away. Then it was upon me releasing hundreds of thousands of hailstone pellets. Before a minute had passed the ground beneath me was covered in little white hailstones, and the puddles of water on the rocky path around me now looked like they were filled with icy frogspawn. For about three minutes I thrilled in this connection with nature. Then the hailstorm moved onwards down Deepdale and towards Fairfield and the ice climbers, who in their precarious situation perhaps thought differently about the hail shower than I did. Then again people who ice climb probably get their own thrills from being in such places in extreme weather.

Not all the finest experiences are had up high and that day in Deepdale was one such occasion at low level, which will always remain etched into my mind. When I rejoined Stan we were both filled with the joy and invigorating energy of the hailstorm. Yet although on the same path and only a few hundred yards apart, we had each had our own separate and unique experience in the hail.

Glaramara is a fell blessed with one of the most evocative sounding names in the Lake District. It is a beautiful name, sounding like a mountain out of Tolkien's mythology and promising high mountain splendour. In certain cases the name of a fell gives a clue to its nature. Glaramara sounds fascinating and is. By contrast Sallows and Ling Fell are pretty much on acquaintance like their names would suggest. At 2560 feet a climb of Glaramara is a worthy day's achievement. It is much higher for instance than the more celebrated Langdale Pikes. Yet all too often Glaramara is either climbed as a prelude to the higher summits of Great End, Esk Pike and Scafell Pike, or as an epilogue to a day on these higher fells. It stands aloof from the time honoured routes up Grains Gill and to Sty Head Tarn and for every hundred people that trudge this way perhaps only a handful will have Glaramara as their main objective.

It is perhaps one of Glaramara's charms is that it is a high fell by Lake District standards (the 46th highest of the 214 Wainwright Fells) and yet manages to escape the crowds that are often associated with the higher fells. It is therefore a worthy objective for the lover of quieter places. No higher praise and recognition can be given than the fact that Wainwright included Glaramara as one of the fells in his *Favourite Lakeland Mountains* book.

Wainwright's endorsement was more than enough for Stan and I to add Glaramara to the ever growing list of fells we wanted to climb and on a bitterly cold day in February 1995 we set out to make the dream a reality. This was a dull glowering winter's day, the kind where the clouds flirt just above the highest summits without ever actually lowering sufficiently to impinge on them or rob them entirely of their views. It was a day where the only colours in the landscape were different shades of grey and black and white. As we walked up Grains Gill, the cliffs on Great End stood out starkly, the white of the snow and the black of the gullies combining to create a scene that looked like an etching.

Tarns always make good stopping places and I have often stopped and sat by the delightful Sprinkling Tarn, spending a few minutes eating a sandwich and looking at Great Gable and Great End. Today however the detour that we made from the route to Esk Hause to visit the tarn took on the air of a pointless ritual. I have known various degrees of cold, but that day at Sprinkling Tarn with an icy wind whipping up the fallen snow into our faces, has to be the coldest I have ever been on the fells. The iced over tarn received about thirty seconds of our attention before we trudged back towards Esk Hause. There are a myriad of paths around Esk Hause, which is a true Spaghetti Junction in the fells. The path onto Allen Crags and Glaramara branches off slightly before Esk Hause. Esk Hause and the area immediately surrounding it is renowned as the wettest place in England, and the volume of drifted snow in the col beneath Allen Crags that day testified to this. It was here that my Ordnance Survey map was violently torn from my hands by a gust of wind. Now any fell walker who wants to adopt a good attitude towards the hills and their environment should never leave litter on the fells. Even though this was an accidental littering, I still had to try and retrieve my map. Stan and I raced after the map only to encounter several foot of drifted snow, which covered us up to our waists and which we had to wade through like treacle. The map was tantalisingly in view, however, and Stan got there first and retrieved it before another gust of wind would have blown it out of all reach.

Glaramara is not as celebrated as some of the other high Lakeland Fells. However Allen Crags, which is in fact higher than Glaramara, is positively neglected. I would doubt if anyone visits Allen Crags for its own sake and yet its view of high mountains, in particular of Great End and Great Gable, deserves better attention. The sheer cold that day and the ever present prospect that the cloud base might lower, meant that we, like most people, did not give Allen Crags much time and instead headed on for the main objective of Glaramara. The high level ridge between Allen Crags and Glaramara is a joy to tread. On that day, covered in snow and ice, it represented one of the bleakest and most wintry, yet eerily beautiful scenes that I have encountered. It was about as close to a snapshot from the wastes of Antarctica as I will probably ever get. The small tarns along the ridge were so thickly frozen that their waters were entirely solid and opaque. What a contrast to the same tarns that sparkle gloriously in the spring and summer warmth.

Although the summit of Glaramara was bitterly cold, it merited us spending a few minutes there. The view from Glaramara's rocky summit is very fine, particularly down to the Jaws of Borrowdale, with Derwent Water and Skiddaw behind. The higher mountains of Bowfell, Great End, Great Gable and the Scafells' make a fine array. The Langdale Pikes look unusual in profile and wisps of cloud were flirting with Pike o'Stickle on this February day. This is a view predominantly of mountains rather than of distance, yet there is much beauty and drama in its intimacy.

Instead of carrying along the ridge to Thornythwaite Fell, we instead decided to make a quiet escape route off the flanks of Glaramara. I am not entirely certain that we took a pathed route off the flanks, as all paths were obscured by the snow, but the route that we did take provided a debut for bottom sliding. Over the years on the winter fells bottom sliding has provided me with some of my most exhilarating and frankly childlike moments on the fells. It is as simple as riding down snowy flanks using one's posterior as a toboggan. Now before I tempt people to try this, I must say that it comes with a health warning. It should only ever be attempted on broad grassy fell flanks, where there are no crags anywhere in the immediate vicinity. Don't try it over a sheer vertical drop. Even a moderate but lengthy and uniform incline will make you pick up a surprising speed. It is also important to be able to clearly see the way ahead of you and therefore plan where you are going to slide. Ideally it is best to be able to clearly see where the route flattens out so that you know where you are likely to naturally stop. Any flattening or gradual rising of the ground should halt your progress. It is best not to use legs as brakes as these can easily get twisted underneath you. Ideally you should have an ice axe so that if you do find yourself going too fast or getting into a nasty situation you can arrest your slide before a fall. If done safely and with due consideration of the terrain, this can be an exhilarating and quick way to descend, but please take care.

Coming off Glaramara is an example of perhaps where not to indulge in this activity, although we did live to tell the tale. We knew that the slope we had chosen was fairly free of crags, although we were mindful of Hind Crag nearby. However, when Stan chose to inaugurate the bottom slide, I don't think he realised how quickly he would end up going. I saw him slide with joyous whoops down about 100 feet of fellside, before coming to a lip of snow, which his body crested and then disappeared over. I had no idea whether Stan was safe or not, but luckily a few seconds later his cries of delight and exhortations for me to follow him told me that he was undamaged. So being a young fool I followed him. To begin with all was fine and enjoyable, but as I headed towards the lip of snow and the unknown drop beyond, a surge of primal adrenalin hit me. Without an ice axe, as I was in those days, there was nothing I could do to stop myself, and as I crested the snow lip I briefly knew what it was like to be airborne, before being deposited safely into a little snow filled hollow which acted like a soft cushion and arrested my fall. I will always remember that exhilarating experience, but in hindsight it was probably the reckless enjoyment of a young fool, which could have easily turned to danger. It's nice to be free on the fells and if due consideration to the terrain is taken such indulgence in the snow can be both enjoyable and safe. In life there are always risks and although I have bottom slid on a number of other occasions, I have since always tried to ensure that I minimised those risks. However, it is easy to get into danger if you chose the wrong slide, so make your snow slide choices wisely and, unlike me in the early days, always take an ice axe. The Mountain Rescue Service does not need any additions to their call outs.

Once any rambler has done a number of walks, the question will inevitably arise as to which is the finest walk or walking experience that he or she has had. In my early fell walking days I found it fairly easy to say which walks were the finest I had done, but having now been doing this hill walking lark for nearly 20 years and having done many hundreds of walks it becomes more and more difficult to chose the top 5 or 10 walks and almost impossible to chose the greatest or finest experience. The criteria are also difficult to decide. Is a winter walk, with snow on the fells and peerless views, finer than a classic summer expedition that ends watching the sunset at nine in the evening? Does a day of solitude in the Northern Fells score more points than a day on Helvellyn's edges shared with couple of hundred people? How do you compare an experience on Fairfield where the mist has briefly parted and given you a surge of joy and excitement, to a day where the views are with you from start to finish? Some days are memorable, without having any single classic or exhilarating moments. Other days may have one brief moment that makes for a classic day. The truth is that it is almost impossible to list a top 10 of my walks. Instead after all these years walking there are simply walks that I remember as representing the pinnacles in my walking career so far. Some fell walking days gradually dwindle in the memory. The best days are the days you never forget. These days remain as clearly etched in the mind years after as when you first did them. In February 1996 Stan and I did the Kentmere Round on a splendid snow plastered day. At the time we were convinced that it was the finest day's outing we had had in some seven years of hill walking. Nearly a dozen years later it still remains one of the finest days I have had in the hills, if not the finest. Other days have matched it, but I cannot think of any that have surpassed it.

The Kentmere Round was the last of Lakeland's celebrated high level horseshoes that I did and one of the last times I would rack up five or more new Wainwright fells in one day. Of all the Lakeland rounds, Kentmere is perhaps the least celebrated and least visited. This is not due in any way to an inferiority of walking or views to be had, but owes more to the fact that Kentmere village, the traditional start for the round, is isolated at the end of a minor dead end road and several miles from any significant habitations or major roads. The fells of the Kentmere Round also lie in the far east of the Lake District, an area which tends to attract less attention than the craggier more celebrated fells to the west. As a rule of thumb the further east towards Shap and the A6 that you travel the less walkers you are likely to meet. Even the drive down the Kentmere valley is both beautiful and symbolic of leaving civilisation to enter nature's realm. This narrow road drive is for me part of the whole Kentmere Round experience.

So imagine, if you will, a glorious frosty and starlit night in winter. The car pulls over into a parking space in the Kentmere valley for an overnight stop. Only a nanny state, in my view, could object to a couple of harmless walkers parking overnight in such a remote place, where not so much as one other car disturbed us. Imagine getting out of the car at midnight to see an array of stars overhead, shining bright in a jet black sky. Stars you never realised existed in your normal light polluted urbanised environment. Imagine thick snow laying on the roadside and crunching unmistakably beneath your feet. Imagine seeing dark shapes, where no star light shone and then realising that these were the outlines of the high mountains around you and imagine waking to a glorious dawn with the sight of a snow plastered Kentmere Horseshoe awaiting you, the rising sun turning the wintry fells rose pink. All this before the walk had even begun.

Over my years walking the fells, I have noticed that most walkers seem to start their walks around nine or ten in the morning and finish their walks around five or six in the evening. I am not decrying that in any way, and it does fit in nicely with the creature comforts of cooked breakfast and evening meal and pub. However before and after these popular times exists a quieter zone of time. This provides an ever so slightly antisocial walker like me with the chance to get onto the hills without having a line of walkers following me, and then later to stay on the hills long after the hordes have descended. Additionally sunrise and sunset are some of the most profoundly beautiful events in the fells and the occasions when I have either been on a high fell to watch the dawn or left a high fell at dusk having seen the sunset, have been some of the most serene and at one with nature that I have had.

Setting off up Garburn Pass at six in the morning on a sub zero degrees winter day, our sprits could not have been higher. The stony path is the sort that attracts running rivulets of water, but that morning all the water had turned to thick ice. Sometimes a pass or a col (Scottish equivalent) can provide one of the highlights of a day. Until we reached the top of

Garburn Pass we had been enclosed in the folds of the fells, although the views were impressive towards Shap Fells and the Howgills, which stood out bathed by the rays of the rising sun. However at the top of the pass the views opened out and ahead of us we saw the Coniston Range lit up pink with the dawn light and looking magnificent in its snow robes. The snow was lying thick at Garburn Pass and the route ahead to the first summit of the day, Yoke, while perfectly obvious, was devoid of path and covered by deep snow drifts.

It was not so much a walk as a thigh deep wade in snow to the summit of Yoke. One particular moment will forever stay with me, when instead of snow underfoot I felt something harder like wood or metal. A few seconds of digging about with feet and hands by both of us revealed several flat pieces of wood, with a metal grill on top of them. For a moment or two we wondered what this could be. Then it dawned upon us. The snow was so deep here that it had banked right up and over a dry stone wall, and we had just trodden onto the flat top of a wooden wall stile, with its metal grill on top to provide some grip for walkers. The snow therefore must have been banked to around six feet here!

The first high summit of any given day on the fells is always a highlight. Yoke, while not the best view of the day, still had a very fine prospect, which was enhanced by our minds and bodies being at their freshest. Up on Yoke the winter sun had now risen. The clarity and intensely bright light of an early winter morning made for an enchanting view across the snowy skyline towards the Coniston Round and Scafells, while south was a grand prospect of Windermere (best seen from the slightly lower south cairn), the homely undulations of South Lakeland and the seascape beyond. Ahead and around us we could see most of the rest of our walk including our next objective Ill Bell, as well as Harter Fell and Kentmere Pike, all under heavy thick snow coats. It was a scene that called us onwards and promised excitement and wondrous views with every step. We knew at this point that we were living one of those classic walking days. Although it briefly occurred to us both that this could possibly be our finest ever day in the hills, the mundane criteria of ratings and rankings seemed petty when immersed in the reality.

I have to confess that we had a wonderful high speed bottom slide off both Ill Bell and Froswick, although I would not necessarily advise this as there are fearsome crags on the Kentmere valley side. We took the risk that day, steering our snow slide course well clear of any crags and had a great time, but the safety caveats I have referred to earlier must again be borne in mind!

The fells of the Kentmere round contain some of the finest and most extravagant cairns to be found anywhere in the Lake District. Ill Bell's small neat and rocky summit contains several beautifully made and graceful cairns, each of which is slender and several feet high. However, for sheer extravagance of cairn, the beacon cairn on Thornthwaite Crag beats them all, protruding some 14 feet into the air and perched on a rocky plinth to add an even greater impression of stature. Its layers of stone are pieced together perfectly, like a completed Jenga puzzle. I recall all 14 feet of that cairn being covered in thick hoar frost and ice that February day.

Nan Bield pass provided a welcome break from snow trudging. I said earlier that when planning winter walks consideration must be given to the fact that thick snow both slows a walker down and tires out the legs and feet quicker than normal walking. If there was a low moment that day it was the somewhat dispiriting climb from Nan Bield onto the great mass of Harter Fell. Many boots had worn thick steps into the snow, but it was hard work and the legs lacked energy. However, low moments in the fells are, in my experience, often followed by high ones and the view that greeted us at the summit of Harter Fell was arguably the finest and most infinitely clear that I have ever seen. It would be impossible for me ever to visit Harter Fell above Haweswater again and see a finer view. It was simply overwhelming and for stark winter beauty it ranks as possibly the finest I have seen. The snow covered undulations of Yoke, Ill Bell and Froswick formed the near scene, with their great plunges down to Kentmere Reservoir. Behind this grand prospect a myriad of familiar fell shapes, all decked out in snow, poked their heads up along the skyline. From this angle the top of Great Gable looked like a thimble, very different from its more familiar graceful outline as seen from Wastwater. But it was to the east that the panorama was at its most vast and clear. The Pennines, by some curious freak of clarity, seemed closer than they had ever seemed before and the towns and fields in the valley of the M6 corridor were also sharply clear. I recall that the brilliant winter sun, reflecting on the snow covered summit of Harter Fell, made us feel quite warm and it may sound slightly outrageous but my face felt a little sunburnt.

If Thornthwaite Crag wins the prize for the most beautiful and tallest cairn in the Lake District, then the collection of ironmongery mingled with a few stones that marks the summit of Harter Fell would probably rank as one of the scruffiest and ugliest cairns (Starling Dodd's cairn is also a contender). If Thornthwaite Beacon has a level of classic artistry that could be compared to a great sculpture by Michelangelo, then the cairn on Harter Fell is like some sinister twisted vision from the hands of an avant-garde sculptor. Nonetheless Stan and I spent a wonderful hour basking in the winter sun by that cairn and absorbing every aspect of the spectacular view into our consciousness. For this reason the Harter Fell in the Far East must rank as one of the finest summit experiences on my round of the Wainwrights.

It is quite normal for the excitement of a mountain walk to gradually taper off after the high point of the day has been reached and as thoughts turn to tiredness of limb and the desire for food and comfort. However, what made this day such a memorable one was that the joy and excitement continued as we crossed over the summit of Kentmere Pike, which has a dry stone wall running almost over its highest inches. The

A frozen Carl Side Tarn

views towards the fells we had visited earlier, Yoke, Ill Bell and Froswick continued to captivate us as the sun began to set and the colours on the fells shifted gradually from brilliant whites back to shades of pink. Late in the winter's afternoon we reached our final Wainwright of the day,

Shipman Knotts and the excitement continued as we had our first ever bird's eye view of the wild and remote valley of Longsleddale, a valley that was to be walked down for the first time much later in our Wainwright round. Longsleddale may well be regarded as where Lakeland ends and subtle contours more reminiscent of the Pennines begin, but the crag of Goat Scar is every bit Lakeland, and if Longsleddale is an end, it is a very beautiful and worthy end.

As we descended from Shipman Knotts the sun began to set brilliantly out to the west, the skies turned hues of orange, purple and light green and the rich colours on the snowy fells mirrored them in a grand natural display. This had been a walk that had everything and where virtually every moment from start to finish had been exciting and spectacular.

I hope that in this chapter I have provided a flavour of the unique and special qualities of walking that can be had in the Lake District under winter conditions. When snow covers the hills the days spent on them are to be cherished. Although there is a higher degree of attention to safety, weather and navigation required in winter conditions, I have always found these aspects add to the excitement of the situation. There is quite simply nothing finer than crunching those final few feet to a high snow covered summit and seeing a spectacular view of winter white fells arrayed around you.

Why Do People Bag Hills?

A hill bagger, in his or her purest form, is a person who collects summits and ticks them off on a list. The aim is to collect all the summits or ticks on a particular list. Where this book is concerned the bagger's list encompasses the 214 Lakeland Fells described in Alfred Wainwright's seven *Pictorial Guides*. However bagging is not limited to the Lakeland Fells. There are Munro baggers, whose intention is to climb all 284 of Scotland's peaks over 3000 feet. Then there are baggers of Scottish Corbetts and Grahams, of Welsh three thousand footers and even of all the tors on Dartmoor. In this beautiful island there are potentially well over 1000 hills to be bagged, enough for a lifetime.

Now as a self-confessed out of the closet bagger, I have often taken a good hard look at myself and my, at times, almost overwhelming desire to achieve a tick on some list. I can honestly say with hand on heart that all of the light hearted quips and jokes that are made about baggers are to some extent true. Pure bagging, in terms of ticking hills off a list, does indeed have a kinship with train spotting and stamp collecting. Dressed in my somewhat shabby, fashionably incorrect, hills walking attire, I cannot deny that I sometimes also closely resemble a train spotter.

Baggers are to a considerable degree selfish people, sometimes to the extent of alienating companions and becoming almost obsessed with their task. On my personal journey there have been good weather walking days when I have bagged say Ling Fell and Sale Fell, in order to tick them off the list, when I could easily have found myself on a favourite high mountain like Great Gable or Helvellyn having a superior experience. So there is also a self-defeating element about bagging at times, when the achievement of a tick becomes almost more important than the quality of walk had on that particular day. There have been times when I have been oblivious to the weather gathering ominously about me as I have focused on the tick. At times the humble bagger experiences something close to the summit fever experience had by climbers on Everest, as we grimly determine to grab our tick from the elements no matter what. More than once, while in the midst of my Wainwright round, I have had the feeling that the task was like a huge elephant on my back. At times I have had to put down the elephant and do a favourite fell that I have already done. Had I not done so, I might have gone bagging mad. Now I have completed my round of the 214 Wainwright summits it has indeed been nice to get rid of the elephant, at least in terms of bagging in the Lake District. Yet strangely, being a die hard bagger, the bagging urge still remains. I have done nearly 100 of the fells at least twice and have found myself already thinking about a second round of the Wainwright fells. After a lifetime of bagging I can imagine a bagger wonders whether there are hills to bag in heaven.

However, as well as acknowledging the undoubted personality defects of any bagger, I would also like to explain the more positive values of bagging. There are other reasons that dwell behind the obvious tick. During my time on the hills it has been my privilege to meet many walkers who were at various stages of bagging the Wainwrights. In the early days it might be that hoary old man on Blencathra who I admired for having nearly completed them all. On other meetings the conversation might be about the charms and qualities of a particular hill, which both I and my fellow bagger had climbed, or one which he had climbed and enjoyed and I still had to do on my list. More recently as I have neared completion of my Wainwright round, bagging has enabled me to have a good all round knowledge of the Lake District, which has more than once been of help and guidance to other less experienced walkers.

One factor that has been almost universally common among the baggers I have met is that they were harmless, self-effacing types. They have been the kind of unobtrusive and undemanding types that you don't mind meeting on the fells. If we baggers appear curmudgeonly it is generally not because we are Scrooge type characters, but because our reasons for walking are not social ones. Most of the baggers I have met have either been alone or with just one or two other baggers. Bagging is by nature a fairly lonely activity. However, on the many times I have engaged in conversation with fellow baggers it has nearly always been interesting conversation. Most baggers who I have talked to also have an innate mutual understanding of that point in any chat on a fell, where a person wants their solitude back. So despite the obvious failings of a bagger, which most of us baggers readily acknowledge, I would also sing the praises of the many baggers I have met both in the Lake District and Scotland. I would rather meet a bagger than a clueless walker who climbs a fell without any idea which fell he is actually climbing. I would much rather have a conversation about the merits of Brae Fell with a bagger, than have someone making small talk to me about where I am staying in Keswick, where I work and even once about the contents of the sandwich I was eating. I have also noticed that baggers have a love for the hills that manifests itself in that key word on the hills, respect. Baggers seldom litter the fells. Baggers don't tend to erect unnecessary cairns or add stones to existing cairns. Baggers don't tend to scrawl things like 'Bob luvs Belinda' on the summit shelter or adorn the walls of a bothy or hut with smutty prose.

While the tick list may be at face value the reason behind the baggers motivation, there is far more to bagging than that. There are no doubt people within the species of baggers who do simply touch a cairn and then dash as quickly as possible back to their accommodation in order to tick the hill off the list, never to return again to the hill. However, these are in my experience a minority. For the majority of us the list of hills to be bagged merely acts as an overall framework for a lifetime of appreciation and enjoyment. Some baggers, myself included, started out climbing the high and famous Lakeland fells without any intention to climb them all, yet somehow got gradually sucked into the addictive world of bagging.

I met an old man once in Scotland who had climbed many Scottish hills but had no desire at all to complete all of them. He had climbed his favourite hills more than one hundred times and would occasionally make a foray into a new hill or area, not driven by ticks, by driven by his own needs that day. He did not care for doing a dull hill simply because it was on a list and to a certain degree I admire him for not allowing the hills to become items on an agenda. But on the other hand surely whenever we step into the hills on any given day we are slave to some extent to an agenda. Even if you wild camp for several nights on the fells, you still have to plan your route to some degree and the hills you are going to climb and places you are going to stop. So why should one agenda be any less valid than another? I had a wealth of respect for that old man in Scotland, who probably had more climbing in his legs than I will ever have, but unlike him I do feel the desire to climb that dull rounded hill on the list. If it remains unclimbed I will always wonder what its ascent might have been like. I will wonder how the view may have subtly differed in its beauty and composition from the views from other neighbouring hills I had climbed. As my Wainwright round progressed, as well as having the obvious desire to climb all the fells, I also had a feeling that if I stopped short of climbing them all, my knowledge of the Lake District would be less than I wanted it to be. It is as if some great jigsaw puzzle had been laid before me, with all the pieces at first scattered and hidden, but then gradually turned over and each slotted into its place in the overall scheme of things. So having climbed say High Seat in the Central Fells, there was an obvious desire within me to climb Ullscarf next door to it. Having bagged both I can now see that although close to each other, each has its own different qualities both of terrain, atmosphere and view.

Each person has their own individual criteria within the framework of a love of the hills. For example, in my own personal computer spreadsheet of the hills, which I am sad enough to keep, I record whether, on the first ascent of a hill, I have actually seen the view. And those hills that I have climbed and not seen the view from become priority fells to go back to on a clear day, at some stage in the future. For instance although I have climbed High Crag of the High Stile range, I have yet to see a clear view from it.

Another personal maxim of mine throughout my Wainwright journey has been to make sure that it never became about having to do a new fell every day. Recently I have contented myself with around 10 new Wainwrights a year, sometimes more, sometimes less. This has usually left me with a number of other days each year where I could do an old favourite, or explore a different aspect of a fell I had climbed before, or just do a low level exploration along new footpaths. I have had a conscious desire to try and strike a balance between the self-imposed task or ambition to bag them all and not making that desire restrict the sense of freedom that can, and should, be had in the fells. In my view completing the Wainwrights should be a constant task of joy and not a schedule that enslaves its owner. While I can accept the fact that some people complete their round of the Wainwrights in a few months or even a few days, I have preferred to tease it out for nearly 20 years, while at the same time desiring to complete the round while I was still relatively young.

All of which shows that although baggers may have the same end goals, there are many different ways of achieving that goal. No method is any less valid than another. It is all about personal choice and that is the way it should be. No-one is likely to cover you in wreaths of flowers or roll out a red carpet when you complete Wainwright's fells. But by the same token no-one is likely to berate you over how you go about completing the Wainwrights.

Another reason behind bagging, which I have alluded to earlier, is the achievement of a personal ambition. Without the achievement of doing the Wainwrights the extent of my own personal achievements to date would have only gone as far as obtaining various promotions within the realm of the Financial Services industry. The Wainwrights have provided me with an altogether different ambition that was not linked to money or status. This has been, if you like, a selfish ambition, but one that through being selfish has maintained my sanity and provided stress relief throughout years of commuting to and from London and being huddled into a carriage on the Jubilee Line. Wainwright believed that life without ambition was 'just aimless wandering' and for me the desire to not just aimlessly wander on the fells is another part of my reason for bagging. It is also good to indulge in aimless wandering at times and I admit I sometimes like to begin walks not having decided which walk or mountain I am going to climb and letting my momentary whims guide me. But it is also fantastic to have certain goals and achievements in the hills to work towards. Wainwright set himself the personal goal of climbing, describing and illustrating all the routes up all the Lakeland fells. He was dogged and determined in this aim but he simply could not have achieved his single minded task if he had just wandered aimlessly in the hills.

Over the years of adulthood as my responsibility and stress levels have inevitably increased, visits to the hills have provided my mental and spiritual battery with a top up boost. The air of the Lake District replenishes and cleanses both my physical and spiritual lungs. I find now that if I am away from the hills for longer than two months I start experiencing withdrawal symptoms, and if the gap between visits to the hills lasts for longer than around four months, which is rare, I find myself getting the hills equivalent of seasonal affective disorder. Perhaps in this case SAD could also stand for summit absent distress.

I suppose some people give up on completing all the Wainwrights because they feel that they will have to visit quite a few dull hills or places where the scenic beauty is diminished and the craggy mountains are replaced by mere rounded foothills. I agree that there is a certain amount of that. No one would have an overwhelming desire to climb Little Mell Fell, Sallows or Ling Fell if they were not part of the Wainwright round, although perversely I find their very lack of redeeming features to have a certain quality of its own. However, dull Wainwrights are rare and I can honestly say that there have been few Wainwrights that on closer inspection have not either matched up to, or in a lot of cases exceeded, my expectations. Gems such as High Rigg, Black Fell, Binsey, Crag Fell and Great Borne are just a few places that without the framework of the 214 fells in Wainwright's Guides, might not immediately suggest themselves and yet each one has provided me with a special memory. Even the three miscreants quoted above provided their own unique memories. On Little Mell Fell I had half an hour of solitude under blackening skies. On Sallows I had low mist through which I got the occasional eerie view down towards

Bowness Knott and Great Borne from Crag Fell

Kendal and on Ling Fell I reclined among the heather and chatted about nothing and everything with Stan. So another reason for bagging all the Wainwrights is that every fell in fact has some merits, even if those merits are sometimes more due to the weather or your companion, than due to the qualities of the fell itself.

My final justification for bagging the Wainwrights is a simple word, but one that has so much depth and meaning. That word is love. Just as two people in love will want to explore and have an intimate knowledge both mentally and physically of each other, such is the same with me and the Lake District. And because of that my love of the Lake District extends beyond just bagging the 214 summits. I will not rest until I have an intimate knowledge not just of each fell, but of every square kilometre of land within the Lake District National Park. Wainwright described his affection with the Lake District as a love affair and to many baggers and non-baggers alike this will ring true.

Alfred Wainwright may well have been the first person to explore and climb all of the Lakeland fells, even though he did so as a pioneer rather than as a devoted follower. AW did not stop until he had chronicled every boulder and scree fan and contour on every fell, until he had annotated every route, no matter how dull, up every fell. The Lake District to him was an obsession but an obsession in the healthiest sense. In this chapter I have tried to explain some of the reasons behind tick bagging a list of hills. In summary I suppose there should be a little depth and a lot of love behind the surface of bagging. If not, we baggers may as well just accept we are little more than train spotters in another guise.

Solitude and Silence

Most hill walkers have a special place or area, somewhere that for them provides an experience that they simply cannot find anywhere else. For Wainwright that most special of places was Haystacks and for me that special place is the area of Skiddaw Forest, the Uldale Fells and the country referred to simply as Back o'Skidda. The fells here lurk relatively neglected behind the vast facades of Skiddaw and Blencathra; a rolling mini-wilderness of heather and course grass.

My special place may seem odd to those who have merely looked at this area on the map or made a fleeting acquaintance with these rolling hills. There are few crags, few soaring outlines and plunging drops, nothing especially high, or especially dramatic and rocky and only one jewel like Lakeland tarn. Some may sneer disdainfully at this area and dismiss it as atypical of proper picture postcard Lakeland. Their qualifications for judging it so may only be that they have glanced at the area from Skiddaw's mainline or Blencathra's summit, or perhaps once wondered through it along the Cumbria Way. If they had perhaps taken time to discover its hidden qualities, time to come under its slow and subtle spell, they might think differently.

The charm of the fells Back O'Skidda lays not so much in any one feature, crag, precipice or summit view, but more in the unique feel and atmosphere of the area as a whole and its sense of space, freedom and silence. The lonely miles and the sound of silence call you back when you are absent. Whenever I plan a week in the Lake District, I will always plan at least one day in the Northern Fells, even though I have long since 'bagged' all of them.

For me this area behind Skiddaw and Blencathra is synonymous with solitude and solo excursions. It is a place best experienced alone, when the sound of silence can balm and relax you into an almost meditative state. From a practical point of view it is also a good place for a relatively inexperienced walker to start doing wild solo walks. That is not in any way to underestimate its wildness, as it is quite possible to get very lost out here. But though it is a wilderness of sorts, even at the heart of the Northern Fells you are in fact no more than about 4 miles from civilisation and the wide path of the Cumbria Way, cutting through the centre of the area, provides a safe get out clause if you get caught in bad weather.

My first encounter with this area was on the Cumbria Way, whose route led me round the side of Lonscale Fell, and on to Skiddaw House and Dash Falls, via the heart of Skiddaw Forest. It was a glorious April day of light winds, pleasant warmth and little puffy white clouds. I had never before experienced such miles of seeming emptiness, but as soon as I rounded the side of Lonscale Fell and started heading north on the rocky path above the Glenderaterra Beck, with the view to Great Calva and Skiddaw Forest ahead of me, I knew that I was going to love this place. Here you step into another time and another world. Here is a place whose pulse beats over eons of time and for whom the short span of mankind means nothing.

My first solo expedition into these rolling lonely fells, in May 1993, was also the first time that I had ever done a full day's outing alone in the hills. The thought and excitement of striking out on my own made me plan a massive walk. Starting from Keswick, I was to walk to Threlkeld and then climb up Blencathra via Halls Fell, (a part of this walk I have already described), before venturing out onto Bannerdale Crags and Bowscale Fell and then using the Cumbria Way for a quick return route. I began with a wonderful walk beneath Blencathra's impressive front, looking up at the dramatic Gategill and Gategill Fell from below, before heading up the narrow arête of Halls Fell. It would still have been a sizeable walk if I had just chosen to head back down Blease Fell and walk from there back into Keswick, but instead I had other plans on my mind. Having attained the summit of Blencathra early in the afternoon, the rolling fells behind it were at my mercy. I wanted to leave behind the crowds and enter an altogether different world. I wanted to experience the joys of walking solo in a lonely place for the first time.

As I headed from the summit of Blencathra to the top of Foule Crag and then descended towards the Glenderamackin col, the people faded away like morning mist, until I found myself utterly alone. Just after dropping down the fan of scree from the summit ridge of Blencathra, there is a sharp little prominence of rock, a wonderful vantage point that I visited for the first time that day, but have visited many times since. From here is a bird's eye view, across a vast yawning chasm, to a side on profile of Sharp Edge and Foule Crag. Often the edge takes on a fearsome dark hue with the sun behind it, and it is interesting to watch the little figures heading along the crest, while one relaxes and reclines in a safe vantage. This little rocky perch has an accommodating little flat area just adequate enough to make a natural seat. It is one of those special little lonely places that the Northern Fells contain, but it is not a place for parties of people, so take my advice and go there alone.

As I left the vantage point and turned my back on the celebrity of Sharp Edge and Blencathra, I got a true sense of exploration. No doubt thousands upon thousands of walkers had in fact traipsed this way before. But I was now alone and heading into a vast empty landscape and it was easy to entertain pleasant illusions of being a lonely pioneer. Although walking in the Lake District is always a delight, there can be times when the sheer volume of people accompanying me up a fell does detract from the raw experience of a natural environment. It is an impossible conundrum as everyone has, and should have, the right to roam on the open access of the fells. However that very right, priceless though it is, can at times spoil the very essence of why we come to such places.

Out behind Skiddaw and Blencathra however a vast quiet area awaits for the walker who simply wants to get away from people. This is not necessarily because he or she is antisocial. Indeed I have partied with the best of them in my time. It is more because within many of us there is a need occasionally to be alone and in being alone to cleanse our minds and experience a certain oneness with nature. However I would add that even the fells Back O'Skidda have become a little more popular since I first walked there 15 years ago.

On my first few trips Back O' Skidda, I hardly met anyone and if I did it was just the odd solo walker. Meeting anyone was a rarity and the odd person one encountered did not really detract from the overall sense of solitude. Recently however I have detected a subtle but gradual increase in popularity of even this Lakeland backwater. Don't get me wrong, these fells are still comparatively lonely and, although numbers of walkers have increased, they still remain relatively unpopular. The difference is more subtle than a sudden influx of hordes of walkers descending on the area. It is perhaps that a dozen or so years ago I did not expect to meet anyone out here, and if I did it was an exception rather than a rule. Whereas before there were just vast acres of loneliness and solitude out here, these days I have to hunt out particular fells and ridges in more and more isolated situations to obtain that true solitude. The difference is that even in these fells now solitude can no longer be taken for granted.

If that sense of solitude ever completely disappeared here, I believe that this area would have lost its greatest quality. Quite what the answer is to the slow but relentless increase in human traffic on the fells, I don't know. Restrictions and quotas of walkers on each fell would be both highly difficult to manage and more fundamentally a breach of our freedom to roam. However, there should still be some places where a walker can reasonably expect to be alone, or at least relatively undisturbed. My only personal advice would be if you want to go in a party or large group, go up a popular fell where parties are an accepted norm on that fell, such as a Scafell Pike or an Old Man of Coniston. If you want to go to the wild and rolling fells around Skiddaw Forest, respect their solitude and the needs of your fellow walkers and go alone, or at most with one other companion. If every walker adopted this practice, the lonely corners of Lakeland could remain relatively lonely for the foreseeable future.

The flat top of Bannerdale Crags is not the most inspiring of places, but I have nonetheless always found it to be a fine place for a contemplative stop. Sharp Edge and Blencathra still dominate a large portion of the view and block out many of Lakeland's better known summits, but there is a fine prospect out towards the Eastern and Far Eastern Fells and an even finer prospect looking towards the flatlands stretching away to the M6 corridor and the Pennines. But Bannerdale Crags is about more than just its view, as is this whole area. It is about the experience of solitude, that feeling of almost travelling back in time to an era when the fells were largely untrodden. Sharing a summit with a hundred other people it is hard to get any feeling of getting back to one's natural primitive roots, but here in the Northern Fells that essence of man combining with nature can be keenly felt. The first time I sat by the little pile of stones that marked the summit of Bannerdale Crags a feeling of peace and oneness with nature washed over me and cleansed me. I knew then that these fells would lure me back again and again, with their age old subtle charms.

Now although I have said that the fells Back o'Skidda lack in crags and drama, Bannerdale Crags does its best to buck this trend. The fell gets its name from the mile long rim of crags that dwells beneath the flat summit area and extends almost all the way to neighbouring Bowscale Fell. It is true that this is not really in the same league as, for example, Scafell Crag and is composed mainly of flaky rock and steep grass, rather than sheer slabs and walls of rock. However a walk along the narrow paths on the rim of the crags still provides an exhilarating half mile or so of drama. And this line of crags is parted by one of the hidden gems of the Northern Fells, a spur of slate rock which forms the East Ridge of Bannerdale Crags.

Many times when I have been leaving the Lake District via the A66 towards Penrith, I have looked back towards the East Ridge, which tries its best to compete with Sharp Edge, and longed to climb it. Wainwright's comments and recommendations about the East Ridge in his *Northern*

Fells Guide merely increased the desire, but it was not until November 2006 that I finally climbed Bannerdale Crags by this route. My walk began at the tiny but attractive hamlet of Mungrisdale. Whereas some walks need a few miles of leg work to get off the beaten track and into the wild and lonely places, this walk had solitude in spade loads. After just a few yards I left the minor road and having shut the gate behind me, a world of solitude was immediately entered. That day started cold with ice formed on the path, but as the sun rose in a clear blue sky, the day became decidedly warm for early November. Ahead of me was the huge pyramid like end of The Tongue and to the left of that the rising sun was keenly highlighting the East Ridge of Bannerdale Crags, defining its lonely drama for me. Eventually, by the river that heads on to the village of Scales, I left the good low level path and took a minor thread of a path heading up towards the East Ridge. A wide grassy promenade leads to the base of the East Ridge. Even though the human traffic has increased in the Northern Fells over recent years, this promenade is still one of those places where you don't expect to meet anyone and I didn't. The silence was profound and was only interrupted, as I began walking up the East Ridge proper, by the noise of the slate rock tinkling beneath my feet, waking up this lonely place.

Now although the East Ridge looks quite fearsome when viewed from a distance it is in fact a very easy but nonetheless highly enjoyable route. There are no awkward obstacles to be overcome and its charms are more to do with its situation and solitude than with any real sense of exposure or rush of adrenalin. It is quite simply a divine place to be. About half way up the ridge, providing a good excuse for a stop, is a ruined stone hut. This is a remnant from the workings of the Bannerdale Lead Mine and a reminder that, even in the wildest parts of Lakeland, ruins from an industrial past are present. However, as with many other ruins in Lakeland, the hut almost seems to have become an organic part of the ridge it sits upon. I sat in the hut, hoping for a few minutes to bond with the hut and the ridge in an organic unity. The minutes I spent there, although not time spent on a summit or a new Wainwright, were some of the most precious and energy boosting I have spent in the fells. I had passed over two hours entirely alone, a rare thing in modern Lakeland. I can recommend the East Ridge of Bannerdale Crags, but the experience will be richer if you go alone.

That November day I headed from Bannerdale Crags onto Blencathra and from there down to Keswick. But back in May 1993 on my first encounter with Bannerdale Crags, I had a much longer and more remote

The East Ridge of Bannerdale Crags

route in mind. Having sampled the delights of the path above the rim of Bannerdale Crags, I headed up onto Bowscale Fell. Here I encountered my first walker since the summit ridge of Blencathra. We exchanged a few pleasantries and he imparted a little knowledge to me, and then we moved on our respective ways and gave each other our solitude back. It was already four o'clock in the afternoon as I reached the shelter on Bowscale Fell, but although it was a long way back to Keswick, I did not want to hurry. It was not important to get back for tea time, or a pub meal, it was only important that I judged my walk so that I got back before dark. The presence of Sharp Edge and Blencathra loom majestically from Bowscale Fell and there is a good view into the heart of Skiddaw Forest and also across the valley containing the River Caldew to the impressive grey flanks of Carrock Fell. Up here on my own, in the late afternoon sunshine of a May day, I felt truly isolated and out on a limb, yet at the same time deeply cleansed of all stresses and worries. Within such isolation one can truly lose one's sense of self and gain a sense of perspective on the petty problems of human day to day existence.

Before I headed back on the return journey to Keswick, I had one final treat that I wanted to at least see, even though there was insufficient time to visit it. Bowscale Tarn, once a favourite spot for tourists in the Victorian age, has these days become rather more neglected. It appeared from a study of my map, that I should get a sighting of the tarn by visiting a lower cairn on Bowscale Fell and a quick five minute grassy romp brought this jewel of Lakeland into view. Although contained in a dark hollow, the tarn sparkled beneath me in the late afternoon sunshine and presented by this beautiful lonely scene, I could almost believe the legend that spoke of two immortal fish that inhabited those diamond studded waters. Not a bad place to pass an eternity, although, being fish, I doubt, if the legend is true, that they appreciate that.

The map seemed to show a nice red dotted path leading down from the col between Bowscale Fell and Bannerdale Crags, following Blackhazel Beck, before meeting and crossing the River Caldew. A faint path was duly found at said col and was followed for a short while before it disappeared, providing me with my first taste of the grim reality that paths shown on maps are not always paths that are easily found or even exist at all on the ground. This is especially true Back O'Skidda and if that path did continue, I certainly never found it again. Instead I found myself heading down the type of steep grassy ground that a human being is not really designed for. However Blackhazel Beck was still beside me and I could clearly see the River Caldew ahead of me, so all seemed well. However, my naive presumption that the red dotted path would make an easy ford of the River Caldew was somewhat far from the truth. Instead I found myself wading around in bog by the banks of the Caldew. The solid stone path of the Cumbria Way lay just a few feet away on the other side of the river, but it appeared that it was only going to be reached by wading across the river. For a while I experienced that type of floundering walking along a boggy river bank that makes me question, at the time, why I love fell walking so much. Then I struck gold in the form of a Land Rover track. However this was to prove a fool's gold, for where the track forded the River Caldew, although a 4 wheel drive vehicle weighing several tonnes would have had no trouble crossing, the depth of the water and the strong current which I could clearly see, meant that this was going to be an awkward moment for this walker. As I waded knee deep in River Caldew, I could feel the tug of the current trying to haul me away. I had wanted to be close to nature that day, but this was getting a little too close! Eventually I made it to the other side and the wide solid comfort of the Cumbria Way path, with nothing more than hurt pride and water filled boots. Basking in the glow of an all day walk and having overcome my awkward moment, the crossing now merely seemed to have been a necessary initiation ceremony into wild solo walking in the Northern Fells.

It was by now nearly six o'clock in the evening and still around seven miles walking back to Keswick. Even lonely Skiddaw House, which I could now see, was a distant object two miles away. I usually find that the walker's mind, when already quite tired but still faced with long distances, copes best by breaking the return journey down into stages. I could see Skiddaw House and so that represented the first stage. I decided that I would motivate myself by moving non stop till I reached Skiddaw House, but would allow myself ten minutes rest when I got there. Once I left the grey bleakness of Skiddaw House behind, my next objective was to get to where the path turned around the side of Lonscale Fell, where The Vale of Keswick could at last be seen. The thought of that homely view motivated me for the next couple of miles. Once there, I focused on the car park at the top of Gale Road and from the car park it was about getting into Keswick and the by now half hallucinatory lure of fish and chips. The last mile or so down to Spooney Green Lane was in almost pitch black darkness. By the time I reached the streets of Keswick, I had been on the walk for twelve long but unforgettable hours.

Recalling the last few miles of this walk makes me think about the pros and cons of solitude versus companionship on a walk. That day I found that while I was on the outward journey I was immersed in and loved the solitude. Yet once I reached the Cumbria Way and the long return leg back to Keswick I would have been grateful of company. While the feeling of reaching a summit all alone is both profound and unforgettable, it is also fantastic to reach a summit with a companion and have someone to share the sense of elation and exhilaration with. While Wainwright chose to make his exploration of the Lakeland fells on his own and no doubt experienced countless times that profound sense of isolation, I often wonder whether there were times during his solitary task of completing the seven guides when he longed for someone with him to share a particular moment. I have a great love of going solo, but for me it compliments the times that I go walking with my close companions. Sometimes I meet up with my walking comrades at an agreed summit, each of us having had five or six hours of going solo and we then share companionship for the return walk, when it is most wanted.

Recalling the walk from Skiddaw House along the Cumbria Way to Keswick also makes me think of a fell that dominates this route and which, over the years, has become one of my favourites. This is Lonscale Fell. Now in the realms of hard fact Lonscale Fell is really no more than a flank of Skiddaw. If it were in Scotland it would hardly warrant a mention and would not be a separately classified summit. But so often in the hills the bare facts do not tell the whole story, for Lonscale Fell, although forever attached to Skiddaw and only a couple of miles from its busy main line route and summit, may as well be a million miles away.

Although Lonscale Fell is generally about the more subtle attractions of heather and grass and loneliness, just like Bannerdale Crags it has its own secret. Few travellers along the busy A66 can have failed to notice the fearful drop of crags from the summit of Lonscale Fell and from this angle it appears a most graceful and almost separate fell. However, this steep face of Lonscale Fell actually contains a perfectly safe, although a little exposed and very dramatic, route onto the fell. This is the north-east buttress of Lonscale Fell and is a secret gem of a place. It is more challenging and steeper than the East Ridge of Bannerdale Crags, but nowhere near as tricky, or potentially dangerous, as say Sharp Edge. In one respect it perhaps out performs any of Lakeland's many ridges with its sense of isolated situation and height. Walking along the slightly exposed and rocky section of the Cumbria Way beneath Lonscale Fell the drops down to the Glenderaterra Beck and the sense of height are already impressive. However once you head off the Cumbria Way path and make your way up the steep end of the north-east buttress, this sense of height increases with every hard won step. The bodily motions to be experienced going up the north-east buttress are more akin to scrambling than walking, but a type of scrambling that is less to do with rock, than with hauling oneself up extremely steep heather slopes. A little over half way up the north-east buttress is a little natural shelter, and a wonderful stop can be had here to fully appreciate the sense of height. Beneath you the grey path of the Cumbria Way winds its course far below and then even further below the Glenderaterra Beck makes its sparkling progress, while across this yawning chasm squats the massive hulk of Blease Fell, lending the situation an even greater sense of exposure. But the exposure is immensely satisfying and in my three ascents of Lonscale Fell by this route so far, I have met no-one and felt truly at one with that ridge and its fantastic situation.

The ridge eventually flattens and trends above some fearful crags to the fantastic East Peak of Lonscale Fell. Although in height this is not the true summit, which lies on a flat area to the West, East Peak is in my view the spiritual summit and the finest viewpoint on Lonscale Fell. The true summit, although a few metres higher, lacks the sheer drop that gives East Peak such a fine sense of a worthy mountain top. In all my visits to Lonscale Fell I have perhaps spent a dozen hours of my life relaxing on East Peak, but maybe only a few minutes on the true summit of Lonscale Fell.

East Peak is a fantastic place for a quiet peaceful contemplation of the Northern Fells. In many visits to this place I have rarely encountered anybody. From this airy vantage the vastness of Skiddaw Forest can be truly appreciated. Looking into the heart of the Northern Fells the predominant colour is the brown of the heather, but it is surprising how beautiful and varied this brown can be, as it ranges from deep browns and light browns to sandy browns, depending on the weather. This landscape is perhaps at is finest on days of alternating sunshine and cloud, when the sun lights up areas of the heather in fleeting hues of gold, while the shade colours other areas a more sombre deep brown. But this is not just a view into the wildness of the Northern Fells, it is also a fine view into Lakeland, especially down the natural rift of St John's in the Vale towards Thirlmere and beyond to Loughrigg Fell. This is the geological fault line that divides the Lake District in a north to south direction.

I have often found myself alone on East Peak and indulging in the kind of activities that are best appreciated alone. I am a great fan of classical music and often find that certain pieces of music can combine with certain landscapes in a kind of symbiosis, which for a while can intoxicate both the ears and the eyes. The last time I was on East Peak I found myself conducting some Sibelius in a stress relieving frenzy using my walking pole as a baton. It may sound crazy and I would certainly never dream of doing this within sight of another person. However there are times when I think it does everybody good to express their emotions and joy freely. You often hear about people so stressed that they just want to shout out loud. Instead of shouting out loud I just use my times of solitude to indulge myself and relax. The great poet Samuel Coleridge Taylor used to enjoy dropping himself off precipitous crags, just to test the extent of his personal risk taking by letting nature take its course with his life and soul. Next to that my ways of heightening my own experiences in the wilds seem positively bland.

From East Peak it is but a short walk to the true summit of Lonscale Fell. If like me, you have drunk in the view and the solitude on East Peak, there will be little on the flat summit of Lonscale Fell to keep you long. However, if like me, you are also prone to carrying Wainwright's guides with you on your walk, you may be surprised to find that the small pile

Back o'Skidda from East Peak Lonscale Fell

of stones which he shows as marking the summit in his 45 year old guide book, has been recently replaced by a prominent and sizeable cuboid shaped cairn. Although, I first thought this neat cairn was entirely new, I have since read that it is actually a re-erected cairn, presumably from various stones lying nearby. So perhaps at one stage there was a cairn like this marking the summit. However this neat cairn was certainly not there when Wainwright wrote the Northern Fells guide and seems to have sprung up or been re-erected in the last few years. It is one example of a number of cairns in the Northern Fells that have recently been enlarged or added to, or simply built from scratch. Where once were just small untidy piles of stones, humble, unobstrusive and therefore in fitting with these subtle lonely places, there are now some much larger structures, which in my view are totally out of character with the area. The cairn on Bannerdale Crags seems to have doubled in size in the last few years, and most absurd of all there is now a large cairn marking the top of Mungrisdale Common of all things, a fell of which Wainwright said 'any one of a thousand tufts of tough bent and cotton grass might lay claim to crowning the highest point'.

I am not a fan of cairn building for the sake of it. I acknowledge and accept that man's works are all over the fells, but these are by and large the works of an industrial past when people had to make a living out of these fells. A large cairn is fitting on something such as Great Gable or Scafell Pike and ancient cairns crowning rocky summits do often add something to the mountain. But why a large cairn on Mungrisdale Common? Why can people not just leave the wilds of Mungrisdale Common pristine and cairnless? It is a bleak and featureless place and that is its appeal for a lot of walkers who go there. Why can walkers not be allowed to merely guess at the highest tuft of grass on Mungrisdale Common like Wainwright must have done, rather than have it announced with an in your face cairn? It is almost as if these cairn builders want to in some way urbanise the raw wildness of such places.

The re-erected cairn on Lonscale Fell can in most weathers and types of light be clearly seen from the main line up Skiddaw and I have no doubt that walkers who have not even heard of Lonscale Fell and don't really give a jot about it, will find themselves heading off towards it purely because there is a big neat cairn there. Should such walkers really be encouraged onto a sacred and lonely place of wildness such as Lonscale Fell? Surely Lonscale Fell is a place for the keen walker to discover and enjoy, rather than for the casual walker to be guided to by its large neat cairn. Why is there a desire to make things neat as if the Lake District was the local landscaped park? If a cairn is untidy or a summit is just marked by one stone or even by nothing, why not leave it that way? Personally, I think there should be a public ban on further cairn building or additions to existing cairns in the Lake District!

Thankfully the Uldale Fells are pretty much free of such cairn enlarging and being still further north and further out from popular Lakeland, these fells have a unique feeling of their own. They are far removed from the crags and high mountains of Wasdale, Langdale and Eskdale, but they have a certain appeal and a certain quality of rolling calm loneliness. They provide an experience that can be just as special, in its own gentle way, as time spent on Great Gable and Bowfell. For these reasons one of my favourite fells is Great Cockup.

Now I doubt very much that many walkers would rank Great Cockup as one of their favourites among Wainwright's 214 fells. Many may think me crazy to even try to elevate Great Cockup into the ranks of other favourites of mine like Pillar, Great Gable and Haystacks. Even the name lacks the elegance of the popular fells, and speaks of some abortion of the landscape, an unwanted and unloved cockup. Yet for me there is something almost monastic about the simple pleasures to be had on Great Cockup. Once the gate near Horsemoor Hills, which has a sign announcing the Uldale Fells, has been closed behind you, the world of man and civilisation is left behind and a calming world of peace is entered. A beautiful track winds up from the base of Great Cockup. The track eventually leads to the gap of Trusmadoor. However if you want to climb Great Cockup, leave the track where it begins to flatten out and simply head up the heathery flanks. This is a bit of a slog, but I have often found a certain satisfaction in just wandering up some steep heathery shoulder devoid of paths. It is almost as if before the contemplative joys of the summit, a certain amount of purging of mind and body through hard exercise is needed. Eventually things flatten out and you find yourself on the wide lonely ridge that leads between Little Cockup and Great Cockup. A further steep pull on grass leads to a defined top with a neat pile of stones to mark it. This is not the actual summit, which lies 300 yards to the east on a flat area, but it is another example, like Lonscale Fell, of a hill's spiritual top not actually being the highest point. This west top, for want of a better description, has more of a sense of height and drop than the flat plateau containing the true summit. I cannot imagine wanting to spend much time sitting by the pile of stones that marks the true top, but this slightly lower point calls out for a stop. It even has a little natural grassy sitting area a few feet below the cairn.

Now I am not going to pretend that the view from Great Cockup rivals the great views to be had from the high mountains in the heart of the Lake District. The charms of the view from Great Cockup are more pastoral than dramatic, and yet it has a silent peaceful beauty. It is the kind of view of patchwork fields and farmsteads and copses of trees that can be just as absorbing to study as a panorama of craggy mountains. The subtle undulations and contours contained in this view have for me a powerful and meditative quality. Due to its situation on the Northern edge of the Lake District, it also provides a wide ranging view of the Cumbrian plains that stretch away to the Solway Firth, with the instantly recognisable Criffel standing proud as the first hill in Scotland. How summits and views can be measured has been, and will continue to be, a subject for debate among walkers, but although few may agree with me, I consider an hour spent alone studying the intimacies of the view from Great Cockup to be just as worthy a tonic for the soul as the grandest mountain panorama to be had. I doubt that Great Cockup will suddenly become the new Great Gable as a result of readers noting my words of love. Those that do go there and enjoy its unobtrusive charms will be likely to be the types of solitary walkers who would have sought it out and found it anyway, regardless of my praise.

A circular walk of Great Cockup alone can be done by descending steeply to the narrow cleft of Trusmadoor and from there picking up a faint track back around the flanks of the fell, which eventually rejoins the original path at the start of the ascent. This is a lovely lonely promenade. Whether you are just doing a circular walk of Great Cockup, or intend to carry on to Meal Fell and other greater things, Trusmadoor is a place worthy of a stop. It is another of those places that are surprising to find among the generally rolling landscape of the Northern Fells. The ground that drops down from Great Cockup, on the one side, and from Meal Fell, on the other side, is very steep and although there are only rashes of stone and rock here, the whole impression is one of drama, albeit on a modest scale. Furthermore, because within this wild declivity almost all views are obscured by the sizeable mounds of Great Cockup and Meal Fell, the sense of isolation here is acute. In fact, although not the wildest of Lakeland places in terms of distance from a road or habitation, Trusmadoor is in my view one of the wildest places in terms of feeling and atmosphere. I have often stopped here and emptied my mind by doing nothing more complicated than lying on my back, closing my eyes and letting the gentle sound of Burntod Gill wash its natural music over me.

While it is tempting to have a long snooze at Trusmadoor and then just head back along the flanks of Great Cockup as I have done on lazy days, such actions do not a Wainwright bagger make, especially when Meal Fell stands above you and provides another tick on the list. As you climb Meal Fell there is a real feeling of already being in isolation, but heading even further out on a limb. Meal Fell is perhaps a little pudding like, but in fairness it is quite a slender graceful pudding. The summit of Meal Fell has a massive wall shelter and a ring of stones that gives the impression of an ancient hill fort. It has mouldered nicely into the fell itself. It was here, on my first visit, that I had one of my most profound hill walking experiences. I have sometimes found that the time spent on a hill can be divided into various sections. I'll explain. On first reaching any new summit there are feelings of excitement, joy and relief. This is usually followed by some refreshments, study of maps, photos, a detailed study of the view, etc. However, having done all the usual things that one does on the summit and having drunk in the view from Meal Fell, I stayed longer, much longer. I became eventually oblivious to the passing of time and as a gentle breeze stirred the coarse grass around me, I became conscious of an experience beyond the obvious delights of view and summit. It was as if for a time I had connected with the very essence of the fell, become a part of the fell, a part of the wind that blew across it and a part of the gently rustling grass around me. I had lost for a few precious seconds all sense of self and made a brief and primal connection with the landscape immediately beneath and around me. Time does not always allow us such luxuries and profundities on the fells, but it is occasionally worth spending the time to discover a unique experience that lies beyond the immediate appeals of the hills we climb.

Although I cannot sing the praises of the Northern Fells highly enough, I would also be the first to admit that among these fells are a few candidates for the title of dullest Wainwright. Bakestall is one 'fell' that did not really do it for me. It seemed merely a bump on the long descent north from Skiddaw's summit, stuck on to its parent rather than being unique or individual. Although Mungrisdale Common's very lack of redeeming qualities has some allure, proper fells would feel affronted if it was included in their company. Perhaps the new cairn is an attempt to give Mungrisdale Common some much needed status. Having left Meal Fell, the next objective in Wainwright's *Northern Fells Guide* is Great Sca Fell. Despite having a name synonymous with the two highest and craggiest mountains in England, this fell has very little in common with them and the wide flat expanse of its summit must also mean that Great

Sca Fell ranks among the lesser lights of Wainwright's 214 fells. Indeed the summit of the slightly lower Little Sca Fell has far more to recommend it, having both a sizeable hoary cairn, a low wall which acts as a wind break and a finer view than the parent fell. Indeed it seems that the inclusion of Great Sca Fell in the *Northern Fells Guide* book owes more to its geographical situation as the high point of three radiating spokes of the Uldale Fells than to any physical attraction of the fell. Great Sca Fell seems little more than a bland shoulder of the higher fell, Knott.

I first visited the summit of Great Sca Fell in September 1996. Had I not been bagging Wainwrights, I have no doubt that Great Sca Fell would have scarcely lodged in my hills memory banks, but because I was bagging Wainwrights, Great Sca Fell will forever be etched into my subconscious. For this unassuming football pitch summit of a fell became my 100th Wainwright. It was not by choice. It just happened that way. So despite there being little in the view and terrain to celebrate about, my time on Great Sca Fell, which was spent entirely alone, was nonetheless conducted in a mood of celebration. This, though, was a more muted celebration than those had upon reaching 200 Wainwrights and when I completed them all.

From the summit of Great Sca Fell, both Longlands Fell and Brae Fell can be easily reached by separate connecting ridges. Brae Fell is yet another lonely outpost of Lakeland. Its northern slopes mark the end of the high ground of Lakeland and because of this the views north towards the Solway Firth are particularly fine. More intimate in the view is the lonely landscape of quiet farmsteads stretching beneath the fell, a landscape that seems to have almost stayed rooted in the past, while advancement and progress has marched its ceaseless course elsewhere. Brae Fell was another summit where I passed an hour in quiet contemplation, but I did not have the summit entirely to myself. After about fifty minutes alone a middle aged man arrived, wearing a handkerchief around his head to block out the September sun. Something instinctively told me that this was also a Wainwright bagger. So I checked out his credentials by describing my walk that day over Great Cockup, Meal Fell and Great Sca Fell, at which point he checked me out by asking me whether I was 'climbing them all?' Now this slightly cryptic question is almost the Wainwright baggers equivalent of a secret Masonic ritual. Those who are initiated into the world of Wainwright bagging know exactly what this question refers to and answer 'yes', before proceeding to say how many they have climbed. Experienced hill walkers who are not doing all the Wainwrights just ignore the question, as bagging is beyond their comprehension. The totally inexperienced return the question by asking 'all of what?'

And on Great Sca Fell, I perhaps revealed the saddest aspect of my bagging persona, as I replied, "Yes, I have now done 101 Wainwrights and today Great Sca Fell was my hundredth'. I was perhaps expecting an acknowledgement of my achievement as it seemed a pretty worthy one to me, but what the man revealed next was the equivalent in Poker terms of me having laid down two pairs, only for a Royal Flush to suddenly be revealed. For this man then proceeded to tell me that Brae Fell was his 213th Wainwright and tomorrow he would be concluding his round on Lank Rigg. So instead of him congratulating me on being roughly half way round my journey, I had to humbly acknowledge and congratulate this man in advance of his impending completion and achievement. However any jostling for position in the Wainwright bagging league was a purely friendly thing and this man was another of those unassuming solo walkers whose presence enhances a walk for a few minutes. The unwritten code of baggers told me that having had an hour on Brae Fell, with fifty minutes of it entirely alone, it was now time to leave this man to have his own time and space. I left with thoughts of my own completion, little knowing that another 11 years would pass before I finally caught up with the Wainwright tally of the man on Brae Fell.

Longlands Fell vies with Binsey for the title of most northerly Wainwright. A glance at the Ordnance Survey map appears to show that Binsey is ever so slightly further north than Longlands Fell. However both share the same feeling of being right on the very edge of Lakeland. Although less of a fell and more a grassy hill, I am fond of Longlands Fell, whose grassy flanks make walking easy. The descent down to Longlands from the summit of the fell is pure joy for tired feet.

Knott dominates this group of fells. It is a great sprawling mass of a fell with its roots extending far and wide. Even before I first climbed Knott its name spoke to me of a wild, unyielding place that commanded a certain respect. No-one could be bothered to waste time thinking of a flowery poetic name for this fell, such as was bestowed on say Glaramara. While it is true that Knott's summit is a flat as a bowling green and as extensive as a cricket pitch, its view somehow manages nonetheless to contrive to have a sense of height and distance. Knott has become something of a favourite of mine, although I accept that even Wainwright himself did not have much of worth to say about the fell. To me though it epitomises the wild nature of the Northern Fells and so it has become a kind of place of pilgrimage. It does also have a sense of command and aloofness from its immediate neighbours and this is not surprising given that it is actually higher than celebrated fells like Pavey Ark or Pike O'Blisco. One time on Knott I recall the mist being so close above the summit of the fell, that if I stood up to my full six feet of height I was within a shroud of mist, yet if I bent down I could see the expansive view under the mist. This again demonstrates that sometimes the weather conditions that we experience on a particular fell as much determine our perception of that fell's merits as the actual terrain does.

Although I would confess that I can sometimes be a little antisocial on the fells, compared to my friend Stan, I am positively welcoming to fellow walkers. Stan does not like to share the fells with anybody except his nearest and dearest and he will quite deliberately go out of his way to avoid people. When he first walked on his own from Great Sca Fell to Knott, a solitary walker approached him along the narrow grassy path that descends from Knott. Even though this walker was alone and was probably a fellow bagger who might have had something interesting to say, Stan did not want to lose his sense of aloneness or have to engage in pleasantries. So instead of taking the path, he took a right angle to the path and traversed some very boggy ground and peat hags purely in order to avoid human contact. Although I would probably never go to those lengths to avoid one person, I can see Stan's point. One of the very reasons that walkers go walking is to get away from people and it is far more respectful to see someone from a distance and make a decision to avoid them, than to carry on walking up to that person and then ignore them when they say 'hello' to you. I have often said a cheery 'hello' to a walker only to have a dismissive look and no response come back at me, or even worse be totally blanked as if I did not even exist. Avoiding people approaching from afar is not rude in my book, but it is rude to ignore someone who actually greets you on the fells. If you break your ankle five seconds after you have scorned someone, they might end up being the person helping you off the hill and to safety.

If I have to grudgingly admit that Knott is a bit of a giant blancmange of a fell, its neighbour Great Calva is a far shapelier thing. The conical profile of Great Calva must be seen and admired by many thousands of travellers along the A66 each year and I expect that many of them could neither name it nor have any desire to climb it. From the A66 Great Calva's distant profile looks a bit like that of an extinct volcano, although it isn't one. In a landscape of rolling unassuming fells it is the odd one out, with its clear and defined twin summit.

Great Calva sits at the northern end of the geological rift dividing Lakeland in two from north to south and its summit therefore provides a beeline view down the rift stretching towards Thirlmere and as far as Loughrigg Fell near Grasmere. In common with its neighbours Great Calva lacks any crags, but whereas Knott and the fells to the north are largely dominated by grass, the terrain underfoot on Great Calva is almost exclusively heather, which gives the fell its unique dark brown hue when viewed from Skiddaw Forest. Great Calva's summit has a true mountain feel about it and I would rate it as the finest summit in the Northern Fells, outside of the Skiddaw and Blencathra massifs.

Earlier on I mentioned that although I enjoy the solo experience, I usually find that once I am saturated with views for the day and have reached my last summit, I often wish that I could have a friend to share the final few miles of the day with. Now Great Calva provides an ideal central meeting point in the Northern Fells to enact such a plan. I can recall Peter, Stan and I all setting out from different starting points with the aim of meeting up on Great Calva at around 3 o'clock in the afternoon. I began from Stone Ends farm beneath Carrock Fell where I was dropped off by Stan. I then approached Great Calva via Carrock Fell, High Pike and Knott. Meanwhile Stan drove the car around to Bassenthwaite to approach Great Calva via Great Cockup, Meal Fell and Knott and Peter set off from Keswick and along the Cumbria Way to climb Great Calva from Skiddaw House.

The Rake Trod route onto Carrock Fell heads steeply up and then follows the line of crags before a final pull to the summit. This route is a little hidden piece of drama and I met no-one as I ascended this way and enjoyed the airy drops down to Stone Ends and the patchwork fields and scrubland that so characterise the flatter terrain around the base of the Northern Fells. Although I encountered a plague of flies on the summit of Carrock Fell, I still managed to enjoy the fantastic views to be had down the valley holding the River Caldew. This is a wild scene more reminiscent of parts of Grampian Scotland than the Lake District. I can also testify that the River Caldew is better viewed from on high than viewed while wading through it! Carrock Fell will also interest anyone with a passion for ancient history, as its summit is ringed by the walls of an ancient fort.

Two miles of wild, pathless and a bit boggy ridge walking lie between Carrock Fell and High Pike. This is the sort of terrain that is merely tolerated by some walkers for the sake of getting to a certain summit, but it has a haunting beauty and peace for others. Your reward for traversing this ridge is High Pike, one of the most ornately decorated summits in the

Lake District. What other summit can boast not only a massive cairn, but also a triangulation pillar, and most curious of all, a stone bench. This bench informs us that it is a monument to Mick Lewis, a young man from the tiny hamlet of Nether Row 'who loved all these fells'. Although I am not a great fan of benches on wild lonely summits, and would certainly rail against any more such occurrences, this bench has been here for almost 50 years and was there when Wainwright wrote his guide books, so I suppose it has almost become a part of the landscape and its history. I also must confess that it does provide rather a nice place to park oneself for a spot of lunch or reverie and I spent so long up there that I almost fell asleep!

Some time later Peter and Stan spotted a tiny solo walker coming towards Great Calva from the summit of Knott. Without binoculars they could not be entirely certain it was me but in these lonely parts it seemed likely. Once I reached the boggy morass that lies between Knott and Great Calva, Stan and Peter knew for certain it was me. I was late for our arranged meeting and as I struggled flustered up the final 500 feet to the

Looking South from Great Calva

summit of Great Calva I was heckled by both brother and best friend shouting 'Where the hell have you been?' and 'Get a move on'. It was all in jest of course, although at the time I could have punched them both as I was jeered and cajoled all the way to the summit! I suppose I deserved the abuse though as my desire to spend an hour reflecting and being generally arty on each previous summit had meant that I had arrived forty-five minutes late. However I also had to point out that my walk had in fact been longer than either Stan or Peter's and, of course, much more arduous.

Once I had regained my breath and sense of humour, there was great shared joy to be had both in the summit view and, perhaps as importantly, in recounting in turn the highlights of our respective walks. After another half an hour we headed down the heathery slopes towards Skiddaw House, before heading on to Bassenthwaite via the sparkling waters of Dash Falls and the sombre Dead Crags of Bakestall. What a wonderfully accommodating, yet at the same time wild and lonely thing, Great Calva is.

Souther Fell was the last Wainwright summit I completed from the *Northern Fells Guide*, which then became the first of the seven guides from which I completed all the fells. Completing one of the guides is a pleasant milestone along the journey to completing the Wainwrights; as if one piece of a great cake has been consumed. Souther Fell is something of a loner and the fact that it did not lend itself to being part of a bagging round probably explains why it got left until last. But there is something spacious and free about the stroll across its flat top when approached from the hamlet of Scales. The summit is right at the northernmost end of the fell and it could be argued that an ascent from Mungrisdale is both shorter and more direct. But by the time I did Souther Fell in April 2000, I had come to realise that a highly pleasurable thing to do with those odds and sods that I was tidying up, was to try and combine them with an ascent of one of the high mountains. And so having reached the summit of Souther Fell and enjoyed half an hour there alone and windswept, I headed straight back along the summit ridge to Mousthwaite Col and from there up onto Blencathra. This way, what could have just been a half day getting a tick, was turned into a fine day of mountain walking, with the bonus of a tick and a visit to one of my favourite mountains.

If Souther Fell is a bit of a loner in the Northern Fells, then Binsey is a definite outcast, sitting as it does outside of the cauliflower shaped mass of the Northern Fells proper. Yet on climbing Binsey one soon realises that Wainwright was absolutely right to include this outpost of Lakeland in his fell guides. For although its approaches are short and simple and of grass and heather, its summit and view are worthy of many more centrally located and celebrated fells. Perhaps because of its isolation from any other fell it has a unique atmosphere about it. Looking from its summit northwards over rolling moorland to the Cumbrian plain, there is a distinct feeling of being at the end of Lakeland and of there genuinely being nothing worth climbing after Binsey until Scotland is reached. This is not a sad feeling, more a wistful reflective one. I first visited Binsey in July 2001 and I could not help feeling that so many hills, stretching south all the way to Hoad Hill, were not just geographically behind me, but also behind me in terms of memories. The summit has a peculiar ancient feel about it, dressed as it is with a number of cairns including a great tumulus to mark the highest point (as well as another trig point).

The view from Binsey is also unusual and surprisingly extensive. Pike O'Stickle in Langdale clearly pops up its thimble like head. Even the Coniston Fells can be seen in the far Southern distance. Seeing the south of Lakeland from its extreme north serves as a reminder that in fact the Lake District covers a quite small area and yet somehow, like Doctor Who's Tardis, seems to contain so much more than its mere physical dimensions on a map could ever suggest.

And here on Binsey my account of the Northern Fells reaches a fitting end. I hope that I have managed to capture something of the timeless quality of these fells. It is an area that is unique. It is close to civilisation and a substantial town and yet manages to convey within its sanctuary a feeling of a vast and spacious wilderness. It is an area that has had its share of the human footprint of industry in the past, yet should now be preserved and left unspoilt and free from further human modification. If some may feel that I have bordered on being controversial and even petty with my dislike of cairn building and such like in this area, it is only because I love it so and want to see it remain as it is for generations to come.

An Unanswerable Question

For the first few years of my hill walking career the Lake District had full reign over my passion for the wild places. But by 1992 the call of a more mountainous and much wilder place could be resisted no longer. Being a sad hill bagging type I once worked out that the entire area of the Lake District National Park could be fitted into the mountainous area of Scotland about 40 times. There are obvious physical differences between Scotland and the Lake District, in terms of the size of the mountains, the wildness of the mountains and the sheer number of mountains. However since Stan, Peter and I first climbed in Scotland and for the last fifteen years of walking both there and in the Lake District, there has been an on and off, but nonetheless continuous debate about the respective worthiness of Munro bagging and all things Scotland, versus Wainwright bagging and all things Lake District.

Now let me firstly say that the clue to this chapter is in the title. This debate, both interesting and fascinating and the subject of many heated arguments, is one that has no definitive answer. However what I hope to do in this chapter is to put my own perspective on the merits and drawbacks of both areas and in doing so conclude that perhaps in the mind of a committed lover of the British landscape and wild areas, both areas are mutually inclusive and complimentary.

I'll begin with Scotland. As I have previously mentioned, although my experience of Munros is not vast and there are others infinitely more qualified to write books about Scotland than me, I have nonetheless done over 50 Munros (Scottish Mountains over 3000 feet) and a fair spattering of Corbetts and Grahams as well (those mountains between 2000 and 3000 feet). I have read that if a hill walker has done 50 Munros, in different parts of Scotland, he will have a reasonable knowledge of the Scottish Highlands. Having now done 50 odd Munros the immediate difference between that task and the task of doing the first 50 Wainwrights becomes obvious. It is a lot harder! In the Lake District you can potter around above Whinlatter Forest and bag four fells towards completing the 214 Wainwrights, without venturing anywhere near the 2000 foot contour. However in Scotland a round that includes four Munros, such as the Carn an Tuirc round in the Grampians involves maybe two to three times the effort and a lot of pathless trudging.

In the Lake District there are just four mountains above 3000 feet, but in Scotland there are 284. While a round of the 214 Wainwrights is a fantastic lifetime experience and involves effort and commitment, there is no question that it is a much less arduous task than completing the 284 Munros. In fact I would say that the effort taken to gain the 50 or so Munros I have climbed to date is nearly comparable to the amount of effort taken to climb all 214 Wainwrights. It is not just a height thing. There are a number of other reasons why the Munros are an altogether tougher experience. In the Lake District the vast majority of fells have a clear path leading you from the start of the walk to the summit of the fell. Even wild parts of the Lake District such as Upper Eskdale and the Northern Fells have a network of paths and tracks through them. If you stray from a path or get lost in the Lake District the chances are you will soon find the path again, or another equally good one and that nothing more than pride will have been damaged. However, although some very good paths do exist up Scottish Munros, they are an exception rather than the rule and where they exist they are a welcome luxury. The typical experience, path-wise, of a Scottish Munro is that it begins with a good path that promises much and is perhaps not far off the standard of a good Lakeland path. If you have studied your maps or guidebooks the night before you will know that this is more than likely a stalkers path, whose reason for existing is not to get you on to Ben Whatever, but to get deer stalkers, who have paid a princely sum of money to shoot some deer, to where the deer are likely to be. So quite often at the head of a valley the stalkers path will either mysteriously end, or continue over and into the next valley. On such occasions the Munro bagger is usually then confronted with perhaps a thousand feet, or sometimes more, of pathless ascent over either bog, heather, rough grass, boulders, rocks or various combinations of the type of terrain that a person's feet seem ill designed for. Although I have had many such slogs in my time, the peculiar thing about us Munro baggers is that we tend to selectively forget the pain bit and remember much more the views and summits. And indeed once you have completed your slog and got onto the ridge of your Munro, your reward will make all the effort seem worthwhile. You suddenly feel that the slog is good for you, that it has cleansed both the physical and spiritually body. Slog toughens you up and makes you gnarled, hardened and experienced. These may be your thoughts, until you are next faced with a 2000 foot heather trudge up a Munro!

It cannot be denied that while there are some vast panoramas to be had from the likes of Scafell Pike, Helvellyn and the other high Lakeland peaks, there are vaster and wilder panoramas to be had in Scotland. For example, on a very clear day on the summit of Ben Macdui, Britain's second highest mountain, I could clearly see the jagged peaks of the Cuillin ridge on Skye some 90 or more miles away as the crow flies. In addition, due to the vastness of Scotland, you will often find that the view you see is entirely new and valleys and areas of wilderness you have never before contemplated are thrillingly presented before you.

Despite not having as vast or wild views, I have never found the views from the Lake District fells to be in any way inferior to those from the highest Scottish Munros. It has been more that they compliment one another. Where the Lake District perhaps scores highly is in the intimacy of its views. Take, for example, the view from Low Fell in the Fellbarrow Group near Loweswater. The fell is only some 1300 feet high and the walk to its summit just a pleasant two miles of gentle incline on good paths. Yet is there anything in Scotland that can surpass the sheer beauty of form, shape and composition that comprises the view from Low Fell. Looking down the full length of Crummock Water, the eye is drawn

Crummock Water and Buttermere from Low Fell

further towards Buttermere, Haystacks and Great Gable, while the scene is perfectly framed by the steep walls of Mellbreak on one side and the massive flanks of Grasmoor on the other. In the foreground the patchwork fields, dry stone walls, little farmsteads and dotted cows and sheep only serve to add a rural charm and homeliness to the sylvan beauty. This type of view is perhaps something that is unique and defining to Lakeland.

The argument Wainwrights versus Munros always has a counter balance though, and although there may not be many Low Fell's in Scotland, there are also many types of view to be had in Scotland that simply cannot be found in the Lake District. Take for example the view from Ben Stack, a solitary Graham (mountain between 2000 and 2500 feet), which stands proud and aloof from its neighbours, in the far north of Scotland. The view from its narrow summit ridge is surely one of the wildest prospects that you could find in these islands. In fact anyone who had spent their life in the South of England would be hard pushed to comprehend that this landscape of a thousand lochans, bare rock and indented tortuous coastline was a part of the same island. Its vast and uncompromising nature is at once slightly frightening and at the same time profoundly beautiful. It is the opposite of sylvan beauty, but it gives just as much to the soul and spirit.

The life of a hill walker would be a lesser life without those special views to be had in the west of Scotland of coast, island and sea. The Lake District does have some glorious seascapes from its fells, such as the stunning view from Black Coombe (an Outlying Fell but surely as worthy as many of the 214 true Wainwrights). However, there is nothing to match the sheer feeling of open seascape and rugged wildness that can be had from the likes of Bla Bheinn on Skye or Ben More Coigach in Assynt.

While there is plenty of slog to be had in the Lake District, the day's walking will invariably end with a well made path that leads to a town or village. Often there will be a shop or a pub at the finish. You can have a truly wild experience on say High Seat in the Central Fells and a couple of hours later be sitting in a pub, with a pint and a meal, in front of a roaring log fire. In Scotland the walk back from a summit can often be long and arduous. I can recall amazing views from the summit of Ben Wyvis out towards the North Sea in one direction and the Fannichs and An Teallach in the other, but the descent from the summit was totally pathless. At first large boulders presented themselves beneath our feet, the kind of boulders that move and shift as you painstakingly try and negotiate them. Then lower down at valley floor level, instead of a nice pub, there was about four miles of pathless peat hag to negotiate, in a kind of no mans land. Reaching the car was a profound moment of bliss, but our accommodation was still over an hours drive away and we ended up with fish and chips at 8.30 in the evening. This is all part of the Scottish experience. The mountains are generally uncompromising, but the rewards are great and the experience and achievement memorable. I would not swap all the pathless slog I have had, and will have, in Scotland for anything. It may sound clichéd but it is character building.

I have mentioned the solitude and loneliness to be found in areas of Lakeland such as the Northern Fells, but there is a type of solitude to be found in Scotland that is on a different level. I recall a day spent solo climbing a pair of Munros called Stob Coire Sgriodain and Chno Dearg. From the moment Stan dropped me off until the moment he picked me up some nine hours later I met no-one. In fact the only person that I saw was Stan, as a tiny figure on the neighbouring mountain range of the Easains, which were his chosen ticks for that day. The hour or so that I spent on Stob Coire Sgriodain's wonderful summit looking at the dramatic plunge down to Loch Treig, has to be one of the most profoundly peaceful I have spent in the hills. Walking between Sgriodain and Chno Dearg, I encountered a vast herd of deer, a rarity in the walker's realm of Lakeland. Here it seemed that it was I the walker that was out of place and the deer who ruled.

Yet with increased wildness and isolation inevitably comes increased risk. Distances can be great in Scotland and whereas a descent into a wrong valley in Lakeland may just mean a hefty taxi fare back to the car, or a long road walk, in Scotland it can be an altogether more frightening prospect. The day I climbed the Munro Creag Megaidh by Lagganside is perhaps the perfect example of the highs and lows of Munro bagging, although with a little more care and a touch less arrogance it would probably have turned out differently. Walking up Coire Ardair, on a glorious late September day, Stan and I had little idea of the wonders and worries that lay ahead of us in equal measure. Upon reaching the summit of Creag Megaidh the cloud began to roll towards us from the north. But this cloud, instead of covering the summit and enclosing us in its folds, hung below the summit and rolled into the distance, creating a carpet of false landscape. A temperature inversion, where a sea of cloud forms below the ridge of a mountain, is surely one of the most amazing natural phenomena to be witnessed by a hill walker. Although the inversion we had on Creag Megaidh that day was not a total panorama of inversion, the view north was entirely composed of a uniform layer of cloud. It was a defining moment in my hill walking career, and ever since then I have hunted and chased the right conditions for inversions, just as some people in The United States chase and hunt twisters and tornados. Inversions are rare things. I once read that they occur roughly once in a thousand days of hill walking. During Christmas 2006 I had no option but to indulge with the family in turkey and spuds at home in Kent, while the Lake District had several successive days of temperature inversion, which I could only witness with a sad sigh on the websites that post pictures from the Lake District each day. As if to rub salt into the wound, I have since met no fewer than three people, including my bed and breakfast proprietor in Keswick, who witnessed first hand those inversions. I have yet to have a full inversion in the Lake District, but Stan and I are now on high alert during the autumn and winter months, when inversion conditions are most common, and our time will come.

The thing about even partial inversions, such as the one we had on Creag Megaidh, is that they have a wonderfully hypnotic effect. Time almost seems to stand still as the mind becomes engrossed in the subtle shifts and changes in the cloud blanket below. We stayed and stayed on Creag Megaidh until the early evening sun began to give the inversion clouds a pink hue, but eventually we had to leave the summit because we had planned, and were determined, to bag another two Munros that day.

All went well up to the summit of the second Munro, Stob Poite Coire Ardair. From there a long high level ridge continues for about three miles to the next and final Munro of the round, Carn Liath. This ridge maintains height and rarely drops below the 3000 foot contour. Although the summit of Stob Poite Coire Ardair was clear and we basked in late evening sunshine, the cloud and mist of early autumn had now obscured the ridge ahead of us to Carn Liath. In our arrogance we thought that this would be no problem. We would just stick to the ridge and follow the path that seemed to head on from Stob Poite and sooner or later we would come across the cairn marking the summit of Carn Liath. Now I must confess that at that point in my walking career I was not exactly great at navigation on the hills. I always had a compass with me, but invariably its only use during the day would be to highlight which direction we were looking in, rather than to navigate our way off a hill. I had no idea how to accurately locate my bearing in mist and the cheap compasses we had were of little use in this regard. It was perhaps inevitable that once we got into the mist problems occurred. The path which had been clear did a typical Scottish thing and vanished. Suddenly we were up over 3000 feet on a wild ridge and with only a vague idea that we should head in a roughly easterly bearing using the compass. In the thick mist all sense of perspective in the landscape was lost. I have a feeling that we ended up very close to the summit of Carn Liath, and we certainly did reach a cairn of sorts, but I cannot be certain we actually made the highest point. In any case by this stage it was past 6.30 on a September evening and all thoughts of bagging another tick seemed trivial as thoughts of basic needs, such as survival and the desire not to spend a night up at 3000 feet, took over.

So we made the decision that we needed to descend and begun to do so. However by this stage all sense of direction had deserted us and having descended about 800 feet and come out of the cloud, the rather sickening truth dawned upon us that the view ahead of us was not one that we immediately recognised as being the same Coire Ardair route we had walked up that morning and which we needed to reach to get back to the car. It then became obvious that we had in fact come off on the wrong side of the ridge. By this time the mist was lowering still and the light was gradually fading. We were faced with the prospect of either carrying on down the wrong valley, but at least being able to see our way ahead and get lower down, or the prospect of going back up nearly 1000 feet into the mist to get to the ridge and try and locate the correct route down. We made what I consider was one of our few sensible decisions during that day and decided to just get down off the mountain and to a lower less exposed place, regardless of where that meant we ended up.

The Glenshirra Forest is not somewhere that is in any way, shape or form accommodating to a walker. It is comprised of giant peat hags and bog. Normally I would pick my way carefully over such ground, but it is surprising what a sense of urgency fading light gives to a walker. Stan and I literally bounded from hag to hag and through bog and over tussock. Time was of the essence and the only stop that we had lasted about a minute while Stan informed me that he recognised the slim ribbon of road, some three miles distant, that represented our objective and hope at that time. It was the Corrieyairack Pass road. A quick study of the map told us exactly where we were and it dawned upon us that even when we got to the minor road, the car was still some 30 miles away! At times such as this the scale of the overall problem is too great to contemplate and instead our minds focused on the immediate objective and that was to get to the road. Our map showed that the road was the other side of a river and that the river appeared to have a bridge that crossed it. We made good time over the Glenshirra Forest to the river, but when we got to the bridge it was like a number of bridges marked on maps in Scotland, in a state of ruin. Thankfully the river was not in spate and we got no more than wet feet from crossing it. Upon reaching the road, although it was nearly dark and we were many miles from the car, we still let out a huge whoop of joy, for our minds had become purely focused on getting off the mountain and getting to the road meant safety.

This was not however some major road, where we would perhaps be likely to hitch a lift and as we began walking the *élan* of reaching the road, was replaced by the more sobering thought of a walk on tarmac through the night with no food or drink. Just as hope was beginning to fade however, we saw the lights of a car approaching us. We waved it down and it stopped. We were invited by a couple of gnarled Scotsmen to a lift in the back of their truck, which though it contained sundry tools and had no seat, was luxury for our tired bodies and aching feet at that moment. We told the men our sorry story and they informed us that we were lucky they were passing. They told us they had been working repairing the road at the top of the pass and that it was likely that no-one else would have passed us that night. They eventually took us all the way back to Laggan where at about 9.30 in the evening we called for my brother to come and pick us up. He was ever so slightly annoyed and I can't blame him, as we were staying near Aviemore and he had a good 80 mile round trip to pick us up and then drive us to collect Stan's car. We finally got back to our wooden lodge at 11 o'clock at night and by this time I was suffering from dehydration and it took about two litres of drink and a hearty late meal to get me back to somewhere approaching normality, although I was still profoundly tired.

That single day about sums up the highs and lows of my Scottish hill walking experiences to date. Yet it is strange how in some ways a low can become memorable. I now look back to the Glenshirra Forest with a certain nostalgia and fondness. Although we should never have got into that situation, nonetheless the challenge was met and it certainly toughened me up and also made me realise the need to improve my navigational skills. Hard walking is what Munro bagging is all about and yet that very hardness gives a tremendous satisfaction and sense of achievement.

I have mentioned that for me the Lake District has a feeling of homeliness about it and although the size of its mountainous area can be a limitation when compared to the vastness of Scotland's Highlands, it can also be an advantage. The 214 Wainwrights have taken me just under twenty years. I am still a young man and yet I feel that I have gained a certain intimacy with the Lakeland Fells that I have not yet gained with

Scotland. There are so many wonderful Scottish mountains that I have only climbed once, and if I intend to bag all the Munros and as many Corbetts and Grahams as I can, the majority of the mountains I climb will never see me on their summit again. To date there are only two mountains out of the 85 odd that I have climbed in Scotland that I have climbed more than once. In the Lake District there are nearly 100 that I have climbed more than once and many favourites that I have climbed on half a dozen or more occasions. So the compact nature of the Lake District is also one of its assets. It is just the right size to get to know intimately in a lifetime. There is a joy to be had in getting to know every feature of a fell, to walk up every ridge route on to a fell and to witness that fell in every season and under every type of weather. I only wish a lifetime were long enough for me to get to know every one of Scotland's fabulous mountains so well. But then that is a bit much to ask for a guy who lives in Kent and works in London. Best not be greedy.

At the beginning of this chapter I said that there was no answer to whether Munro bagging is better than Wainwright bagging or vice versa. Each area has aspects that are unique to it and they both compliment each other. The only answer is that I would never wish or chose to be without either, but if was forced to exile myself forever from either Scotland or the Lake District, I would find it desperately hard to imagine never setting foot in my beloved Lake District again. Scotland provokes within me feelings of excitement and thrill and wildness and exploration and stamina, but it does not perhaps evoke those deep rooted feelings of comfort and intimacy with a natural friend that I find in the Lake District. And yet to ponder a life without those wonderful mountains north of the border, without the thrill of reaching a wild Scottish summit and seeing a vast new panorama, would perhaps also be unimaginable.

The Lure of Langdale

There can be few more impressive aspects of a mountain landscape than the head of a mountain valley, where the valley floor sweeps up majestically and imposingly to dominant craggy mountains above. And among the impressive valleys in Lakeland there are few that conclude with such an awesome spectacle of mountain architecture as Langdale. Langdale, like Wasdale and Borrowdale, is an iconic word in Lakeland. The floor of Great Langdale is a small oasis of flat land, hemmed in on all sides by steep contours. These contours rise up to some of the most celebrated summits in Lakeland: Bowfell, Crinkle Crags and the Langdale Pikes. If Borrowdale is all pastoral beauty, then Langdale is all savage mountain beauty.

Many people refer to the Langdale Pikes as if they were one mountain, but there are in fact several separate Wainwright summits to be bagged

The Langdale giants from Loughrigg Fell

here. The Langdale Pikes do share one thing in common. They seem to have conspired to achieve two of the greatest illusions in the Lakeland Fells. Firstly, I always find it impossible to believe that even the highest of the Pikes is a mere 2400 feet, for they seem in stature to have at least the height of Bowfell or Great Gable. From the head of Windermere, the mountains around the head of Langdale dominate, but I have always felt that the Langdale Pikes perhaps compel the eye and command the attention even more than Bowfell and the Crinkles. Once seen or climbed they become instantly recognisable. Driving up the M6 there is a rise in the road, just past Lancaster, where the first proper view of the Lakeland fells is had and even from this distance the Langdale Pikes are instantly recognisable and give nothing away in terms of presence to their higher neighbours. From within the heart of Langdale itself the sweep from valley floor to Pike O'Stickle, Loft Crag and Harrison Stickle is surely one of the most awesome sights in Lakeland. The feeling when beneath the Langdales is one of a massive presence, almost overwhelming and more than a little imposing.

Unfortunately this is where the second illusion intrudes. If the Langdale Pikes had similar steep walls on their opposite side, they would not only be some of the finest mountains in Lakeland, but would perhaps even rank with the likes of Liathach in Torridon for their pure mountain architecture and impregnability of form. But unfortunately the Langdale Pikes are a two dimensional sham. The geological term 'crag and tail formation', describing the way mountains often have one craggy steep side and a opposing smooth and gently contoured side, was never more aptly used than for the Langdale Pikes. Once up within their summits it will be seen that they are nothing more than an imposing front for the vast plateau like wilderness of the central spine of Lakeland.

And yet this simplified view does not do the Langdale Pikes justice. What is not an illusion is the fact that each of these summits is a worthy mountain summit in its own right, with a classic mountain feel and the area contains perhaps the finest and most perfect of all Lakeland's mountain tarns. Few will forget the first time they see Stickle Tarn with its stunning and slightly frightening backdrop of Pavey Ark. The fact that the tarn is dammed by a wall and therefore technically artificial detracts nothing from the scene. For me, Stickle Tarn is one of those special Lakeland places that evoke many contrasting memories.

The first time I visited Stickle Tarn was on a boiling hot May day in 1991. On reaching the tarn it was so hot I found a rock large enough to hide behind, changed into a pair of swimming trunks and spent the rest of the day walking on the Pikes in nothing more than my trunks and walking boots. This was a one off display of youth and now, approaching middle age as I am, it is likely to remain a one off. In fact I only mention it as a direct contrast to another time I stood by Stickle Tarn one late January day. The same place, the same natural features arrayed before me, but there the similarity ended. Stan and I reached the tarn as the first light of a January dawn hit the face of Pavey Ark. The Ark had a covering of snow, although the sharper crags and features protruded darkly through this white covering. The sun's first rays lit up the face of Pavey Ark, first with a deep pink glow and then later in fantastic hues of gold and orange. But this was not to be a blue sky day of winter wonder. The sun's presence was merely a dawn greeting and with the speed of weather change that can happen in the high places in winter, dark clouds began forming over the Pikes, clouds which hung fit to burst with snow. We carried on for a bit, heading for the Wainwright of Blea Rigg, but soon the snow came down in thick swirling torrents and the mountains around us disappeared. I had already been in a white out once and it was not an experience I wanted to repeat and so we headed back to Stickle Tarn and down the path to Dungeon Ghyll. This was one of those times when I have failed to reach a summit and yet still had a classic memorable time on the fells (the weather did however clear again later in the day and we bagged Loughrigg Fell!).

On another occasion I stood by Stickle Tarn and scarcely noticed its calming waters, as my eyes were fixated by a rising slanting crack in the cliffs crossing the face of Pavey Ark. There is something all consuming about the prospect of climbing Jack's Rake for the first time. I had done Striding Edge and Sharp Edge, but they were merely classed as scrambles, whereas Jack's Rake is officially a rock climb, albeit the easiest of the easy. As I stood by Stickle Tarn there were two choices, the easy and normal route onto Pavey Ark, which I had enjoyed on several previous occasions, or the thing of terror that I had set out to do that day. What helped was that I had Stan with me, who had already done Jack's Rake on his own a couple of years earlier. What did not help was the fact that it was raining. Wainwright says in *The Central Fells* that 'Jack's Rake is just about the limit that the ordinary common garden or fell walker can reasonably be expected to attempt'. And that day this fell walker definitely found his limit. Having said that, it was not quite as bad as I had thought it would be. Yes, there are fearsome drops down to Stickle Tarn and yes, my ungainly body found itself in positions that made it look even more so.

However the blessing of Jack's Rake, for a novice climber like me, is that the rake hugs a line across the face of Pavey Ark and the face of the mountain acts as a kind of comfort blanket. Despite the mild terror and thoughts that I had not yet written a will, one cannot but be impressed by the feeling that, as a walker, you are in the very womb of the crags of a mountain, a place that would normally be the reserve of the climber. Although the heavy rain and the necessity of using all limbs made it impossible to carry Wainwright's guide book and follow his description of Jack's Rake, I still mentally ticked off the features I had memorised from the guide the night before. First the three ashtrees which seemed so out of place in this world of rock. Then Great Gully where the pinnacle that marks the end of the climb comes into view and finally the summit wall, upon reaching which all terror was replaced by relief and immense satisfaction in equal measure.

Now I could enjoy my favourite thing about a fell, its summit, and Pavey Ark has a wonderful summit. Not only does the cairn sit close to a massive plunge, thereby giving the view perspective, but the immediate scenery is that of a true mountain. It is a chaos of rock, but a beautiful chaos. Pavey Ark has a stunning view of the Langdale Valley snaking its way towards Windermere in the distance. As with the other peaks that comprise The Langdale Pikes this is a view of depth and the flat and perhaps slightly drab moorland behind, that forms the 'tail' of these 'crag and tail' mountains, in no way detracts from the true mountain feel on Pavey Ark's summit.

The same is true of Pavey Ark's neighbour Harrison Stickle. Harrison Stickle also has a mountain feel about its summit and this is heightened by the fact that there is a divine little scramble to attain the summit ridge (although this can be avoided). The summit of Harrison Stickle is to me unique in the Lake District. It is not particularly narrow and not particularly small in area, yet standing on this summit is a bit like standing on a magic carpet, with a feeling almost of no longer being part of the land beneath you, but being raised above it. The feeling of height looking down the Langdale Valley confirms the illusion that is the Langdale Pikes, for here we are only at 2400 feet and yet is there anywhere else in Lakeland that feels higher.

Loft Crag has a glorious shagginess about it and once again its small perched cairn, placed above the climber's only terrain of Gimmer Crag and the magnificent rock and mountain scenery, are those of a true mountain. Maybe because it lies between the high point of Harrison Stickle and the truest of the pikes, Pike o'Stickle, my experience is that the summit of Loft Crag tends to attract less visitors and those that do come seem to be keen to move on quickly to the enticing prospect of neighbouring Pike o'Stickle.

The thimble that is the summit of Pike o'Stickle has a pleasant habit of popping up in views from other summits. Whereas a keen walker may struggle, when identifying peaks in a view, to work out his Ullscarf from his High Raise, or even his Scafell from his Scafell Pike, few will fail to instantly recognise Pike o'Stickle. Its unique knobble is the culmination of a 2000 foot sweep of majesty rising from the floor of Langdale and from its summit one can best appreciate the immensity of this drop, as the tiny silver thread of Mickleden Beck weaves its course below. Wainwright tells us in his Central Fells guide that there is a scree route up this seemingly out of bounds sweep of land. However, contained on this inhospitable route are evidences of a Stone Axe factory, which just show the lengths that ancient man was prepared to go to in order to craft the tools needed to hunt and survive. This route up Pike o'Stickle is another reason why completing the Wainwrights is merely the end of the beginning, and it is one on a list of must do ascent routes now that I have completed the 214 fells. This is a list which to my delight keeps growing.

If the Langdale Pikes create an illusion of being amongst the highest of Lakeland's mountains, then the two great mountains at the head of Langdale need no such spells. Crinkle Crags and Bowfell together form a massive and terminal wall of rock, the kind of wall that makes a halt to all roads and cars and says 'get out and walk'. These two Lakeland giants are often linked together on the same walk via the high col holding the Three Tarns, but they each have much to explore and admire and I personally think of them as separate mountain expeditions.

Crinkle Crags is another of those mountains that is recognisable from a far distance, with its knobbly skyline standing out just as that of the Langdale Pikes does. Indeed there are certain similarities of terrain between the Langdale Pikes and Crinkle Crags. But whereas each of the Langdale Pikes summits counts as a separate Wainwright, your only reward for traversing all of the five Crinkles will be one solitary Wainwright. Never mind though, for this is an outing to make even the most ardent of baggers realise that there is more to life than how many ticks can be had in a day. As befits one of Lakeland's highest mountains Crinkle Crags can be climbed from several directions. Even from the Landgale Valley, there are those who will prefer to climb it via The Band and Three Tarns and those who will prefer to climb it via Red Tarn. Personally I feel that the Crinkles are better appreciated when done south to north, with the view of the Links on Bowfell and a stop at Three Tarns to end the day. The great thing about fell walking though is that the choice of route is yours.

On the wide and grassy path that leads up to the Crinkles there is little to indicate the drama that is ahead, but once on the first of the Crinkles the terrain becomes rocky and glorious throughout. Between the first Crinkle and the second and highest of the Crinkles, is one of the more awkward spots to be found on the Lakeland ridges. Called the Bad Step, in approach it seems to be an impossible barrier to progress and I remember a couple turning back at this point the first time I climbed the Crinkles. In reality it is not as bad as its name implies. There are a number of choices, including a bypass path which skirts all difficulties. If you want a little excitement added to your walk you can climb the 10 foot rock pitch of the Bad Step, which although almost vertical has the worn hand holds of generations of walkers. Or you can do what a thinner me did first time and squeeze between the two chockstones that seem to bar progress. There is just enough room for a person of average girth to get through this gap. This tunnel through the rock appears to have formed since Wainwright wrote the *Southern Fells Guide* in the late 1950's, although he does mention it in his much later book *Favourite Lakeland Mountains*. However, I would have to lose some weight before contemplating the squeeze through the chockstones again, or I might end up like Winnie the Pooh wedged in Rabbit's front door until I lost sufficient weight to get unstuck. Then again if this did happen, perhaps I could write a book about it and call it *The Crinkle Crags Diet*. It could hardly be less masochistic than cereal and salad and think of the situation and the isolation to be had during the long nights on the fell waiting to get thinner!

Having negotiated your way over, through or around the Bad Step, the summit of the second and highest of the Crinkles awaits. This is not perhaps one of the finest views from a high Lakeland summit, the nearer and higher summits of Bowfell and the Scafells ensure that, but there is still a very fine prospect to be had, particularly in a southerly direction, where the Duddon valley is superbly viewed as it winds its delightful rural course out to the shimmering Irish Sea.

The remainder of the Crinkles ridge is a constant delight, with continuous vantage points for the dramatic plunge down into the Langdale Valley, as well as numerous small tarns and pools. It is also extremely rocky terrain and in places there are massive potholes in between the vast rocks and boulders. I can recall actually clambering down one such hole the first time I climbed the Crinkles, and as I stood

The Eskdale side of the Crinkles

in this rocky hole the main ridge was completely above the level of my head. There is some wonderful aimless exploration to be had between the fifth and last Crinkle and the natural sanctuary that is the Three Tarns.

When a walker has passed a pleasant cloud free summer's day on a fell it is always fascinating to see the same fell under very different conditions. I remember setting out on a winter's day from the high starting point of Wrynose Pass and heading for the Crinkles neighbouring Wainwright of Cold Pike. Red Tarn had a wafer thin skin of ice on it, and as we climbed higher the snow line was soon reached. Just before we entered the mist I recall seeing the Crinkles in a very different mood. The top of each of the Crinkles was under a thick glowering body of cloud, and beneath this the crags plunging from each of the Crinkles stood out fierce and deep black. One imagined the lair of a dragon, a terrible place where man should not venture and yet these were the same Crinkles that had been my warm and relaxing playground on other days. That view was the highlight of an otherwise slightly disappointing day on the fells. The rest of the day was spent finding our way to the summit of Cold Pike almost entirely in thick mist. Now I don't mind mist at all and it can provide some amazing experiences when it shifts and clears, but when it does not clear and you have climbed something high, the appeal tends to wear off. That day on Cold Pike something even worse happened, a near clearance. For a few seconds a watery sun tried to poke its way through the pea soup mist-come-fog. For another couple of seconds a tiny hole appeared in the cloud bank and we stood transfixed by the sight of the conical summit of Harter Fell in Eskdale. But it did not last long enough and nor was it revealing enough to be a classic experience. Instead the tiny window of view quickly disappeared and the mist rolled back. It was not a bad day on the hills and there had been a few fantastic moments, but it left one feeling what might have been. A few years later I started my passion for hunting temperature inversions on the hills, where a sea of cloud is below you. I know now that at such times it is best to be up as high as possible. I can only surmise, but it seems highly probable to me, that if Cold Pike at 2300 feet was literally just below the cloud base, then had we instead done the Crinkles at 2800 feet, we might have witnessed a truly awesome inversion. Perhaps this is one of those occasions in my 'bagging' years where the desire for a new tick has meant an inferior experience than might have been had from its higher but already climbed neighbour. What makes it worse is that, in keeping with my own set of criteria, I must revisit Cold Pike because I have yet to see more than a fraction of its view! Still perhaps I could combine an ascent from Wrynose Pass, with an ascent of the next door fell Pike o'Blisco, a beloved fell whose relatively lowly stature is defied by its uniformly rugged character. Mountains are not decided by rules of height. I have climbed heathery puddings over a thousand feet higher than Pike o'Blisco that are not proper mountains.

Every now and again in a hill walking career a day is had on a particular fell that is as near to perfection as can be. At such times it is tempting to never redo that fell again, for how could it match up to the perfection already had. Prior to March 1997 I had climbed Bowfell twice, both times in warmer months and both times with the usual crowds that one of Lakeland's highest peaks attracts. I had enjoyed the delights of the walk and the summit views, although felt that the mountain had more to offer me in both regards. Then in March 1997 a day arrived that was to reveal Bowfell to me in all its glory.

Stan and I had driven up to Great Langdale over night and grabbed a couple of hours of sleep in a lay-by, before setting off up Bowfell in virtual darkness. Just before Stool End Farm the metalled farm track crosses a bridge over Oxendale Beck. The embers of dawn caressed the dark water below. As we climbed up Lakeland's famous Band, the first rays of a wonderful sunny day hit us, although there was thick ice in places on The Band and the sun gave out little warmth. This time we were to visit Bowfell's secret. As with Pillar, Bowfell has a high level traverse designed for climbers to get to their crags and rock faces, but also perfectly accessible by the ordinary walker.

Bowfell's Climbers Traverse is quite a bit shorter than Pillar's high-level traverse and if I were honest I would say that the traverse on Pillar is a finer rollercoaster through the heart of a mountain. But Bowfell's Climber's Traverse does pack a lot of fun and a little mild terror into its short length. The scenery is immense and the feeling of being in a privileged place for a walker is the same as on the Shamrock Traverse. Before long you are beneath the immense face of Cambridge Crag, which towers above and leaves you feeling small and slightly exposed on the narrow path beneath. Here we came across a waterspout marked in the Wainwright guide, an odd feature to find in such a place. Its water was clear and at a temperature that must have been barely above freezing it was chillingly cold to the touch. At this amazing place the route splits into two choices, although the obvious route to keep the interest and adrenalin going is the route that slants up between Flat Crag and Cambridge Crag, rather than the route between Cambridge Crag and Bowfell Buttress, which is more of a slogging chore. The better route between Flat Crag and Cambridge Buttress also provides a close up and rather scary view of the Great Slab, an immense and roughly diamond shaped flat rock face, tilted at such a nasty angle as to prevent any thoughts of trying to stand on it. That day you could clearly see thick ice on the face of the Great Slab. I have often found it satisfying, but also vaguely terrifying, to be in a relatively safe vantage place, but with the prospect of almost certain death just a few feet or even inches away. However that day I was to learn that even in places of relative safety there can be danger. As we climbed up the icy defile above the Great Slab, trying to be cautious and careful, I had a slip forward. I am a little notorious for loosing my footing on walks, often to the amusement of Stan or Peter or anyone else I am walking with, but today Stan was not laughing as he saw me heading face first for the ground beneath me. At such times one has to marvel at the set of automatic reflexes from the central nervous system that makes one's hands somehow land in front of one's face before it hits the rock beneath. I like getting close to impressive rock scenery, but that day was a little too close for comfort. I was lucky to get away with nothing more than slightly grazed hands, rather than a smashed face. As it was this turned out to be a minor blip in a day of perfection and although a little shaken, I continued to walk over the final rocks to the high eerie that is the summit of Bowfell.

Although it was cold and icy that day, there was no snow to be seen on the winter hills. And yet as we sat by Bowfell's summit cairn that did not matter. It was just past eight o'clock in the morning, the sun shone in a peerless blue sky and there was not a breath of wind. The view from Bowfell was as perfect as it could ever be and the clarity was immense, as over 100 Wainwright summits were arrayed in the glorious early morning light, along with a sizeable arc of pale blue sea. Perhaps most stunning of all was the sparkling jewels of the Three Tarns nestled some 600 feet below us. And amazingly on this the sixth highest of the Lakeland fells, we were totally alone and had neither met nor seen anyone since we began the walk. There is something truly primeval about being in such a place undisturbed. I am glad that the majority of walkers like to have their cooked breakfast and seem to start heading on to the hills at around half past nine in the morning. At such times, with nothing but nature and the company of a close friend who knows how to appreciate the silence and grandeur as I do, we glimpse something of our ancient roots, when our lives were lived in harmony with nature, as opposed to current times where our lives are largely lived closeted from nature.

It was only after an hour of unsurpassed elation, followed by unsurpassed peace and meditation, that we saw the first solo walker of the morning trudging past the Three Tarns. It was time to make way and give this fellow early bird his moments of peace on the summit, before the hordes inevitably arrived. As we headed back down The Band, we passed the familiar procession of people heading for Bowfell's highest inches and realised that the Lake District, although it may often seem small and crowded, is in fact big enough to accommodate both the hordes and the lovers of solitude. All you have to do is understand that the hills don't have watersheds of time or season. They are open all hours.

Encounters on the Hills

One of the great delights of walking the wild places of Britain is that inevitably you will stumble upon some of this country's varied wildlife in its natural habitat. I have always found such encounters to be uplifting and at times a reminder that there are still places on this crowded island where nature is king and not man. I don't claim to be any wildlife expert, but part of the aim of this chapter is just to illustrate the kind of natural experiences that can be had on the hills, experiences that in some cases form a lifelong memory and which are often as special as views and summits and ridges. At the same time, and by contrast, I would like to mention some more of the human encounters that I have had on the hills, some annoying, some illuminating and one in particular very special in a number of ways.

Wainwright was passionate about Lakeland's sheep. Indeed in one of the more unusual of literary gestures he dedicated Book Four, *The Southern Fells*, to the hardy Lakeland sheep. Some may find this quirky, but I am inclined to consider this a very apt dedication. For where would Lakeland be without its sheep. The imprint of these weather worn animals lies all over the district, from the picture postcard white dots in the patchwork fields when viewed from on high, to the amazing sheep tracks that are such a feature in places such as the Northern Fells. There is a great tendency to think of sheep as rather stupid animals, useful for meat and wool, but devoid of grey matter. However anyone who has stumbled upon a sheep track and admired the way it contours perfectly around the side of a fell cannot but admire what in essence is the most logical route around any object. In this regard sheep are practical. They are not interested in ephemeral things such as summits, as anyone who has mistakenly taken a sheep track thinking it was a man made path will know. For sheep tracks often end mysteriously in dead ends, or what us humans with our drive to get back to civilisation construe as dead ends. In reality they are probably just places where there is good grazing.

So in some regards sheep are practical, although this needs a little qualification. For many is the time that I have been climbing a high mountain, such as Bowfell, or The Old Man of Coniston and witnessed sheep in places that defy logic or sense. I recall coming down Rossett Gill and seeing a solitary sheep perched precariously on a narrow ledge of grass, with crags and drops all around, seemingly quite happy while his fickle quarry of food lasted. How that sheep ever got down from there I do not know. Perhaps it didn't get down, for sheep casualties are an unfortunate fact of hill farming. How it got to this plinth of grass amidst a chaos of crags in the first place was another matter.

Although sheep sometimes get themselves into positions where it is impossible to help them unless you have ropes and climbing things, I have always tried to do my bit for the sheep. On one occasion I came across a sheep whose head had become trapped in one of the square holes on a metal fence. The sheep was doing its best to free itself, but as it made its frantic gambit, it was clear that the wire around its head was not only uncomfortable but in danger of garrotting the poor beast. Luckily the farmhouse was near at hand and I braved an assault by a couple of sheepdogs, to knock on the door. It was worth the effort, for once I had explained the situation the farmer quickly rushed out and with a heave and a push, which I would have felt awkward administering myself, he freed the animal. The sheep ran away, startled for a few seconds, before resuming its familiar calm munching of grass, as if nothing had happened.

If Lakeland's sheep are an inherent part of the character of the landscape, deer are a much rarer sight. I have had some notable encounters with deer on the fells, usually when I have deliberately strayed from the paths. However, if you really want to see deer in large numbers on the mountains, Scotland is the place. Having said this, I remember a day in the Central Fells when I had just bagged the lonely summit of Ullscarf, something of a connoisseur's peak. In fact, I had imbibed the solitude to such an extent that as I left the summit, I had a desire to remain alone and take the term 'open access' to its truest meaning. So I left the path that leads to Greenup Edge and instead made a pathless way on tussocky grass and heather, above the steep contours of Lining Crag. Now it is a fact about deer that they are often initially hard to spot, as they merge chameleon like with the heathery, grassy landscape and it was not until this particular herd poked their heads above the rim of the crags and into the open sky, that I suddenly realised I was close to about fifty deer. Away from the man made highway of the path and amidst heather, bog and tough grass, it seemed briefly as if I had intruded upon someone else's home. So I watched for a few minutes in spellbound silence, took a picture of the deer silhouetted against a backdrop of fell and sky and then left them to it.

The summit of The Nab is perhaps one of the most prized among the Wainwrights, but this is not because it is particularly high or craggy, although it does present an impressive wedge when viewed from

Deer, off the beaten track, on Ullscarf

Martindale. It is more because it has an aura of natural secrecy about it. The Nab is a deer sanctuary, a place reserved for deer to more or less do as they please, except when the stalkers are in town. My first knowledge of The Nab came from Wainwrights *Far Eastern Fells Guide*, and at the time he wrote the guide The Nab was out of bounds for a fell walker and effectively a trespass. Wainwright made the trespass in the name of his commendable desire to document every inch of the Lakeland fells and comments that he probably got away with trespassing 'due to his marked resemblance to an old stag'. He warned that other trespassers 'must not expect the same good fortune'. This is all very well to say, but now that the pursuit of Wainwright bagging has become popular, The Nab represents something of a dilemma.

As a result, The Nab was one of those odds and sods of the fells that kept getting left out of plans and ended up as part of something of a mopping up exercise. It was to end up being my 208th Wainwright. The problem, particularly for a non-local, was trying to establish whether 50 years on from Wainwright's guide books, The Nab was still out of bounds.

I consulted other more recent guide books and they seemed to include descriptions of getting onto and off The Nab, with little or no mention of trespassing. All seemed well, but despite also searching on the internet I was unable to establish for certain that it was now permitted to go onto The Nab.

Eventually the Wainwrights that were left began to run out and as I had decided some years before that the Nab would definitely not be my last Wainwright, it ended up having to be done, trespass or not! So on a largely overcast day, when cloud formed a low curtain over the fells and my newly acquired GPS unit came into its own, Stan and I found ourselves heading for The Nab. We were doing a horseshoe of a route that also included the as yet unclimbed Beda Fell, as well as the once before climbed Rest Dodd.

I had previously been on Rest Dodd on a hot day in August and today's all enfolding mist and drizzle was a stark contrast. The summit cairn on Rest Dodd felt wild and the drop off its steep nose down towards The Nab did not look that inviting. But before our proposed encounter with The Nab and its wildlife, we had a human encounter worth relating. As Stan and I sat in the elements, soaking in the wildness and not particularly worried about anything, a rather uncertain couple of men approached us, regaled in top of the range walking gear. Now I am a great believer that expensive gear doth not an experienced walker make and these two were a prime example of my theory. They greeted us and informed us that they were doing Wainwright's Coast to Coast walk and asked where exactly they were, which was not encouraging. They had a quite large scale map of the Coast to Coast route, which seemed in the main to just plot the course of the route and had little relevant detail other than that. This map was not as poor as some I have seen, but surely an Ordnance Survey map would have been more appropriate. From memory I did not recall the Coast to Coast walk actually going over Rest Dodd, and when we informed this pair that they were in fact on the summit of Rest Dodd, they seemed at first to doubt us, as if it was us that had got it wrong, and not them. However once they saw the contours on our GPS unit and compared them to the Ordnance Survey map that we had with us, they realised they had perhaps been quite near to heading in completely the wrong direction. They then pointed in the direction of Ramps Gill and asked whether they could contour down there, which was virtually the opposite direction they wanted to be heading. From previous visits to this area we were able to describe to them the direction and terrain heading off Rest Dodd and the rough bearing to get them back on The Coast to Coast and down to

Haweswater. They left us on Rest Dodd and a few seconds later were enveloped into the mist. Whether they made their overnight destination or not is something I will never know, but I do know that if they had not met two rather shabby looking walkers on Rest Dodd they would have headed many miles off course. Now I am the first to admit that I have made many mistakes on the hills and my navigation has at times been pretty poor, but if anything both my own early experiences and these guys experience serves to highlight the need to have a proper map and some decent navigational aids and skills.

Anyway back to the deer. There was a peculiar eerie feeling as we headed off Rest Dodd into the mist and the general direction of The Nab. We were still not totally sure that some gun wielding deer estate manager would not be there to greet us, although in our hearts we knew the increased popularity of the fells since Wainwright wrote about the Nab would probably mean we had nothing to fear. In fact we were in for a memorable treat.

A few minutes into a very steep descent off Rest Dodd a sturdy dry stone wall is reached and, where a stile headed over the wall, a placard confirmed that we were about to enter The Nab Deer Reserve and that as long as we stuck to the permitted paths and stayed quiet we would be fine. The feeling crossing that wall can only be described as one of privilege. We were now just below the mist base, which hung behind us in deep shades of grey over Rest Dodd and the other higher fells. As we tramped and squelched over the eroded peat hags towards the Nab summit, our thoughts were not of terrain or view or even summit, but simply of the utter peace and tranquillity of the place. And like being in a cathedral or a library it seemed natural and wholly appropriate to say little to each other and for anything that was said to be in a low whisper. Then about half way along the ridge we saw them, or more accurately they saw us. When I say a herd of deer, some might think perhaps of 20 or even maybe 50, but I'll swear we saw at least 100 deer that day and unlike the deer on Ullscarf who seemed content to graze away while I watched them, these deer decided to make a steady line away from us and down into the retreat of Bannerdale, not startled by us, but nonetheless desirous to be away from these humans. After that the rounded summit of The Nab was a bit of an anticlimax, for truly the tick was just that and the memorable experiences had all been before the summit itself. However without the fundamental objective and desire to tick of The Nab it is arguable that such an experience would not have happened.

Stan heading towards the Nab

These are the memories of deer that stick in my mind in the Lake District, and although I have had many other encounters in Scotland with great herds of deer, perhaps the ones in the Lake District stick in the mind because they are by comparison quite rare experiences and so savoured all the more. Scotland did though provide my closest experience of deer, or should I say of a single stag. It was on an aborted attempt to climb the Corbett of Rois Bheinn, in the west coast region of Scotland called Moidart. Heavy rain had barred our progress and we were rather dispirited as we trudged our way back through the low and rough hinterland beneath the mountains to the hamlet of Lochailort. At such times though, the wild places can sometimes and suddenly lift our spirits with the unexpected. As we rounded a corner, not more than 10 feet from us a huge stag stood proudly, replete with a fine set of antlers and looking the spitting image of the Monarch of the Glen. For a few seconds it stared a powerful stare of primal instinct towards us before bolting over a hillock and immersing itself in the wilderness that was its home. This event lasted just a few seconds but it had made the day and it somehow did not matter that the required number of ticks had not been gained or that a wonderful view had not been seen.

If Lakeland has a symbolic animal apart from its sheep, it must be the red squirrel. These native squirrels are for me the true squirrels of the British Isles and each time I have spotted a red, I have been entranced. Over the years I must have had as many as 20 sightings of red squirrels, ranging from a quick flash of red tail bobbing in the distance, to a pair of reds dancing and leaping in the trees directly above me for several minutes, as I started a walk up Rosthwaite Fell. Natural wooded areas seem the best places to see red squirrels, rather than man made forests such as Whinlatter. A good place I have found is the lovely walk that accompanies both banks of the river that holds Aira Force. Winter is a good time, as the leaves are bereft of foliage making these elusive creatures easier to spot. Red squirrels are to me altogether more attractive than their grey cousins, being smaller, more colourful and having that wonderful bushy tail. I have been encouraged that in recent years I have tended to see more red squirrels rather than less. Let's hope that the Lake District forever remains the domain of the red squirrel.

And so to a few human encounters. I have often thought when standing in a crowded carriage on the Jubilee Line that while perhaps twenty percent of the people crowded in with me might interest me in conversation, there would also be perhaps twenty percent who would profoundly irritate me if I had to talk to them. I have generally found this rule is applicable to walkers met on the hills.

Time spent in the hills is to be savoured and there is enough room for everyone to enjoy the fells even on crowded days. However, there are a small minority of walkers who seem, to put it bluntly, more interested in their own egos than in trying to blend in harmoniously with their surroundings and the people they are sharing their walk with. For my first example I must go to Scotland. Imagine having just slogged for many hours to reach the hard won but amazing summit of Ben Eighe in Torridon. You arrive sweating like a pig and find a spot where you can recline relatively undisturbed. There were perhaps a dozen other people on the summit that day. I did not have an issue with that and expect people on high and famous summits. I believe that if I want solitude I should not expect it here but should go elsewhere. However I did not expect what happened within about twenty seconds of my arriving. I had barely had time to gain sufficient breath for conversation and was starting to soak in the fabulous view towards the Letterewe wilderness, when the view was replaced by a man's face leaning over me. He was eating a sandwich and immediately began asking me the usual time honoured questions about where I was staying, what route I had taken, where I was heading. When he asked what I thought of the view, I very nearly said that I could not tell because his leering face was in the way of it, but despite wanting my own bit of space and time, I am too polite to do this. The point is that such seemingly friendly gestures on the hills are in reality very annoying. It is one thing to strike up a conversation with someone who seems to be looking for one, or even to venture a few words from a respectful distance, but to invade the space of a walker who is doing nothing more than trying to relax and enjoy the view is, I feel, very rude. If a rule book of etiquette on the hills is ever written this type of behaviour would be in the 'do not' section. Thankfully after a few minutes the man moved on to another innocent walker and being the type he was, he did not stay on the summit for very long. I don't mind socialising on the hills and I am happy to an extent to engage in conversation, but socialising is not a reason for me to go to the hills and if I did desire to strike up a conversation, I would never do so without being encouraged or invited.

All of which leads me to my second story, which relates to a time on the summit ridge of Blencathra. Again, the actual summit had perhaps fifteen to twenty people crowded around its quite small area. I stayed for a little while and made polite conversation with a handful of people about the merits of the view and the various routes up. Nothing irritating about that and again I would be truly curmudgeonly if I expected to meet no-one in such a famous place. However as with any lover of solitude, I wanted to share some reflective moments up on the high ridge. As it would be very impolite to ask everyone to leave the summit so as I could selfishly indulge my solitude, I instead removed myself from the summit equation and walked along the ridge to the almost equally fine rocky vantage that is the summit of Gategill Fell. People passed behind me on the path every few minutes and I said hello to them if they said hello to me, but for a while no-one seemed interested in disturbing my relative peace on Gategill Fell's top. The plan seemed to have worked and everyone was happy. I was not spoiling anyone else's enjoyment and they were not spoiling mine. I was enjoying the gradually fading light of a November evening, knowing that I could just romp down Blease Fell and was contemplating the ever more colourful hues on the fells that encircled Derwent Water. Then a man disturbed my reverie. At first I was not too bothered as he seemed to have a keen interest in the hills and at such times I generally don't mind giving any little knowledge of the area I can. So when he pointed to the distant Coniston Fells and asked me what they were I was happy to oblige, thinking perhaps that he would then go away content. Even when he then pointed to the neighbouring Crinkles and Bowfell and asked me to identify them I was reasonably happy to oblige, although I was beginning to get a nasty sinking feeling. After about the tenth time of being asked 'What's that one over there?' I began to feel like I had become a Wainwright guide book in human form. By the time we had reviewed the entire Southern Arc of the view and were proceeding towards the Coledale and Newlands round I had frankly had enough. I contemplated giving this man an impromptu present of the *Northern Fells Guide* that was in my rucksack, to prevent other innocent ramblers falling into his trap. However I value my hoary old *Northern Fells Guide* to much. So instead I reluctantly informed him that I had to go. When he then asked me which way I was heading off the fell, I began to envisage being followed back to my self-catering place and perhaps even having to give up my bed for this man. Luckily though this was just the wild imaginings of a near maddened fell walker and I breathed an almost audible sigh of relief when, having informed the man that I was heading down Blease Fell, he then informed me that he was heading down Scales Fell, pretty much in the opposite direction.

In essence I believe that we each owe it to each other on the fells to be considerate and think before we intrude on someone else's moments of peace and escape. I don't go to the fells to make friends or be sociable. I believe in being polite to others on the fells, but never intrusive. And for a final few words on the subject of sociability on the fells, Wainwright is a very good person to turn to. He was a man generally more concerned with mountains and animals than with people. As well as dedicating one of his seven pictorial guides to the sheep of Lakeland, he also dedicated the *Northern Fells Guide* to the 'solitary wanderers on the fells'. In making this dedication it is almost as if he recognised that in those of a solitary nature there exists a kind of common bond or kinship.

I am also reminded of Wainwright's interview for the radio programme *Desert Island Discs*. AW was asked what he would do if he met another solitary walker on a summit. Surely one would at least have to say hello? His reply was short and sweet 'no I don't think you do.' This type of answer has perhaps served to foster a view that Wainwright was just a grumpy old man content only in his own company. However I am more inclined to the view that within his philosophy of silent contemplation of the fells, he was not so much being anti-social as simply saying that the best and truest way to enjoy the fells is alone. It is not an insult to humanity, just a plain and simple fact.

This is perhaps why, when I come on to the subject of more positive meetings with people on the hills, most of my recollections are either of a solitary walker that I have met, after hours of lonely walking, or of a walker whose very presence or personality has left a marked impression on my own feelings about the hills.

High on the summit of Esk Pike, I met a gnarled old man, looking to all intents and purposes the image of Private Fraser from Dad's Army and with a look on his face that matched. It was winter and it was just him and me on the fell. I decided to just say a brief hello and then remove myself to another part of the summit. But to my surprise, when I did say hello, the man's face suddenly changed to a more genial demeanour and he started talking about his life on the hills, almost as if he was in some way using me as a vehicle for his nostalgia. I did not mind, for this man had walked the hills for many years, just like Wainwright. He had walked in Scotland and Ireland and Wales as well as just about everything hilly in England. And it was not with a boastful tone that he spoke of his life in the hills, but rather with a tone of awe and wonder. I remember him imparting to me that life passes quickly and to cram all the wild experiences you can into it. It seemed to me as if through his countless years of walking the hills, something of the essence of the wild places, of their very spirit perhaps, had infused into him.

I recall meeting another such person while climbing Morrone above Braemar in Scotland. This man was a veritable encyclopaedia of local knowledge. As we passed conversation about the mountains that I was hoping to climb that week, and I pronounced each mountain name in a dreadfully Anglicised accent, he politely corrected each name into its proper Gallic tone. It transpired that this local man had lived and breathed his local hills for many many years and had lost count of the number of times he had climbed them. Something of the peace and calm of the hills radiated from this man and he was not at all irritated by this keen youth quizzing his knowledge, although I knew and sensed when to move on.

My final recollection of a memorable meeting was for me perhaps the most memorable of all and certainly the one with the most far reaching of consequences. Now I have said earlier in this book that no hill is boring. Standing waiting for a delayed train at London Bridge is boring and I would infinitely rather be on the most squat and dull of fells than be doing my daily commute to London. But the two Mell Fells in Lakeland's eastern fells are, to put it in a different way, perhaps not the most interesting of hills. In fairness to Great Mell Fell, it at least has a little more to offer than Little Mell Fell, which is a contender for the title of dullest Wainwright. Great Mell Fell is higher, a longer more varied walk, and even has some rather interesting trees, contorted by the wind, on its flanks. Nonetheless even though Great Mell Fell is only a couple of hundred feet lower than notable fells such as Eagle Crag and Raven Crag, it would probably not even get a mention in this book if it were not for the unusual occurrence that happened during my ascent.

It was on a short holiday to the Lake District in October 2000 that my brother Peter and I set off to climb Great Mell Fell on a rather dull and slightly drizzly day. We parked at Dockray and as we walked under a monotonous grey sky, towards the looming wedge of Great Mell Fell, it seemed as if this was not going to be an especially memorable day in the hills. It was as we left the minor road to head up a rather muddy lane leading onto the fellside proper, that we noticed a four by four vehicle and a group of four people busying themselves with various items of filming equipment, cameras and the like. One of these men stood out to both Peter and I, with that kind of instant recognition that dawns on us when we see someone well known. I had known that face and beard for a decade, stretching back to when I was a teenager and encompassing all the many hills I had climbed in between. This was a man who along with Alfred Wainwright himself had inspired me in the earliest days of my hills education and whose videos with AW had been watched by me hundreds of times. It was none other than Eric Robson.

Now I have never been one to start asking for autographs and begin fawning over celebrities and I can imagine how irritating that might be for them. However I could not resist a quick 'Hello Mr Robson', to which Mr Robson replied with a like response, but in those deep tones that characterise his voice and which were so familiar to me from the videos with Wainwright. We began our climb and left them to their filming business. Now my brother is not perhaps the quickest of walker's up the fells and soon Mr Robson and his crew had caught us up. We more or less shared the climb up and arrived at the summit at roughly the same time. Although I was conscious of not disturbing their filming, there was little I could do, for as much as they wanted their footage, I wanted my new tick. They were a friendly bunch, although I do recall that one of them, the cameraman I think it was, did not consider that climbing the fells with heavy equipment was particularly enjoyable. Can't say I blame him, with a heavy camera on his back!

I recall having a reasonably lengthy chat with Eric Robson on the summit of the fell. It was hard to know what to say to someone who had known and worked with Alfred Wainwright and who himself was something of a legend to me. I found myself wanting to say so many profound things that might be worthy of such an occasion, things that AW might have come up with. But I think I ended up speaking a load of garbage, along the lines that I considered that a fell could only be truly ticked off the list of Wainwrights if the view had been seen. I knew what I had meant to say, but I ended up saying it in a way that sounded just like all those types of baggers who are only interested in the ticks. The types I don't really identify with. If this had been a job interview I would have failed to impress. I tried to help the researcher to identify a tiny knobble on the distant horizon and even cocked that up. I said it was Great Gable and it turned out to be Dale Head (an understandable mistake, but a devastating blow in the circumstances). Mr Robson, despite the useless verbiage that poured from my mouth, remained a model of politeness.

Eventually the drizzle increased, the fells became murky shadows and both Mr Robson and the film crew and my brother and I departed from the summit of Great Mell Fell. That evening in my room I felt that I could have said something a little more profound about the hills to Eric Robson. Nonetheless I knew that meeting him had made Great Mell Fell a Wainwright that I would never forget.

If that had been the end of the matter this chance meeting would still have made it into this book, but over the course of the next seven years things slowly and surely took an altogether unexpected turn. First the video of the walk that Eric Robson and the crew had been filming came out. Called *Remote Lakeland*, it documented a long distance walk around the perimeter of Lakeland, visiting some of Lakeland's quieter, but no less worthy summits. It was interesting to see the footage on Great Mell Fell and realise that my brother and I were at that moment trying to cower out of the camera's line of sight. As a whole it was a beautiful addition to my collection of hills related videos, something to stoke the memories and fuel the ambitions on a cold winter's night, when the rain and wind are lashing my house.

For the next few years I thought little more about my meeting on Great Mell Fell, until in early 2007 I was perusing the walking books section of a Keswick shop and came across a new book by Eric Robson called *After Wainwright*. Here he described each day of the journey depicted on the *Remote Lakeland* video. Stan was with me that day and we both instantly looked to see whether the meeting on Great Mell Fell had been mentioned, thinking it unlikely, but hoping that a line or two about it might be in the book. It was to Stan's immense amusement and my slight chagrin that I began to read not just one sentence but a whole half a page or so about Eric Robson's encounter with me and my brother. Stan's amusement was due less to the fact that his best mate was referred to in print and more to how he was referred to. I had been dubbed a Wainwright Bagger, a 'trainspotter with altitude'. My comments about having to see the view from every Wainwright, which I had meant to convey something more cerebral than the normal philosophy of a hell bent tick bagger, had been interpreted as a rule rather than a personal philosophy. I have to add though that I could see the funny side of it all. My verbal rubbish on Great Mell Fell had come back to haunt me. And despite the aura of spirituality and joy in peace and solitude that framed my love of the hills, I had to admit to myself that I was still in essence a bagger. However in the year or so since Mr Robson dubbed me a Wainwright bagger, I have learnt to embrace being a bagger, rather than trying to disguise the fact. Although, as I hope this book conveys, baggers come in many forms, like I am sure train spotters must do as well.

It was in the bookshop, staring at the inescapable facts of the words written about me, that an idea began to stir in my head. I was due to complete all the 214 Wainwrights that very year and I had always had a passion for writing. Perhaps I should write something about my journey to completing the Wainwrights and by doing so exorcise the baggage of bagging that hung over me throughout my year of completion, both physically and mentally. But as yet it was just an idea, and the idea needed a further spark to give it substance and drive.

In May of 2007, Stan attended a lecture given by Eric Robson at the Theatre by the Lake in Keswick. During his lecture Eric Robson yet again referred to meeting me and my brother on Great Mell Fell and I had now become an 'extreme Wainwright bagger', due to my suggestion that to truly count the tick the view had to be seen. It appeared that I had acquired a sort of anonymous infamy. So when Stan came back and told me about the lecture, I decided that in the spirit of the right to reply, it was time that I endeavoured to contact Mr Robson.

I fired off an e-mail to the Wainwright Appreciation Society, hoping it would wend its way to Eric Robson, who is chairman of the society. I wanted the tone of my e-mail to convey the fact that although I had been sledged Aussie cricketer style about my bagging antics, I had taken it in the spirit it was meant. Baggers are in general an odd bunch and there was a perverse pleasure and no little merriment about being labelled with train spotters. I made brief mention to the fact that I was writing a book about the journey to completion, but the e-mail was not intended to be a plug for my book, it was about trying in some way to claw back my tattered hill walking image!

Although the e-mail was not intended to be about the book, the reply did provide a spur to begin and complete this book. Eric Robson replied in person and as well as thanking me for taking his comments about baggers in good spirit, he also said that he would love to read the book when I had finished it.

Now while all budding writers desire to be in print, I must confess that writing this book has been in equal measure about the pleasure of recounting my journey, even if no-one else ever reads the account and also about the prospect that I might be able to give a little bit of reading pleasure back to a man who, along with AW, had provided such an inspiration to me in the early years of the journey to completion.

Contrasting Experiences on the Fells

The fact that a fell or mountain has the word 'great' within its name, by no means can be regarded as an indication that it is worthy of greatness. Great Mell Fell only appears to be called such because it is higher and slightly less rounded and dull than Little Mell Fell. Great Scafell disappoints in how far removed it is in character to its grand namesake Scafell Pike. However there is no doubting that one mountain in the Lake District, perhaps above all others, is entitled to proudly and justifiably wear the title great – that mountain is Great Gable.

Over the years I have developed an intimate and deep relationship with Great Gable and in particular with one of the many routes to its summit. The route from Seathwaite farm to Gable's summit has become a kind of annual pilgrimage for me. For me this route has everything that a grand day out in the mountains should have. It is not in the main about solitude, but then Great Gable never really is. On this walk I am quite happy to forsake solitude for the constant shifting delights the walk has to offer, and the ever changing and varied scenery. Although I have ascended and descended Great Gable by other routes, to me this route has qualities that recommend it above all others. The walk begins in a valley where the mountain to be climbed cannot be seen and this adds an element of excitement and adventure to the walk. No real sense of Great Gable can be had from Seathwaite Farm, where Base Brown instead is the dominant fell.

The cascades of another Sour Milk Gill (the other more famous one being in Far Easdale) accompany the delightful steep and rocky early sections of the walk, before the upland hollow of Gillercomb is reached. Gillercomb is a rather dreary place, and it almost feels like you are back at ground level as you tread its largely flat course.

If time allows it is worth detouring up onto Base Brown, partly because it is another Wainwright and partly because from just a little way north of its summit great plunging views can be had down to the Seathwaite valley. However if you want to miss Base Brown then a level half mile along Gillercomb and a short and fairly steady climb will lead you to the summit of Green Gable. From here the objective of Great Gable now dominates the view, with the final knobbly and craggy 400 feet rising above Windy Gap. From here Great Gable's summit structure looks imposing. If mountains are judged so by the nature of their terrain, then Great Gable fits the bill. However the one thing that cannot really be assessed from Green Gable is the sheer height of Great Gable. That appreciation will come later.

Green Gable is often given short change by walkers bound for its more famous and more spectacular neighbour. The times I have spent on Green Gable have rarely been spent in isolation, but I have noticed that most visitors seem to only tarry for long enough to touch the cairn and maybe give a cursory five minutes attention to the view. I think Green Gable deserves better and in some ways its view is just as good as that from the main summit of Great Gable. It is more of a perch than Great Gable's summit. Where better can one appreciate the architecture of the upper Ennerdale valley, with its controversial pine forest? Equally fine is the view of the craggy Shamrock Traverse side of Pillar, where on days of shifting cloud and light Pillar Rock stands out like a black fin against the main body of Pillar. This is probably the finest place to appreciate the High Stile range and Haystacks and the way those massive fells cleave and separate the valleys of Ennerdale and Buttermere. Then there is the beautiful sneak view of Buttermere and Crummock Water. It is fun also to try and delineate Blackbeck Tarn from Buttermere, for Blackbeck Tarn appears to merge into Buttermere when viewed from Green Gable's summit. All things considered there is every reason to tally awhile on Green Gable.

However even the most ardent of summit worshippers (or bores depending on your viewpoint), would have to admit that the lure of Great Gable does tend to pull one away from the prospect of resting for a few hours on Green Gable. To get from Green Gable to Great Gable via Windy Gap, Wainwright's advice is simple 'follow everybody else', which I suppose serves to show that the popular mountains were popular even 40 or 50 years ago. Personally I have always enjoyed this last bit of the ascent, which is rocky everywhere and being so close now to a grand objective I don't tend to regard these final few hundred feet as slog.

The view from Great Gable's summit, replete with large cairn and bronze War Memorial tablet, is extensive, with all of Lakeland's highest summits in view. Yet because the immediate vicinity of the summit does not fall away in any direction, the view is one of vastness rather than perspective. Wainwright devotes four pages to showing the summit view pictorially. However, unlike other high fells he does not add a written text to the effect that the summit view is one of the finest views to be had in the district. Earlier on I mentioned that climbing Great Gable from Seathwaite has become something of a pilgrimage for me. But whereas the majority of walkers will crown their own achievement on the highest point of Gable, my personal pilgrimage to Great Gable does not have as its highlight the true summit of the fell. The highlight is instead somewhere that is near to the summit, yet out of sight from the summit. It is a place with arguably the finest view in the Lake District and yet a place where perhaps only one in twenty of the visitors to Great Gable's summit goes to or has even heard of. This place is the objective of my pilgrimage to Gable – it is the Westmorland Cairn.

I have generally limited time spent on Great Gable's actual summit to the mandatory ten minutes scanning the view and taking a few pictures. I am not a fan of busy places in the hills, as you will have gathered by now. Instead I find myself drawn south westwards, where it appears that the ground is going to drop away fiercely, although it does not, and where a tantalising glimpse of Wastwater way down below promises to deliver so much and does.

It is only a short walk to the Westmorland cairn, but the cairn seems an altogether different place to the crowded summit. In several visits to the cairn I have only met a handful of walkers and often had the cairn to myself for long periods of time. In a kind of abstract way it could be argued that the true summit of a mountain does not necessarily have to be defined by its highest point and I certainly feel that in many regards the Westmorland cairn is the spiritual summit of Great Gable. From nowhere else is the sheer height of this mountain, or perhaps of any other mountain in the district, better appreciated. The sweeping drama of the plunge down to the patchwork squares of fields and dry stone walls in Wasdale and the sheer sense of aeroplane style altitude of the view of Wastwater are sights that take the breath away and hold the attention like no other view. Does the massive sinewy build up of Lingmell and the Scafells look anywhere more impressive than from here? When speaking of the natural features of Great Gable, Wainwright describes the view to Wasdale as 'the finest view in the district' and this is surely a reference to the view from the Westmorland cairn rather than from the summit itself.

I am not a great lover of cairns for the sake of cairns, and I think that a useless cairn is a form of litter on the landscape. However surely the two brothers who erected this cairn in 1876 to mark what they considered to be the finest view in the district, had justification in doing so. Such a grand scene deserves a cairn and this ancient cairn perched on a rocky plinth above an abyss of scree and rock, is perhaps one example of where man's imprint has added something to the landscape, rather than taken something away from it.

On one of my visits to the Westmorland Cairn, shifting mists were crossing Gable's face and I arrived at the cairn under a blanket of cloud. I waited for five minutes or so and nothing happened and I began to think that my pilgrimage that day would not have its crowning glory. However, just at that moment the mists parted and the view of Wastwater was dramatically revealed. That moment was one of the most exhilarating in my walking career and it is often the case that the best summit experiences are those where there is a doubt over whether the view will be revealed. Suddenly that doubt is replaced by unexpected thrill.

So if I had to choose a favourite mountain and a favourite mountain place, I can think of no better than Great Gable and the Westmorland cairn. And if I had to chose my favourite route to a mountain, the climb of Gable from Seathwaite would be it, because it leaves the finest view until the very furthest point and during the course of the walk great changes of scenery are seen, along with fantastic valley views. Indeed it seems difficult when contemplating Wasdale from the Westmorland cairn to think that the day began in Seathwaite. And like the best things in life

Great Gable with a cap of cloud

Great Gable will go on giving pleasure down the years. For example I have yet to sample the delights and horrors of the Gable Girdle and Great and Little Hell Gate. These are waiting for me on a future visit.

I suppose it is inevitable after such a high point that things will come back to earth and there is earth in abundance of the lose variety on the route down Aaron Slack. On the plus side Aaron Slack is a very fast and efficient way of descending over 1000 feet from Windy Gap to Sty Head Tarn. It is worth the awkward scree filled descent in order to vary the return route and also because Sty Head Tarn is the perfect finale to a great mountain day. From Sty Head tarn the well trodden and in places delightfully smooth motorway of a path makes an unerring course back to Seathwaite.

Whereas most of my memories of Great Gable are from the warmer climes of spring and autumn, my abiding memory of St Sunday Crag is one of the depths of winter. St Sunday Crag is another of those names, like Great Gable, that promises a great mountain and then delivers one. As I described earlier, my first memories of St Sunday Crag are from when I was on neighbouring Fairfield in the winter of 1993, and the mists parted for a few seconds to reveal the huge wedge that is St Sunday. It was to be almost seven years though before I finally climbed this fantastic but, as yet, not too popular fell.

In the year 2000 Stan and I set out early for our winter trip to the Lake District. Christmas had just passed and we found ourselves aching for the hills even more than usual. A settled and cold weekend in the middle of January gave us all the excuse we needed. However this is the time of year that has the least daylight and by the time we had had our cooked breakfast at our B&B in Keswick and driven down to Patterdale it was already nearly 10 o'clock. That day began with high grey clouds which skirted the highest fells. There was no snow at ground level but we could see that a decent covering of snow began at around the 1500 feet contour and the higher tops seemed to have an extensive covering.

Arnison Crag, the very first fell in the first *Wainwright Pictorial Guide*, was also the first objective of the day. I recall being enveloped in a gentle snowfall half way up the fell. It was the kind of snow fall that has no wind to blow it along and whose silent fall adds to the peace of the hills. It was icy and slippery going up Arnison Crag, but its little rocky summit was adequate reward for our efforts. From here we got our first sense of what the day ahead promised. I remember that under the high cloud covering, the snow on the flanks of Stony Cove Pike and Gray Crag, in the Far Eastern Fells, assumed a peculiar shiny grey colour, rather like that of silver modelling paint. Red Screes had an ethereal cap of sunlit white cloud on it and we could see that the weather appeared to be gradually brightening from the south.

Wainwright does not describe a ridge route from Arnison Crag to Birks and as we waded up to Birks thigh deep in snow and on a very uniform drab slope we could understand why. On Birks we had our first true realisation of the classic winter day ahead, as the full sun came out and revealed the snow plastered walls of Dollywagon Pike and Nethermost Pike, as well as a starkly revealed dark outline of Striding Edge.

Now, as you will be aware, I tend to linger on summits longer than is perhaps strictly necessary, squeezing out every moment of hills pleasure. Even I have to confess that the summit of Birks is a bit of a flat place to dwell for long, especially when St Sunday Crag looms large and inviting ahead. So after only 15 minutes, rather than the usual mandatory half hour, we headed on for the main objective. A short but steep pull led us onto St Sunday Crag and although the view from its summit is obscured by the massive bulks of the higher Fairfield and Helvellyn, on a peerless day of blue sky and sun on snow covered ridges that blemish did not matter. The Far Eastern Fells were well revealed, but still shadowed, with their snow coverings steely grey under a cover of cloud. However, the continuous ridges, crags and buttresses of the Eastern Fells, leading from Red Screes in the south to Helvellyn and beyond in a north west direction were all lit brilliant white. Under snow, mountains always seem to appear higher and craggier than they are, as every feature is delineated and pronounced, and the mountain scene around us had an Alpine feel about it.

Rather like Great Gable, St Sunday Crag also has a place that is perhaps a finer belvedere and a quieter spot than the summit itself. This is Gavel Pike and a delectable little high level ridge leads there from St Sunday's summit. Wainwright gave his stamp of approval to Gavel Pike as a more attractive summit than St Sunday Crag itself and I can only agree. It has those perch like qualities which provide depth and space to the view and which for me give a true mountain flavour. Although Wainwright rates Gavel Pike as a good place for a lunch stop and this would definitely be true in warm weather, on a freezing January afternoon keeping the gloves on was more important than taking them off for a bite to eat.

Nonetheless, Gavel Pike was a splendid place that day and afforded tremendous views of the cliffs of Fairfield in snowy garb and the plunge down to Deepdale, places which had already provided a number of special winter memories for me. A mist had begun to form and hovered about

Gavel Pike and in the void between us and Fairfield, while two crows circled above us cackling away. The scene was not pretty or beautiful in the picture postcard sense of Lakeland, but it was savage nature in the raw. Stan and I became entranced by the shifting mists, which had an almost hallucinatory effect and seemed to call to us to stay longer and continue to witness their ever changing dance. Time was temporarily forgotten until one of us abruptly pointed out that it was two o'clock in the afternoon and we both realised that it was a little late in the January day to still be up at 2500 feet.

As we made our way towards Deepdale Hause and our escape route off the high places, the mist continued to ebb and flow over the ridge. One minute we were in cloud and the scene was one of low visibility and ever darkening hues of grey. The next minute the mist would part and in the direction of Grizedale Tarn we could see the early stages of a winter sunset, lighting up the Central and Western Fells in hues of gold and even green. Likewise our moods altered between ones of slight concern and haste, when in the cloud and mist, to ones of joy and awe when the mists parted. As we descended into Deepdale, first the rose pink coloured mountains and then the approaching night gradually enfolded us and by the time we reached the valley bottom and the relative safety of the level valley path, night was almost upon us. The last three miles were walked quickly and with our head torches on. It would have been slightly spooky alone, but with a companion it was a wonderful and rare experience, well removed from civilisation and with all the other walkers already back at their cars or accommodation. Every now and then we turned off the torches. As our eyes adjusted to the blackness we could see that the blackness was not uniform but had deeper black areas and shapes, which were occupied by the presence of the high mountains around us and pin pricks of light which were the stars above us. We finally got back to the car at just after five o'clock, cold but utterly invigorated.

Mind you not all of my winter experiences have been as pleasant as that on St Sunday Crag. Although winter can provide perhaps the finest landscapes and experiences in the hills, it can also throw up the worst weather and greatest dangers. Of all the weathers that a walker does not want to get caught in, blizzards and whiteouts are perhaps the kings of unpleasantness. I have experienced such conditions on a few occasions in the Lake District, although generally I try to avoid the high places on such days. Here I would like to tell of two such times, one in a place of relative safety where the blizzard was in a perverse way enjoyable and another that was very definitely not enjoyable.

Caudale Moor or Stony Cove Pike, as it is sometimes known, is not a difficult or tricky climb from the Kirkstone Inn. Perhaps it was the shortness of the climb or the fact that we were tired, having just driven for six hours overnight, that made us slightly underestimate the glowering black clouds, full of snow, that hung over Kirkstone Pass and its surrounding fells. Although children and families were sledging on the slopes behind the inn, this was not a fair weather day and the weather omens were bad. But surely this was a relatively safe venture? We had a compass, the Wainwright guide showed a wall to follow all the way to the summit and the climb was a short and slightly cheating pull of only just over 1000 feet. It seemed that the odds of romping up there, bagging the fell and dashing back down were in our favour.

Behind St Raven's Edge we lost sight of the homely inn and lost the sound of the whooping voices of the happy children. All was quiet, eerily and ominously so, as the deepest black clouds I have ever seen hung over us and extended towards the Fairfield and Helvellyn ranges. It began to snow, but rather than an immediately heavy snow, this was to begin with just a few flakes of the light stuff. We were not at this point worried as we had the wall to guide us. As we headed higher though it became more of a battle and both the snowfall and the wind increased. I remember noticing that the wall beside us was now covered with the drifting snows of today and prior days and the wall could no longer be distinguished from the landscape around us, or relied upon to guide us. Still a kind of summit fever took us over and we battled on to a cairn. I am still not sure to this day whether this cairn was or was not the summit and at this stage in proceedings I ceased to care. For by now the wind was beating up into a gale and a blizzard of snow was raging around us. Normal powdery snow is quite pleasant upon one's face, but this was a malicious snow-come-hail and it stung the face like little pellets of glass. I wear spectacles and these were now useless and plastered with snow, but when I took them off the snow was so harsh and stinging on the eyes, that it was much more unpleasant than wearing the snow encrusted glasses. The white of the sky merged with the white of the ground and this, coupled with the relentless snow in our faces, led to what seemed like several minutes of floundering around aimlessly, with little sense of purpose or direction. The compass was not an option as there was no way we would have been able to see to take a bearing in this atrocious weather. This is one of the few times that I have experienced what can only be described as a primitive rush of adrenalin. It was one of those thankfully rare times in the hills when instinct and basic survival take over from enjoyment and relaxation. The only thing to do was to get down and if that meant heading into the wrong valley so be it. Thankfully after about 15 minutes of downward floundering and being blown off our feet, we relocated the wall and the blizzard began to relent. Although I have never been one to shout or make noise in the fells, I think the sheer relief mixed with adrenalin made me shout out a cry of relief.

If there is a lesson I learnt from this day, which is now over ten years ago and seems like part of my long past and reckless twenties, it is that no fell or tick bag is worth risking one's life for or worth the embarrassment of having to explain how the situation could have been avoided to the Mountain Rescue Service. Then again though, by such mistakes we learn. Of course I have since gone back to Caudale Moor in fair weather to make sure I had reached the summit. A committed bagger has to be sure about these things! But having since definitely got to the summit, I am still none the wiser as to whether we actually reached the highest point in that blizzard.

While the experience in a blizzard on Caudale Moor was frightening and unpleasant, there was another time I was in blizzard conditions and the experience was altogether more enjoyable. In February 2004, Stan and I introduced a mutual friend Kevin to the Lake District. We had known Kevin for a number of years and as he was the type of person who liked walking locally and lived in the countryside, it seemed natural that he would be the type of person who would like the fells. This proved to be a correct assessment and for the last four years Kevin has been a welcome addition to the group when he has been able to come with us.

Whereas my introduction to the Lake District was one of a slow build up to the high places, Kevin was very much thrown in at the deep end. His first ever day of fell walking was a bitterly cold experience on Angletarn Pikes and Brock Crags, with frequent squally snow showers, enough to put off all but the true fledgling hill lover. For Kev's second day in the Lake District fells, we planned something seemingly a little easier, a romp up the mainline of Skiddaw.

It was a glorious start to the day, frosty with blue sky. However the luminous grey clouds behind Skiddaw told us that this was a fool's dawn and that bad weather was on its way. Skiddaw granted us its views as far as the final pull onto Skiddaw Little Man. At this point we looked out towards Skiddaw Forest and the white fingers of snow and ominous dark clouds told us that a heavy snow storm was approaching. There was already a decent covering of old snow on the route up to Skiddaw Lesser Man, and before a further fifteen minutes had passed there was a further fresh covering of snow and visibility became poor. Yet up here on Skiddaw we did not worry, as Stan and I knew the place so well. Instead we indulged in snowball fights and generally revelled in the winter wonderland around us. It was as if, up in the snow storm, we had entered another world. Keswick and civilisation lay in a different world far below.

On Skiddaw Little Man's summit things began to get fierce as the wind picked up and the conditions started to resemble the blizzard on Caudale Moor. Coming down the far side of Skiddaw Little Man, on the way to Skiddaw's main summit, things got really bad and it became more of a battle than a thing of enjoyment. For a while, just after the final gate on the mainline, we debated whether to carry on. This was not because it was excessively dangerous, but more because it was so cold and harsh. Then the wind died down slightly and we decided to go for the summit. I remember that my rather cheap woolly balaclava gave up the ghost on the final pull up Skiddaw. It had become so weighed down with the falling and driven snow, that where once there had only been a small hole in it for my eyes, now there was a large gaping hole in it the size of my face.

My face became raw and as we battled the final feet to the summit cairn, Kevin remarked that it was extremely red. The cairn was duly reached and we quickly dived into the shelter. Stan's own balaclava was plastered in a kind of permafrost and we dubbed him 'snowbeard'. Kev on the other hand, the good-looking member of our trio, had each of his delicate eyelashes highlighted by a little covering of snow. This time the blizzard experience had still had its moments of discomfort, but the ratio of enjoyment to discomfort had been tipped in favour of enjoyment and there was little sense of danger.

Stan as Snowbeard on Skiddaw summit

Having said that, as we descended in near whiteout conditions we found ourselves veering off course and towards Carl Side, instead of the main line, and it was only the sudden revealing of Skiddaw Little Man, now on our left, when it should have been to our right, that made us contour back to the Main Line. So it is possible to get slightly lost even on Skiddaw and even when you have climbed it more than a dozen times! The final wonder of the day came as we emerged out of our world of poor visibility and wind driven snow and the view was revealed to us again. Gone were the frosty, but essentially green, landscapes from the start of the day and in their place the Lake District was covered in a layer of fresh snow, with gentle flakes of snow still falling. The transformation was divine, although the car nearly got stuck trying to drive it out of the Gale Road car park. Kev's first two days in the fells contained the kind of experiences that either makes a person hate the hills forever, or makes a person realise that they will always love the hills and their elemental savage nature.

Size isn't Everything

The contrasts of scenery that are such a feature of the comparatively small area of the Lake District National Park are nowhere more pronounced than in the variety of scenery and situation to be found on the lower fells of Lakeland. I can think of nowhere else in this country where there are such a beautiful and varied collection of lower hills. The wonderful rugged nature of Lakeland means that a fell of barely over a thousand foot can have the stature of a mini mountain. But the lower level is not just about crags and rocks, it is also about sinewy paths, woodlands, pastoral beauty, intimacy of view and some hidden remote gems. Although there is no strict definition of what constitutes a high or low Lakeland fell, personally I consider that upland Lake District tends to begin at about 2000 feet. This is generally the height where a fell becomes a mountain, although there are of course exceptions. Using this personal rule of thumb there are roughly 80 lower Wainwright fells, of which in this chapter there is only space for me to describe a few of them. This is not meant to be a definitive selection of the best of the lower fells, but a personal selection of those dearest to me and those that have provided a few memorable and contrasting experiences.

The vast central plateau of Lakeland has at its rim many dramatic buttresses and cliffs. The Langdale Pikes are perhaps the most famous and dramatic example of bold outlines emanating from the bleak central upland behind, but Raven Crag is almost as dramatic. The ascent from the minor road by the western shore of Thirlmere is largely confined in trees. This is a common feature in many of the routes up the lower fells and often endows these ascents with a wonderful sylvan beauty. Here the wood is a coniferous plantation, which opens out for a while to reveal the precipitous face of Raven Crag. On my first climb of this fell I began to wonder how on earth a mortal walker could scale this fell, and even now the view of the crag from below never fails to halt me in my tracks. Luckily for a walker there is a sneaky way around the back to the top of the fell. At about 1300 feet the path comes out to a clearing and from here onwards the route is a joy to follow.

First the path plunges into a dark tunnel of pine trees. I am not a great fan of such plantations, but I do love the primeval darkness that can be experienced when densely packed conifers block out the light. After this tunnel of trees the path twists and turns upwards, crossing over numerous tree roots and becoming steeper and ever more promising. Then the path emerges from the conifers and you are more or less at the top of Raven Crag. The summit itself is a lovely spot, but for me the spiritual summit of Raven Crag and the best and most exposed viewpoint, is to be found by making a short detour down from the actual summit in the direction of Thirlmere. After perhaps fifty yards a small and grassy platform is reached, a perfectly safe place in itself and a wonderful resting point, but situated right at the edge of danger, above a fearful precipice. The walker will know full well that this is the limit of where he or she can go. But what a privileged place it is. While the view in itself is not extensive, with the vast bulk of the Helvellyn ridge effectively blocking much of it, Raven Crag does boast a fine and highly dramatic view of Thirlmere. Indeed this must rank as one of the finest views of a lake from any fell. The overall impression is one of fearful height above the lake. In sunny weather the lake sparkles down below, while in dark moody weather it appears gun metal grey. This little ledge, perched above the plunge down to Thirlmere, has to be one of my favourite places in the district.

As I have said the plateau of the Central Fells gives way to a number of wonderful fells at its edge, but it also contains some of the wildest, boggiest and most featureless of all the Lakeland fells. It will surprise many and even horrify some that Armboth Fell features on my personal list of favourite lower fells. I have to say that prior to climbing it I had also written off Armboth Fell, thinking it would be likely to be one of the dullest fells in the district. Indeed it was a fell that was left till near the end of my round not because I wanted to tease out the anticipation of it, but frankly because there always seemed to be better things to do. Now I have actually climbed it my opinion has somewhat changed, although I accept that many of those reading my reasons may still be unconvinced.

On an impossibly wet day, that had little chance of clearing, it seemed somehow fitting to bag Armboth Fell, before retreating to the creature comforts of a bath, a hot meal and a pint. Now over the years I have learned to love wet days on the fells. Once you get wet there is a certain masochistic pleasure about walking in the rain and mist, and there is also a peculiar satisfaction to be had in wrestling a summit out of a bad day. So to a certain extent and limit I can honestly say that I like bad weather. Sometimes a soaking on the hills feels surprisingly good and I like to experience the elements. For this reason I have never been one to indulge in expensive fashionable gear on the hills just for the sake of it. Yes I do have a wind proof, waterproof, coat but I only tend to use it when it is cold or harsh on the fells. I would never these days for example venture onto the high winter hills without my winter boots and adequate winter clothing and gear. However I also consider that there are times when gear can take over from immersion in the experience of the fells. Let me give an example.

Years ago I was on a climb up Skiddaw's main line with Peter. It was a mild May day but the forecast was one of wind and rain. We had decided to try and battle up Skiddaw via the relative safety of the main line and if we got beaten into a retreat, so be it. As far as gear goes I had a pair of cheap waterproofs and that was about it. They were waterproof to an extent but no more than that and a day of hard rain would leave me as good as soaked. But we did not care. That day we actually wanted to get soaked and to experience the elements. Why else go up Skiddaw in driving rain if not to get such a raw elemental experience? About a hundred feet up the start of the main line a group of walkers passed us. They were dressed in the most expensive and latest hi-tech gear, with their faces barely visible beneath their enormous, multi purpose, all weather proof hoods. It looked as it they were making an attempt at Everest. As they passed us I can remember hearing a derogatory laugh, as if by dint of their expensive fashion they were somehow superior beings to us. So it was with a certain pleasure that later that day, on a rain lashed and windy Jenkin Hill, we met the same group of walkers beating a hasty retreat down the mountain without having got anywhere near to the summit, while we motored on, soaked to the skin, to Skiddaw's wild summit.

Personally, unless the conditions fully justify it, I think there is no need to button oneself up to the hilt in a cushion of all weather gear. Just as driving through scenery does not provide the same level of connection with the landscape as walking through it does, so I feel that walking over protected by gear can overly shield a walker from connecting with the wild experience of nature. If the hills are bucketing down rain what is wrong with experiencing that elemental feeling of being amongst it all? Yes, sense should prevail and if the conditions need all the extra layering and waterproof and wind proofing then it is best to have it. But the main line, on a warm but wet May day, does not need the level of gear that one might take to Antarctica. There are times in the hills when gear seems to become, for a certain species of walker, less about the essential needs of the individual and more about making a fashion statement or a display of wealth to others on the hills. Thankfully this breed is rare! So yes, of course, one should take Antarctic gear if one is likely to meet such conditions and they do exist on the Lakeland hills, but when a simple

An ever shifting Coledale scene from Catbells

waterproof will suffice I cannot see the need for fashion parading hi-tech gear on the hills.

This is somewhat of a digression from Armboth Fell but perhaps will go some way to explaining the appeal of the fell for me and Stan on the day we climbed it. The route we took to Armboth Fell started on the same path that I had used to climb High Tove. It had been over seventeen years since I had been on this path and it was funny how distant memories were suddenly awakened over the sobering distance of time.

As the trees to the left of the path ended and the enclosed nature of the ground changed to one of space and bleak moorland, we headed away from the High Tove path, crossed Fisher Gill and made our way to Fisher Crag. Fisher Crag is one of those Lakeland places that has no bagging classification. It is neither a true Wainwright nor an Outlying Fell. Yet it is too fine a place to be missed and it proves the point that the bagging of Wainwrights is merely a framework for a wider and deeper appreciation and exploration of the wonderful landscapes of the Lake District. To simply bag Armboth Fell and never visit Fisher Crag would be a sort of hill walking crime.

On this, the bleakest and rainiest of days, the summit of Fisher Crag gave us five wonderful minutes of relief. In many ways Fisher Crag resembles its near neighbour Raven Crag. Both are wooded near the summit, although the actual top is clear of trees and both have spectacular plunging drops down to Thirlmere. On this day the experience was not just about the summit and view, it was what the weather did. For those few minutes the rain eased slightly and the clouds, which had been a neutral uniform grey, suddenly and dramatically tore themselves apart over the lake and bubbled and boiled over the massive flanks of Helvellyn. I would have walked much further and got much wetter than I did that day, for those five minutes of hill walking ecstasy on Fisher Crag, watching the elements at play.

As the rain began to pour again and the hills became shadowy and veiled again, we contemplated the bleak moorland that lay between Fisher Crag and Armboth Fell. If there is a path linking Fisher Crag to Armboth Fell we never found it. Instead there was a peculiar kind of energetic pleasure in just putting our heads down and romping at a steady march and in as straight a line as possible in the direction of Armboth Fell.

Having gained the summit plateau of Armboth Fell the next issue concerned which of the several contenders for highest point, poking out of the morass of squelch and bog beneath, was the actual summit. At this point my *Central Fells Guide* was called upon in order to see what Wainwright had to say about the summit. The Armboth Fell chapter in my guide now forever has that wrinkled look that paper develops after a soaking. We were looking for a rocky mound in the middle of the mire, like a crouton floating in some soup. It took a bit of finding, but once we found it there was no doubting it as the true summit.

The rocky mound of the summit is actually rather distinctive, a little bit of proper Lakeland stuck forlornly in a quagmire. This mound is rather like an upturned rowing boat in both appearance and dimensions. It floats forever upside down and stranded in a sea of bog. For all this though I am fond of the summit of Armboth Fell. It has a certain unique quality about it, albeit a very bleak quality. I cannot think of many better ways of getting away from civilisation than a climb to the rocky mound of Armboth Fell, on what Wainwright would have described as an 'impossible day'.

While Raven Crag has tended to provide me with largely dry experiences and Armboth Fell provided an almost entirely wet experience, my memories of Catbells are of mixed weather and contrast. If there was a hill walker's quiz night and the challenge was to name certain fells from their outlines alone, almost everyone would guess Catbells. It is a contender for Lakeland's most popular fell and is both beautiful to look at and beautiful to be on.

The first time I climbed Catbells was on a glorious May afternoon and via the most popular route from Hawse End. Peter, Stan and I had spent the morning rowing out to a little island on Derwent Water. To be fair it was actually Peter who did the rowing while Stan and I just sat back and admired the views. Despite its busy reputation the summit of Catbells was not popular that day and we soaked in views of a sun drenched azure blue Derwent Water and the massive graceful outline of Skiddaw. Relaxation was the order of the day.

On another recent visit I approached the summit via the ridge from Maiden Moor, which I had climbed up to via a largely pathless flank. It was late October and what had begun as a day of sunshine and showers, walking along the busy lakeside path by Derwent Water, had turned into a day of driving rain and solitude up on the Newlands ridge. On Maiden Moor I had only an hour or so of usable daylight left and there was little to encourage me to go on to Catbells, when I could just make an escape from the weather via Hause Gate. However as I left Maiden Moor, Catbells reared imposingly and rather spectrally through the sheets of driven rain and I just thought why not? Catbells summit, a place of relaxation and laziness before, was that day a dark unwelcoming place that did not suggest anything other than the briefest of stops.

Before long I found myself back at Hause Gate and descending the rocky stairway of a path that makes a quick beeline off the fells. On the way down I met a young couple swiftly marching up the fell. They had a certain purpose and intent to their stride and had they not stopped me I would have said nothing to them about the fading light and bad weather, but just have said a brief hello. However they did stop me and producing the kind of low quality excuse for a map that you might find coming free with a packet of breakfast cereal, they asked me the way to the Swinside Inn of all places. At this point it kind of occurred to me that if at 4:30 pm on a horrible October evening you want to be heading for the Swinside Inn, the best thing is not perhaps to be heading up Catbells. So, without trying to be patronising, I merely informed them that they were in fact heading up Catbells and it was still some way to the top and some way further down the other side and then along about half a mile of road to the inn. They were grateful of the knowledge as they did not realise they were climbing Catbells. Their hopeless map contained about four place names on it and one of them was Catbells. It had no contours on it and nothing really to distinguish Catbells, as a high place, from the Swinside Inn, as a valley place. I couldn't really blame this couple. It was in part the map's fault for being worse than useless, but such poor awareness of location and tools of navigation is one of the reasons people get lost on the fells.

Now when this couple simply carried on going up Catbells, I considered that my role in life was not necessarily to save such people from a good soaking, if they chose to ignore my advice. I began to continue down the hill, but after a hundred yards or so the thought of this couple began to niggle and irk me. People have been known to call out the Mountain Rescue from humble Latrigg, so there was no reason why these two might not get horribly lost on Catbells. Although I cruelly considered they might well benefit from such an experience and in doing so end up purchasing some proper maps, I did not want the resources of the Mountain Rescue to be wasted on this couple if I could help it. I also remembered the feeble map I had myself used on my first trip to Lakeland. So I yelled after them something to the effect that I really did not think it was such a good idea heading up a fell they knew nothing about, on a darkening October evening. They stopped and waved to me a gesture of thanks. It then appeared that they were debating with each other what to do and so after a couple of minutes of staring after them I considered that short of trying to physically lift them off the hill, my duty to them was done. After that I headed on, more concerned with my own selfish desires to get back to where Stan was meeting me with the car, than with the couple. I hope they did turn back and follow my route down to the road but I can't be sure.

I don't really like giving advice about what to do and what not to do on the hills. I've been very green and naive at times and even now I'm not immune to the occasional bout of stupidity on the hills. But after my first Cumbria Way holiday, where a guide book to the long distance walk and a small scale tourist map barely sufficed, I realised that proper maps were needed. The Ordnance Survey maps are not only an essential piece of navigational kit on the hills, but they are also a thing of beauty. I have often found myself picking a map from my collection on a dark winter evening in Kent and plotting and planning my future in the hills. If us Wainwright baggers have one thing in common as a breed it is perhaps a respect, possibly bordering on obsessive affection or love for these maps and all they bring to our lives. Train spotters may gain some comfort from this statement!

Stan and I have recently purchased a hand-held GPS unit. It's a sort of Sat Nav for walkers, although it won't tell you to turn right at the next junction or hopefully lead you into a cul de sac when you wanted to be on the M6. Now having used this navigational tool for a couple of years, I have mixed feelings about it. On the one hand when I was on Rest Dodd in thick mist it was able to guide me unerringly in the direction of The Nab. On the other hand it can sometimes be quite inaccurate with heights and I have even known the electronic compass to show south as north. The batteries also tend to get eaten up quickly so it is best to carry spare. The thing seems to be waterproof but there are no absolute guarantees. In conclusion, they are useful and they are fun to have, but I would still always have the map and compass with me. In bad weather they can complement map and compass skills, but I don't think they can at the moment be a complete substitute for these skills.

In the same north western group of fells as Catbells is another personal favourite lower fell. This is Barrow. Barrow is the kind of hill that simply asks you to come and climb it. Everything about Barrow seems pleasurable and accommodating. The path up is clear and at times luxuriantly grassy and makes a beeline for the summit. Yet despite the easy climb, Barrow still manages to have a stature and grace when viewed from the A66 near Braithwaite. The first time I climbed Barrow was on a day when I have to confess I had spent most of the time watching Test Match Cricket. Even though I love cricket, I don't love it as much as hill walking, but this was at the end of a long and hard walking holiday and it was rather a dull monotone day, so the cricket and a general sense of laziness beckoned.

However, at around four o'clock in the afternoon, I suddenly found my hills appetite and energy renewed and the buzz of wanting to do a new hill began to be infinitely more exciting than watching England bowl. By the time I reached Braithwaite, having walked by minor roads and paths from Keswick, I was buzzing with hills fever. Like a drug it took me up Barrow's easy ascent in just thirteen minutes. Now even though I was younger and fitter than I would probably like to admit I am now, this is nothing to boast about. I simply mention it as a reflection of the ease of Barrow. There are more than enough hard and tough hills and so it is only right that some hills should be easy. Barrow fits the bill. Lots of views are hard won, but with Barrow you can have a great view with minimal effort. Not only is it a great place to appreciate the Vale of Keswick, but it is also a great belvedere for appreciating the beauty and drama of the Coledale Round.

On one occasion I was on Barrow's summit at five o'clock on a November evening and, having watched the sunset and lingered for some time, I headed down Barrow's easy path to Braithwaite. The path was lit by nothing more than the full moon light and a route that is normally popular became a place that I had to myself. The lights of Braithwaite twinkled invitingly in the distance, but despite their call I did not rush this palely lit experience. I know Barrow like every other fell has had its times of hellish weather, but for me it has always been the most welcoming of places.

Ard Crags is sufficiently removed from the usual Coledale Round to benefit from a relative lack of popularity. However, although it does not attract the masses, this is not due to any lack of merit in the fell itself. It is a beautiful little fell, with steep flanks leading down to the narrow road heading for Newlands Hause on one side, and steep flanks heading down to the secluded Rigg Beck on the other. In itself Ard Crags is a small climb, a fell that can be bagged in a couple of hours from the road by Rigg Beck. But the first time I climbed Ard Crags I had a much longer day in the fells planned. It was a glorious September day and for the first time in my walking career I had planned to finish a walk on my own and in darkness.

Once the minor road is left behind, Ard Crags looms ahead impressively, with that same upturned hull of a boat appearance that distinguishes other fells such as Yewbarrow and Great Borne. The walk in, beside the stream of Rigg Beck, is enclosed by steep flanks on all sides and one soon feels that civilisation has been left behind. At length the beck is crossed and a grassy path leads up to the ridge of Ard Crags. From here it is only a short pull onto the neat little top of Ard Crags.

Ard Crags small heathery summit is a delightful place to relax. Although steep drops lead off both sides of the summit there is never any feeling of danger sitting on Ard Crags, just a feeling of exhilaration. Some summits were not designed for crowds of walkers and Ard Crags is one such place. Its relaxing charms are best appreciated alone. I recall spending at least an hour on the summit, on a day of warm balmy weather, but just enough of a breeze to keep it from being too warm. The view from Ard Crags is too restricted by the massive bulk of Eel Crag for it to be outstanding, although this bulk is an impressive thing in itself. But what the view from Ard Crags lacks in distant panoramas it makes up for in intimate beauty. The pastoral valley of Newlands is nowhere better seen and the sense of height and drop above this most sylvan of valleys is impressive.

The ridge between Ard Crags and its neighbouring Wainwright of Knott Rigg defines the joys of high level ridge walking, with a mere 200 feet of ascent over the course of the mile between the two summits. This is one of those places where you can, for a few moments, stop looking down at your boots as you walk and look at the scenery around you. Although Knott Rigg is not as worthy a summit as Ard Crags, it is perhaps the more popular of the two and the reason for this is the proximity of the Newlands Hause road and car park. At over 1000 feet this car park provides an easy springboard to Knott Rigg's summit, the kind of pleasant stroll to a summit and back that could easily be done in under an hour. For a few minutes on Knott Rigg I had the summit to myself and admired the prospect of Newlands backed by the Eastern Fells. Then a steady trickle of people began to emerge onto the summit. I find that on days where I climb a popular fell, such as Great Gable or Skiddaw, I acclimatise and expect people and as a result do not hanker after solitude. However in reverse, on days such as the day I first climbed Ard Crags, where the order of the day was solitude, I find myself doing everything I can to maintain that solitude.

As I descended from Knott Rigg the crowds increased and the car park at Newlands Hause was crammed to the brim with cars, an ice cream van and people enjoying a picnic in the warm sunshine. But whereas for these people Newlands Hause was a place to stop for maybe an hour or two, for me, desirous of solitude, there was no thought of stopping for a moment. Crowds are a fact in the Lake District and I accept that and at times am happy to go with it. However I wanted to get back to peace and silence and so I made a beeline beside Moss Beck, heading for Buttermere Moss. It is strange how sometimes a place thronged with crowds can sit less than a few hundred yards from a place of wildness and solitude. That short and steep haul beside Moss Beck separated the popularity of Newlands Hause from the seclusion of Buttermere Moss. Not that Buttermere Moss is anything in particular to write home about. Seclusion and peace are about all that it has going for it, for it is one of those places that even on a dry day holds water. I also found out that day that Buttermere Moss is a heat trap and before long I found myself rather envious of the crowds at Newlands Hause and would have probably swapped solitude for an ice cream.

The haul from the watery plateau of Buttermere Moss to the rocky summit of Robinson is rather dreary but the rewards make it worthwhile. Up till this point I had not been lucky on the Newlands fells, but Robinson, which sits apart from the main Newlands circuit, was an exception.

Robinson's view is not a great view of valleys, the summit is too flat for that, but it is a fine view of mountains.

I left the summit of Robinson at about five in the afternoon and by the time I arrived at Hindscarth all the walkers were making their way off the mountains. On Scope End, which is not a Wainwright, but is still a worthy little top, I watched the sunset over the Coledale Round. I was by now utterly alone and experienced that kind of profound peace that exists in the dawn and the dusk. By the time I reached the old mine road I had nothing but the light of the moon to guide me. That day some of the fells of the Newlands Round finally yielded their delights to me.

Sometimes the same small bit of fell side can provide very differing experiences. High Rigg in the Central Fells, when climbed from the Church of St John's in the Vale, is one of the shortest and easiest climbs to a Wainwright fell. A fit person will do this climb in 15 minutes. My own pace tends to average more like the 35 minutes that Wainwright self-effacingly admits it took him. The first time I took this easy route of ascent was on a winter's day of glowering clouds and imminent snow showers. High Rigg recommended itself to Stan and I that day because it was a new Wainwright that could be quickly done in almost any weather, before retreating to the warmth of a pub with an open fire. That day the summit, although only 1163 feet, was a wild, cold and windswept place. A covering of snow lay on the Helvellyn ridge and Wanthwaite Crags on Clough Head stood out bold and imposing on the white background. However it was too bitterly cold to stop for long on the summit and so we descended back down the path and found a sheltered spot. From here we watched the approaching winter storm as the fells of the Coledale round became immersed in the weather. First Eel Crag became shrouded and disappeared in a fierce snow shower, followed by the rest of the high Coledale fells, until only Barrow stood out, deep black against the raging snow storm. Then even that humble fell vanished and a minute or so later the first flakes of snow began to fall on us. At such times lower fells are a blessing and we managed to get back to the car in less than ten minutes. By the time the wind driven snow came to the little church, we were nestled in the car with the heating turned to maximum.

This same short 450 feet ascent could not have been more different when I climbed it on a warm August day. This time there were dozens of men, women, dogs and children heading up the fell, but for once I was not agitated by their company. For that day I was one of them, as I ascended High Rigg in the company of my wife Jenny, our seven year old

Looking to Helvellyn from High Rigg

son Timothy (six Wainwrights to his name), our three year old daughter
Hannah (High Rigg was to be her first Wainwright), and our month old
baby daughter Gemma in a sling on my front (I'm not sure being carried
up High Rigg counts as her first Wainwright). That day was about the
shared joys of taking my young family up a fell. It was about the joy of
taking the picture of Tim and Hannah posing on the rocks on the summit
and about the delight experienced by my son as he added another fell to
his list and then proclaimed it as 'easy'. It won't be long before he puts
his old man to shame!

Up till then High Rigg had been a fell that symbolised a short climb,
but I thought that the fell deserved better than that and so I decided to
devise my own 'grand tour' of High Rigg, this time alone. Beginning in
Keswick I took the Railway Path that heads inconspicuously out of the
town and then makes its level beeline deep in the gorge containing the
River Greta. It is a fine but popular walk and a delightfully easy way to
start a long day in the fells. Be mindful of bikes though as this is also a
long distance cycling track. The track crosses the river by several sturdy

bridges, each one a delightful spot to tarry. Eventually my self-devised route headed under the A66 and after a little road walking and a short pull on a path over a field, I arrived at the sanctuary of Tewit Tarn. I had so often seen Tewit Tarn sparkling below on my excursions onto Lonscale Fell and Blencathra, but this was my first visit to the tarn. It is a delightful place, replete with a gnarled tree to sit beneath. Here the blue water, with the majestic backdrop of Blencathra's steep face, makes for a perfect photo opportunity.

Low Rigg is not a Wainwright but it is another of those non-classified summits that have merit. If you are coming this way it is worth the effort to attain its quiet top. A short and slightly boggy stroll further and I found myself again at the little church beneath High Rigg. This time I felt that I had done the fell justice and there was a certain sense of satisfaction and reward through effort as I sat by the summit cairn and soaked in the views towards Thirlmere and Raven Crag. On my several previous climbs of High Rigg I had noticed the undulations heading south from the summit of High Rigg. Today on my personal 'grand tour' of High Rigg I wanted to make an acquaintance with this mini-wilderness. For every hundred people that visit High Rigg's summit, perhaps only a dozen or so do the traverse of the ridge. They miss out on much that High Rigg has to offer, as the ridge is a delight with its twists and turns and quiet little tarns in secretive hollows. At the end of the ridge, at over a thousand feet, is a delightful cluster of trees. The path winds between these trees in a heavenly scene, before dropping down to valley level. The path back to St John's church, along the base of High Rigg, continues the joy of this walk as it undulates by a sturdy wall and every corner rounded presents a new and delightful pastoral scene. By the time I had made my way back along the base of High Rigg to the church and retraced my steps back along the Railway Path to Keswick, I knew I had at last done justice to High Rigg and given the fell due respect for the previous times when I had quickly dashed to its summit.

One of the many delights of the walk around Derwent Water is that this pleasant stroll by the lake can be combined with more vigorous excursions into a number of fells. Catbells and Maiden Moor can be conveniently climbed from the west bank of the lake, while the fells of the central spine of Lakeland are at your mercy from the east bank of the lake. Walla Crag is not quite big enough to occupy anything more than a half day, but when combined with a walk around the lake, a full and varied day can be had, with the added merit of a different route of ascent and descent on Walla Crag.

Personally I have always preferred to do the lake first and Walla Crag later in the day. For me the path down the western shore of the lake is more attractive and varied, in its combination of woodland, meadow and open vistas, than the path down the eastern shore. The western side is also more removed from traffic, whereas the path down the east side runs close and at times even right beside the busy Borrowdale road. When the car park at Great Wood is reached a path slants across the wood before heading steeply up Walla Crag. This is yet another of those steep wooded paths that so characterise the lower fells. Here the path runs by Cat Gill and there are couple of mini waterfalls to be seen. The tree covering is dense but occasional glimpses of Derwent Water below raise the anticipation of what lies ahead. Eventually the trees end and there is a short section of steep hauling up rocky steps by a wall. The wall is then followed to the summit of Walla Crag.

Walla Crag is really little more than the craggy terminus of Bleaberry Fell and yet this must rank as one of the finest low summits in Lakeland. The bare summit, which is rocky in some parts and heathery in others, has perhaps the finest and most intimate view of Derwent Water from any fell. From the summit thickly wooded slopes plunge down to the lake in an abrupt downfall. The view of the Coledale round across the lake is majestic, with Ard Crags sharply defined. To the south the valley of Borrowdale is clearly visible and also, to the north, Skiddaw and Blencathra, with Keswick nestling beneath and a full prospect of Bassenthwaite. Even the bleak moorland rising to Bleaberry Fell has a certain haunting beauty about it. Walla Crag is justifiably popular, but one advantage of walking round the lake first is that if you arrive at the summit after four in the afternoon, you might just have it to yourself.

But the joys of Walla Crag do not end at the summit. This is a fell of surprises, nooks and crannies and just as the ascent is wonderful and varied, so is the descent down to Rakefoot. If you have a decent head for heights I would recommend keeping to the Derwent Water side of the wall that runs across the summit, for here the path twists and turns delightfully above steep wooded slopes. In one particular place a steep ravine almost cuts the path in two and a look down this crack in the fellside informs you that this is a place where care is needed. This exciting detour eventually re-crosses the wall and merges back with the main path, from where it is just a short stroll back to Rakefoot. If time allows, scorn the road back to Keswick and instead take the path alongside Brockle Beck which eventually arrives at a farm which sells ice creams! And if you still have energy left at this point it is worth making the five minute detour to the little rocky top of Castlehead, which although not a Wainwright is almost as fine a place for viewing Derwent Water as Walla Crag itself.

In describing walks up Ard Crags, High Rigg and Walla Crag I have consciously attempted to try and illustrate how these 214 Wainwright fells are about so much more than just the summit. Yes summits are often, although not always, the highlights of a day's walking, but sometimes as great a joy can be had in how you actually get to the summit and the shortest route, while getting the tick, often does not do the fell justice.

If ever a fell could leap to my defence, on the occasions I have been dubbed a tick bagger, it is Latrigg. Other than Skiddaw, which I have summited over a dozen times, Latrigg is my most often climbed fell. It is yet another example of a fell which on the face of it can appear bland to climb and over popular to be on and yet which, with a little bit of lateral thought, can provide intimacies and solitudes to rank with the best of them.

The first time I climbed Latrigg was by the short fifteen minute pull from the Gale Road car park. This route will sometimes see hundreds of walkers in a day and other than the advantage of getting to the summit and its views as quickly as possible, this route has little merit to it. Latrigg has far more to offer than its wonderful views of Derwent Water and the Vale of Keswick. In the years since I first climbed Latrigg I have taken on a kind of mini-project, a sub plot to the completion of the Wainwrights, which has been to hunt out every route and path on Latrigg. Yet, despite a number of expeditions, I am still coming across new routes.

There is the lovely grassy promenade to the summit along the high ridge above Brundholme Woods. With a little planning this route can be joined from the Railway Path leading out of Keswick, before a return down the Cumbria Way and back to Keswick. This route to the summit is still quite popular, but less so than the short Gale Road car park route. One November day I climbed Latrigg late in the evening via this route and then took a direct route off Latrigg which plunges down through dense pine forest. Deep in the dark tunnel of these pines the headtorch came on, revealing an eerie evening mist. Here can be found some of Latrigg's quietest and most atmospheric corners. Eventually the path emerges from the pine forest to a wide terrace path, which is a joy to tread with its occasional vistas through the woods and towards Keswick and Derwent Water.

Perhaps the loneliest route up Latrigg is what I might call 'Latrigg direct'. This is a connoisseur's route up the fell which starts normally enough in Spooney Green Lane, but just after the house at Thorny Plats, diverts away steeply from the popular Cumbria Way path up an almost hidden little track. This track winds up through an area of sparse pines, a place in the very heart of Latrigg and a place of solitude. Higher up, the path crosses the wide terrace path described earlier and makes a steep and grassy beeline for the bench on Latrigg's summit ridge. If you want solitude on Latrigg take the direct route on a winter's afternoon. It will seem a million miles removed from the normal impressions of Latrigg.

Latrigg is among my favourite of all the fells and such favourites become places that we want to guard against change and progress. So it was with a rather guilt ridden angst, that I learnt of plans to bulldoze a wheelchair access path to the summit ridge of Latrigg. As I saw pictures on the internet of the newly made gravel path with a bulldozer standing beside it, I felt an odd sense of personal loss and anger. I also read articles on the internet with well known walkers decrying the path as an ugly scar and out of character with the landscape. I even read comments from disabled people saying that they accept that there are certain places they cannot go to and would rather these places remained unspoilt. So I found myself firmly in the sizeable camp that was opposed to this scar on a beloved fell.

However having since actually visited the wheelchair access path and walked along it, I must confess that I have changed my somewhat entrenched position. Yes, the path does not add anything to Latrigg, but in truth it does not detract from Latrigg as much as might be supposed. Throughout the course of this book I have described many places in the Lake District where solitude can be found for the able bodied and where the landscape is pristine. So while us walkers should rightly try and oppose developments on the fells, is it too much of a concession for just a small part of one of these 214 fells to be opened up to those who would otherwise be unable to reach such a place. Latrigg is already a popular fell and for those who want it to be something different there are the lonely routes I have described. Perhaps as walkers and conservers of the landscape we can sometimes become too closed and entrenched in our views. We go to the hills to connect and explore our humanity, but what use is it searching for and finding your humanity in the hills, if you never display it to others. I consider that there is room for a fell where everyone can enjoy a high view; a place that can bring such joys to those who thought they were out of reach. Perhaps Latrigg can accommodate us all.

A Bagging Milestone

Although there are no rules to the pastime of Wainwright bagging, having now completed the 214 Wainwright fells, I would give a sound recommendation to make sure that you try to leave a variety of fells among your last twenty or so. The joy of those last few would be diminished if you ended up with twenty Ling Fells, or twenty Little Mell Fells at the end. Part by accident and part by design I was lucky that my last twenty or so included a mix of high and low fells, as well as remote and celebrated ones. In this chapter I shall describe some fantastic experiences that I had as my Wainwright round drew to a close. In doing so perhaps it will add fuel to my argument for leaving some of the best fells till near the end.

On a sunny crisp February day in 2006, I found myself heading up Red Screes for the first time. Red Screes can be climbed via a rough and steep scramble from the Kirkstone Pass, a short haul of under a thousand feet. But this day we had an altogether grander expedition in mind. Amongst the twenty or so Wainwrights that I had left to complete, were a little cluster comprising High Hartsop Dodd, Little Hart Crag, Middle Dodd and, of course, Red Screes itself. Although not a round that was celebrated or that I had even read described before, I noted that these four new summits could be linked together in a circuit starting at Brothers Water. At this late stage, in my journey through Wainwright's fells, the luxury of four new summits in one day was a singular thing and this was the last time in my round that I would bag more than two in one day!

For this walk I had the 'new boy' Kevin with me, as well as my long standing hills companion Stan. As we parked up at Brothers Water, on a perfect winter day, we were simply itching to start the walk. The approach to this group alongside Brothers Water is as charming as any low level walk in the district, with banks of natural twisty trees rising steeply to one side and the beauty of the lake, backed by the huge shapely wedge of Hartsop Dodd, to the other. There was a skin of ice covering the surface of Brothers Water and we gained some childish delight in skimming stones over the ice and listening to the wonderful chiming sound they made.

After a short distance we came out of the wood and our first objective, the graceful cone of High Hartsop Dodd, soared ahead of us. It is in such places that the *Wainwright Guides* add to the enjoyment of the experience by pointing out the little things that would otherwise go unnoticed.

Wainwright mentions the symmetry between the roof of a barn at the foot of High Hartsop Dodd and the shape of the fell itself and it was fun to stand, as he must have, and observe this harmony of the man made and the natural. The climb of the fell itself is short and uneventful and the summit has little to recommend itself, but does have wonderful close up views of Dovedale and the cliffs of Dove Crag, as well as a nicely framed view of Brothers Water. The ridge between High Hartsop Dodd and Little Hart Crag is straightforward, although oddly omitted as a ridge route in the Wainwright guide (although referred to as such elsewhere within the text). There are a few little tarns between the twin tops of Little Hart Crag and it was interesting to note that whereas at valley floor we had been able to easily break the skin of ice on Brothers Water, up at 1900 feet the ice was unbreakable and thick enough to walk upon.

The summit of Little Hart Crag has sufficient distinction to provide something of the feel of a mountain summit, and although the views are not the finest to be had, there is still a fine prospect south down the wild valley of Scandale, whose beck ran a sunlit silver course towards

Stan relaxing beneath Little Hart Crag

Windermere that day. On the ridge route between Little Hart Crag and Red Screes there is a fine prospect of Little Hart Crag's twin summits from below, but there is little else to be recommended about this ridge route, which is longer than it looks on the map. However it is worth the effort, for the summit of Red Screes must be one of the finest and most interesting in the Lake District. The intermediate and distant views are enormous, with the thimble of Great Gable and the wedge of Pillar's summit towering over the folds of mountains in between and Bowfell and the Scafells in fine profile. The distant views south and south east are simply overwhelming, with a vast panorama of the lower bumps of South Lakeland, the Howgills and Shap Fells and the distant sea. But it is perhaps the intimate close views that most draw the eye. Only when the utmost inches of the summit are reached is the plunge down to the Kirkstone Pass road revealed, with the cars toiling over the pass, seeming small and insignificant below. And for a scene that could encapsulate sheer Lakeland beauty is there anything finer than the view over Middle Dodd and into Patterdale, a scene that truly conveys the height of the fell.

Red Screes is more than just a wonderful viewpoint though. Its summit area is one of the most interesting in the district, with a huge mound of stones, like some ancient burial formation, situated right on the edge of the plunge down to Kirkstone Pass, as well as a trig point and wind shelter. But perhaps the finest and most unique feature of the summit is the tarn that sits in a little hollow, just a few yards from the highest point. Red Screes tarn is one of the highest tarns in the district and the only one I can think of that is such a feature of a high Lakeland summit. On this February day we gained great delight in skimming stones on its thick coat of ice up at 2500 feet. We lingered here as long as the February daylight would allow, revelling in our simple childish play with the ice. Eventually we headed on over Middle Dodd and steeply down the nose of this fell (the Dodds around Hartsop all look steep and are steep). By the time we reached the woods by Brothers Water, the path was lit only by the light of a full moon, and the nocturnal hooting of an owl, in those beautiful woods, drew a close to a wonderful day on the fells.

Ennerdale Water had not been a popular starting point in my round of the Wainwrights. However towards the end of my round, I had the perfect opportunity to rectify this and to appreciate the quiet charms of this corner of Lakeland. Great Borne is rather out on a limb from the popular round of the High Stile range and an approach from Buttermere via the boggy wastelands of Floutern Pass does not have much to recommend it. So instead Stan and I planned a more attractive walk from the Bowness

Knott car park by Ennerdale Water. The great grey flanks of Great Borne, also know as Herdus, are a distinctive feature of the Ennerdale skyline, and Great Borne shares with Yewbarrow the characteristics of an upturned boat.

Resting at the foot of Great Borne and almost entirely covered in coniferous plantation is the craggy summit of Bowness Knott. It is a summit far more often admired from a distance than actually climbed. Although Wainwright's guide to the Western Fells suggests that Bowness Knott will soon be out of bounds to the walker because of the encroaching trees, this has thankfully not proved to be the case and it is worth the short detour, from the Rake Beck approach to Great Borne, to climb Bowness Knott. This is unless, of course, you are the type of militant bagger for whom a non-Wainwright fell is not considered worth climbing. Keep an eye out for a small stile in the fence to your right and then a minor path than heads up through the pine forest, before emerging into the open, a few hundred yards away from the summit of Bowness Knott. If the weather is clear you will be glad that you made the little detour, for the summit of Bowness Knott is one of those places, like Raven Crag, that drops away in crags to a lake beneath. In this case the end of Ennerdale Water is spread out below you and its waters were a wonderful turquoise blue the day we climbed Bowness Knott. Across the lake Anglers Crag mirrors the rockiness of Bowness Knott. Like Fisher's Crag above Thirlmere, Bowness Knott escapes classification as a Wainwright fell, but perfectly proves the point that those who stick only to lists can miss some delightful places. And because it is not a Wainwright and lies off the beaten track, there is the added bonus (no pun intended) of a high chance of solitude.

There were at least half a dozen people ahead of us heading up Great Borne beside Rake Beck. In fact this steep route seems to have become a reasonably popular way to the summit of Great Borne. Yet, if you look in the Great Borne chapter of the *Western Fells Guide*, there is no mention of an ascent via Rake Beck, and instead Wainwright suggests a less direct approach via Gill Beck. It therefore appears that the Rake Beck approach and path has formed since the *Western Fells Guide* was written. In fact the Rake Beck path, which is steep and hugs to the side of the beck in some exposed situations, has the feel of a newly trodden way about it. Altogether it makes for a grand and sporting little ascent on to Great Borne.

Great Borne's summit and view exceeded my expectations. The summit is rock strewn and has a mountain feel, out of character with its mere 2000 or so feet of elevation. In the midst of these rocks is a triangulation column marking the highest point. But it is the view that perhaps most surpassed my expectations, for this is a fine place to appreciate the huge build up of Grasmoor and the other satellites of the Coledale Round. The Ard Crags to Knott Rigg ridge can be clearly seen and there is a grand backdrop of the Helvellyn Ridge.

The great global warming debate continues with arguments for and against the theory that man's pollution is warming the climate and even those who say that man's influence has not had any effect on the climate. I am no scientist or expert but on 29 October 2006, the day we climbed Great Borne, the Lake District saw temperatures of 17 degrees centigrade, while Southern England basked in 19 degrees. I do not expect to be in a T-shirt on the fells at the back end of October, but it seemed entirely appropriate on Great Borne that day. I have noticed that over the course of the eighteen odd years I have been walking in the Lake District, the periods of warm weather have seemed to extend further into the traditional realm of autumn.

On the ridge between Great Borne and Starling Dodd it was interesting to find the spring that Wainwright mentions, a little bubbling of water coming out of the ground on the short pull up to Starling Dodd. If Great Borne exceeded my expectations then the other new Wainwright on our walk, Starling Dodd, rather disappointed. I had always thought of Starling Dodd as being a wild place out on a limb and with quite a shapely cone like appearance. Regrettably Starling Dodd is much better to look at and dream about than to actually be on. I agree with Wainwright that it makes 'little impact on mind or memory'. Its views are similar to Great Borne's but for some reason nowhere near as well presented. Perhaps the most striking thing about Starling Dodd is the array of ironmongery on its summit cairn, bits of which rather resemble a devil's pitchfork, in keeping perhaps with the rather unwelcoming nature of Starling Dodd.

Thankfully we had greater heights on our mind in the form of Red Pike. Red Pike had denied me its views on my previous visit and so it was wonderful to revisit Red Pike and capture those views. This time, pockets of mist swirled around the summit, but this was not an all enveloping mist. This was the type of mist that adds to the summit appreciation, rather than detracts from it. At last I could appreciate the views of five different lakes that can be seen from Red Pike's summit. Crummock Water is the most dramatic of the five, but perhaps most curious is the glimpse of Derwent Water viewed down the Newlands valley. Red Pike was popular that day and, if I am honest, there were a few too many people for my liking on the summit. This included one man who seemed to delight in stripping off his shirt and revealing his bare chest to the assembled summit crowd. However, most of the crowds thronged on the High Stile Range will be headed for Buttermere and that is why the Ennerdale route up or down Red Pike is recommended to the lover of solitude. From the moment we left Red Pike and made a beeline descent down to the Ennerdale Forest road, to the moment we arrived back at the Bowness Knott car park in near darkness, we met no-one. The Ennerdale flank of Red Pike may not be as interesting or craggy as the celebrated Buttermere flank, but there is something grand and sweeping about a descent this way into Ennerdale Forest, with the great bulk of Pillar and Steeple encroaching and the shadows lengthening.

A few days later we were again in the Western Fells for some more off the beaten track new Wainwrights. This time however the approach was from Wasdale and even though this walk was only a few miles from the Great Borne walk it was entirely different in character. One the greatest attributes of Lakeland walking is that within small areas and distances there is so much variety of terrain and scenery. This was also a special day because it was to be the day that Stan and I reached our 200th Wainwright fell together. Unlike our final Wainwright there had been no plan laid as to which would be the 200th summit. The rather dull Sour Howes nearly made it, but in the end the honour of number 200 fell justifiably to Caw Fell, with Haycock forever number 199 on the list.

These two high fells are wild, tucked away from popular routes and deserving of respect. An approach from Wasdale via Nether Beck is a long and fantastic day's outing, with Caw Fell lying out on a limb at the furthest point of the walk. Good weather makes for good feelings and as we walked past the Nether Beck falls on a glorious crisp and sunny November day, my mind was as alive and joyous to every sensation as it had ever been. Having a babbling stream and some waterfalls always adds interest to the approach to a mountain, but after Great Lad Crag the beck peters out in marsh and there is then a long pull of 1000 feet or so up to the col between Haycock and Scoat Fell. At the col a wall is met and it is then only a couple of hundred feet or so of ascent to the summit of Haycock.

Haycock's summit area is one of rocky desolation, the sort of tough rocks and boulders that prevent any paths from forming. Although only a mile from Scoat Fell and the popular Mosedale round path, Haycock still manages to feel distinctly remote. It is perhaps the least visited of all the Lakeland fells above 2500 feet. Even a determined Wainwright bagger, such as myself, kept finding that Haycock, despite being a fell I really wanted to do, kept getting put off for another day. Its ascent either involves a long walk in from Wasdale, or an even longer walk in from Ennerdale Water. It does not suggest itself as part of a round and nor does it leap out in views from other fells as a dramatic shape or outline that must be climbed. It mostly appears as a rather shy dome, hiding away at the back of more popular fells.

Haycock's delights are ones of solitude in a high mountain situation. Where else in the Lake District can you sit on a summit over 2500 feet and feel so removed from society? The view is excellent, particularly towards the massive looking Scafells and towards the west Cumbria coast, which is extensively revealed from this most westerly fell of over 2500 feet. That day however one element within the view did mar it. I noticed what appeared to be a new batch of wind turbines out towards the western coast.

Now in these days of climate change and global warming, there is a danger that anyone being seen to speak against renewable sources of energy will be shouted down in a chorus of boos. So let me be the first to say that I am all for renewable energy and sensible alternatives to the pollution we have been chucking into the atmosphere. But let me also voice an opinion that there is little point in preserving our environment from climate change, if in doing so we end up damaging the pristine nature of places like the Lake District. I have nothing against wind turbines as such, but I feel that there is a constant need to evaluate the benefit of these giant and unsightly beasts, against the spoiling of the unique landscape of not just the Lake District, but the British Isles as a whole. It is also as well to remember that a lot of the drive for new 'farms' of wind turbines and other projects such as hydro-electric schemes is driven as much by political needs and monetary needs, as it is by the needs of the planet. It is no coincidence these eco friendly projects get a large government subsidy for the company that builds them. And yet often these turbines only generate enough power for a few hundred or a few thousand households, a pinprick in terms of the energy usage of a country with a 60 million population. So it could be argued that these turbines merely pay financially and politically driven lip service to the battle against mass pollution. And ultimately all the wind turbines you could ever wish to despoil the Lake District with, would count for little if we cannot get the likes of China and India to reduce their ever growing emissions.

There was recently a wind turbine proposal for the M6 corridor at Whinash that would have seen a farm of 27 four hundred feet high wind turbines dominating the horizon around Shap and Tebay. Yes on the one hand it would have created enough energy for over 100,000 households, but on the other hand the landscape of the area and the views from the wonderful Far Eastern fells would have been considerably compromised by these monstrosities. Is it worth destroying pristine environments for the sake of creating energy for what may sound like a large number of people but is in fact less than half a percent of the population of one small country? What would Alfred Wainwright have thought! Thankfully at Whinash logic has prevailed and the proposal did not get approval. Various celebrities, who I have the utmost admiration for, threatened to chain themselves to the turbines and in the end it was deemed that the detrimental effect on the landscape outweighed the benefits. But for every proposal that gets denied another one gets through, or another new proposal springs up. There is, as I write, a proposal to erect some giant wind turbines at Berrier Hill, which lies just a mile or so outside the National Park boundary, making it more likely to gain approval. If this proposal goes ahead, and it is being bitterly opposed, it will be an eyesore in the iconic view from nearby Blencathra. Does the generating of renewable energy for a few people justify the defiling of part of the essence of a fell like Blencathra?

There are now wind farms that can be seen to the south of the National Park, out towards the west coast and around the Solway coast. I have a recurring nightmare of one day going to the Lake District and finding the entire National Park boundary perfectly delineated by a ring of wind turbines. It is but a nightmare for now, but it does seem that outside the little yellow line that marks the National Park boundary on the maps, anything goes in terms of such proposals.

We should not seek to save one thing by destroying another. Humanity should learn to stop thinking in purely human centred terms. We are intelligent creatures and there must be a way to preserve the planet without eroding the very essence of places like the Lake District. Otherwise, if we save ourselves but destroy our precious wild places, what have we really achieved?

Walking from the already remote Haycock towards Caw Fell is a Lakeland experience like few others. Caw Fell is one of those fells that just sprawls, squat and neglected. It occupies a vast area and in Lakeland terms it is a high fell, but it is hard to ever see it becoming a popular haunt for walkers. There is just too much effort required to reach it.

By the time we reached Caw Fell the sun was already dipping towards the horizon and the car, in Wasdale, seemed a very, very long way away. There are few places in the Lake District that can match Caw Fell for a feeling of uncompromising remoteness. Stan and I would not have chosen Caw Fell for our 200th Wainwright because of its grand summit or dramatic approach, for it has neither. However, for a solitary place to celebrate the milestone and for a cracking view, it will always live in the memory. While the view of the mountains of Lakeland is not great, that was not what so captivated us about the view from Caw Fell. It was the view seawards that compelled. A great arc of the sea sparkled, with the Isle of Man sitting seemingly suspended on top of it. The views coastwards were also incredibly distant. We made out the Solway coast of Scotland and the coast of Ireland. And then something almost mythical was sighted on the horizon. I had seen many clear Lakeland views in my time, but I had very rarely managed to make out the mountains of Snowdonia. Yet a check on the GPS unit confirmed that here they were, some 90 miles away, and seen from a hill as apparently humble as Caw Fell. What a 200th Wainwright present!

It was a long walk back to Wasdale from Caw Fell's summit. We contoured pathless around Haycock and had fantastic views down Blengdale, one of Lakeland's wildest, almost forgotten valleys. Wainwright recommends using the Ladcrag Beck route in ascent, rather than in descent. We should have heeded his words for the Ladcrag Beck route is pathless and quite boggy, not the sort of thing one wants at the end of a long mountain day. Eventually however the nicer terrain of the Nether Beck path was reached and we were treated to pink wispy sunset clouds and a crescent moon rising behind the Scafells, for the last few miles of what had been a grand wild outing in Lakeland.

The central spine of Lakeland begins in the south with the celebrated Langdale Pikes and reaches its northern terminus at the equally popular Walla Crag. However in between these two extremities lies a vast upland plateau, which although it contains a lot of bog, also contains some special summits. Towards the end of our Wainwright round, Stan and I found ourselves needing to mop up two off the beaten track Wainwrights, in the form of Thunacar Knott and Tarn Crag (Easdale). A quick study of the map revealed that these two Wainwrights could be combined in a round starting from Grasmere, with time to throw in a couple of old favourites, Sergeant Man and High Raise.

This walk, which ascends into a wild moorland plateau, begins in contrast with the sylvan and much trodden path to Easdale Tarn via Sour Milk Gill. On a glorious frosty February morning the well made path eased us into the landscape. It is not hard to see why Sour Milk Gill was so called and the path passes close by the falls, with a little branch path providing even closer access. A short distance further Easdale Tarn is reached, one of Lakeland's finest tarns and a popular spot. There was a decent covering of ice on the tarn that day. Many eyes have stared at the tarn and its dramatic backdrop of crags and mountain. Many cameras have taken pictures of this scene. Yet surprisingly few people go on to climb the fell that forms the backdrop. Most head on the well made path towards the Langdales. As we sat by Easdale Tarn and soaked in the atmosphere, an enormous party of teenage school children arrived, making just about as much noise as their lungs could muster. Stan and I quickly headed off, using the faint tracks and bits of path that make their way up Tarn Crag and gradually the noise died down and the party headed on, no doubt bound for the Langdale Pikes. We were left in silence, back in the Lakeland we loved. At length we joined the east ridge of the fell, and shortly before the summit, where a little secret valley separates the true top of Tarn Crag from the summit of the cliffs, we made the detour to the cliff top for the stunning view down to Easdale Tarn. Were it not for Wainwright, such delightful spots would probably be bypassed, as the mind focused on the highest point. Here again on Tarn Crag, as is so often the case, the highest point of the fell is not necessarily the best viewpoint. For the top of the cliffs above Easdale Tarn is a wonderful secluded spot. In fairness though, the true summit of Tarn Crag is also a lovely little belvedere, which feels much more mountain like and higher than its 1800 feet suggest. In fact it must be one of Lakeland's smallest summits, with just room for one person to sit by the cairn. The views back down Easdale and towards Grasmere are the outstanding features of Tarn Crag.

The ridge walk from Tarn Crag to Sergeant Man seems a lot longer than a mile and a quarter. Some ridges are inspiring to walk along but this one is a little dispiriting. If Tarn Crag has something of the mountain form about it, then Sergeant Man is really little more than a rocky bump on the wild central plateau of Lakeland. Yet, outside of the Langdale Pikes themselves, this is probably the most popular summit in this area and as we approached it other walkers started to appear from various routes. Sergeant Man's main merits are as a viewpoint, particularly for Pavey Ark, which in certain lights takes on a dark black and forbidding hue. The view towards Pavey Ark and beyond to the Coniston Fells is one of savage mountain scenery, without a vestige of the pastoral farmlands or little dotted habitations that are so often thought of as typical Lakeland.

From Sergeant Man it was an easy mile, with little ascent, to get to the next Wainwright summit. Thunacar Knott is one of those fells that, if

Wainwright had not considered it worthy of inclusion in his guides, would be visited even more rarely than it is. It is not a fell that makes one jump out of bed in the morning to go and climb it, or a fell that is a must do on any hills agenda. In fact from other fells it is quite difficult to even pick it out. Pike o'Stickle, Pavey Ark and Harrison Stickle are instantly recognisable shapes, but Thunacar Knott is just a tiny knoll on a vast plateau. I was not expecting much from Thunacar Knott, so in fairness let me quickly say that it actually surpassed my expectations. Perhaps it was the glorious light and clarity of February that flattered the fell, but I took rather a fondness to Thunacar Knott. In its shyness there is also a certain spacious feel of wildness. It has a fine cairn and twin summits with a lovely little tarn in between, which was covered with thick ice and reflected its rocky surrounds perfectly. The flatness of the immediate surrounds does not make for a great view, although it's not bad, but the charms of Thunacar Knott are subtle ones that go beyond in your face views. For those who seek it, there is something deeply relaxing and profound about the simplicities of Thunacar Knott.

Having bagged Thunacar Knott the new Wainwrights for the day were done and it would have been easy to have just headed back to Grasmere. But there was an old favourite that I wanted to visit, something of a small detour from the route back to Grasmere, but a detour well worth making.

Of the respective highest fells in each of the seven *Pictorial Guides*, High Raise is without doubt the least celebrated. Indeed with the Langdale Pikes nearby, it is easy to forget that, in terms of height at least, High Raise is the king of the Central Fells. It is however a king that chooses to hide away behind lesser and more attractive subjects and as a result is quite rarely visited. Even peak baggers will often just add High Raise on as an afterthought to a day on the Langdale Pikes. Today however we wanted to make High Raise the ultimate objective of our walk, to revisit an old friend.

High Raise suggests little to recommend it when approached from Thunacar Knott or the Langdales, but this is more than made up for when the summit is reached. Often Wainwright provides a simple arc diagram of the fells in view from a particular summit and he might add a few lines about the best aspect of the view, but for the finest and most comprehensive views he devotes several pages to a fuller impression of the view and lets it speak for itself. The view from High Raise merits a full three pages in the *Central Fells Guide* and I personally think that it is one of the finest views in the Lake District, with the added bonus of being a relatively unpopular place. Think how towering Eagle Crag looks from the hamlet of Stonethwaite and then look down at it, seemingly insignificant 1000 feet below, from the summit of High Raise. Admire the full and welcoming profile of Skiddaw in the distance, with Keswick nestling beneath it and Bassenthwaite Lake and Solway to the left; the roughness of Rosthwaite Fell across the gulf of Langstrath; the precipitous angle of Honister Crag; the wonderful arc of celebrated high mountains from The Old Man of Coniston in the south to Grizedale Pike in the north-west. High Raise is the highest point in the Central Fells and its rock strewn summit and view are those of a commanding mountain. It is a place I hope to still be visiting long after my completion of The Wainwrights has become just a thing of distant memory.

I would like to end this chapter about the wonderful experiences I had leading up to completion, with a couple of walks from Eskdale, a delightful place that time and progress seems to have all but forgotten. Ever since we had purchased Eric Robson's *Remote Lakeland* video and seen footage of his ascent up Green Crag, this fell had become a much anticipated experience on the journey to completing the Wainwrights. When viewed from the wild high road near Devoke Water, the shaggy outlines of Green Crag and Crook Crag arrest the attention, even though the much higher Harter Fell and Scafell lurk nearby. Green Crag in many ways typifies everything that I and countless other walkers love about the Lake District. It is not just a wonderful and surprisingly remote and hard won summit, but its approach via Low Birker Tarn is as beautiful and varied as any in the district.

The beauty begins almost immediately, as a farm road leads to Doctor Bridge, a lovely arching stone bridge spanning the River Esk. Here we encountered a couple who were to be the only walkers we saw on the entire walk and even they were not bound for Green Crag. At Low Birker the farm road is left behind and a grassy path threads its way gradually up through a juniper bush plantation, an idyllic lush place in direct contrast to the later stages of this ascent. The path zig zags through the junipers and at about 800 feet reaches a stone hut without a roof. This is the ruin of an old peat hut and, indeed, the path is an old peat road. The hut was used to store the peat and a quick look around the interior reveals just how well and strongly built this peat hut was.

As you ascend beautiful views begin to open out revealing the calm pastoral beauty of quiet Eskdale, with a dramatic backdrop of some of the highest mountains in England, Scafell, Scafell Pike, Bow Fell and Crinkle Crags. On the sunny February day that we climbed Green Crag, the sea was shimmering and glistening behind the low but shaggy Muncaster Fell.

Shortly after the peat hut the scenery changes dramatically. The pastoral views are left behind as you arrive at a vast upland moorland plateau. This is a lonely corner of Lakeland that does not look that large an area on the map, but manages to have a spacious feeling of remoteness when you are there. Here you get your first views of Crook Crag and Green Crag itself, with both rising dramatically and rather imposingly ahead. The lonely Low Birker Tarn is passed. It is a stretch of water that I imagine could look very bleak on a wild wet day. However on this sunny winter day it revealed a wonderful rich blue colour that, with its wild surround, made for a perfect photo opportunity.

Although it is only two and a half miles from the start of the walk to the summit of Green Crag it seems much further. This walk has a truly wild flavour about it and although short has the feel of a more serious and remote undertaking. Yet again, on a walk in winter, Stan and I began to muse about climate change, as the moorland plateau became a heat trap. With sweat in our eyes and the sun beating down it felt more like May than February.

The view north from High Raise

Although the summit crags of Green Crag look like a serious and potentially terminal obstacle to a walker, this is one of many imposing looking summits in Lakeland where the walker can skirt round the back and breach an obvious and easy line above the crags. As the summit was reached a cold wind whipped up. It suddenly felt like winter in February again, as opposed to early summer!

Green Crag's little rocky platform of a summit has a commanding and spacious feel about it. If you wanted somewhere that epitomised getting away from it all in the Lake District, this would be high on the list. The views are not so much beautiful in a pastoral and typical Lakeland sense. It is more a wild beauty, tinged with a timeless and ever so slightly sombre quality. The wild upper Eskdale faces of the Scafells and Bowfell are wonderfully seen. The prospect westwards, towards the sea, is one of remote upland areas. These bleak hills are perhaps more reminiscent of Pennine landscapes than typical Lakeland landscapes. They are bleak not in a derogatory sense but as something rare to be savoured. These rolling miles of empty space have a wonderful meditative quality about them. The landscape of Devoke Water, Whitfell, Kinmont Buck Barrow and Black Combe is a wild tract that, with the exception of the wonderful Black Combe, I have yet to walk into. It contains no Wainwrights as such, only fells included in the *Outlying Fells Guide*. Yet here is an area that is expansive and beautiful in its wildness and now that it has called to me from Green Crag, it will not be long before I yield to the call and begin what I hope will be an intimate acquaintance of this unique and almost forgotten corner of Lakeland.

We made a short detour and a little rocky scramble to the summit of Crook Crag on the return journey. Having started the walk at one in the afternoon and savoured every glorious step, the sun was setting over Eskdale and the Scafells as we descended back to civilisation. Green Crag may only be a half days expedition, but it packs so much into that half day. It has a stature and remote feel beyond what the bare facts of a map would suggest. I consider that Green Crag ranks as one of the finest of the Wainwrights. It is perhaps the perfect fell walk, being beautiful and varied from start to finish.

Two months later I found myself back in Eskdale on another of those peerless sunny days that seemed to bless us for most of our last 20 or so Wainwrights. This time the objective was an altogether grander mountain. It was a mountain that despite being nearly the highest in England had, from a combination of initial bad judgement and later deliberate planning, been left till almost the end of my Wainwright round. Stan had climbed Scafell for the first time via Lords Rake and the West Wall Traverse, with my brother in 1993. He had since climbed it several further times from Wasdale and he will not disagree with me saying that it is one of his favourite mountains, if not his absolute favourite. Yet despite the fact that this walk would gain Stan nothing in terms of new Wainwrights, I could sense that he was almost as excited as I was in anticipation. This was I imagine partly because it brought us closer to equalisation of the same Wainwrights and therefore closer to our ultimate objective of completing together on the same summit. It was also I think partly because in climbing it from Eskdale, Stan was taking an altogether different route, so for him it was almost like climbing a new mountain. I think though that above all his excitement was because he wanted to show and share with his best friend a mountain that he knew and loved.

For years we had planned to do one of the many routes into wild Upper Eskdale that ultimately reach a high Lakeland mountain. We had had wonderful bird's eye views of Upper Eskdale when we had climbed Grey Friar and Hard Knott, views that made us itch to get into this landscape. While Lakeland contains many mini areas of wilderness, it is perhaps in Upper Eskdale that Lakeland most approaches an area of true wilderness. In many regards Upper Eskdale gives nothing away, both in rugged mountain scenery and enormity of scale, to Scotland's wild places.

As we took the hour long drive from our base in Keswick and over Wrynose and Hardknott Passes to Eskdale we were both feverish to get our boots on and get up close and personal with Upper Eskdale. From Boot it is a long six mile walk to the summit of Scafell. However it is the type of walk that is varied and constantly interesting and time never seems to drag. The Terrace Route beneath Goat Crag and Dawsonground Crag is a delight to follow. Unlike the popular Wasdale routes to Scafell this is relatively quiet. I think we met only two people until we got to the summit of Slight Side. Instead of the intrusive motorway type path that is becoming a common feature on some of the more popular fells, the path for this Eskdale approach to Scafell has an organic feel. Its ups and downs blend with the natural contours of Scafell's wild hinterland. The early stage of this walk is a delight and in dry weather there are many grassy nooks and crannies to recline amongst and absorb the peace and silence. The immediate objective of Slight Side keeps poking its head above the horizon but from the confused landscape of the Terrace Route it seems distant and hard to get to.

Eventually at Catcove Beck the scenery changes and the path crosses a vast upland plateau, with Slight Side now looming and rearing up ahead.

As the day was warm, at Catcove Beck we reintroduced ourselves to the sport of head ducking and the refreshing nature of the experience was just as we remembered. After Catcove Beck the walking is easy for a mile or so on a narrow grassy path, before a steep haul of 1000 foot on to Slight Side. This ascent is eased by the gradually increasing views back towards Harter Fell and Green Crag and into the wild, chaotic and beautiful wilderness of Upper Eskdale and the Great Moss.

Slight Side is really just a lower satellite of Scafell, but its rocky sharp little summit has all the feel of a proper mountain place about it, and the view, especially south and west, is spacious in the extreme. Slight Side's key merit as a viewpoint is for the view towards the coast and sea, which is supreme. It is also a great place to appreciate the vast hinterland of the Scafells. That day the jewels of Stony Tarn and Eel Tarn sparkled in the sunlight on the great expanse of moorland below us.

The ridge from Slight Side to Scafell is one of the most dramatic places in the Lake District, especially if a walker keeps to the eastern edge, where a fearful plunge drops away over Cam Spout Crag and down to the meandering River Esk and the wild valley floor of the Great Moss. It is a scene which in its wild spacious grandeur resembles something from the Wild West of the United States. High mountain rock scenery dominates as the unfrequented craggy backsides of Scafell Pike, Esk Pike, Bowfell and the Crinkles stretch out in awesome array. This is perhaps some of the finest and wildest mountain scenery that England has to offer. As we neared the summit of Scafell the ground became rocky and boulder strewn, but my thoughts were now dominated by the closeness of a mountain that I had waited to summit longer than any other. Fourteen years had elapsed since Stan first set foot on Scafell and now at last it was my turn. I had endured countless mickey taking exchanges from both Peter and Stan, to the general effect that my Lakeland knowledge was tainted by not having climbed Scafell. Now at last it was in reach and it felt strangely appropriate to have left this second highest mountain till near the end. As I stood just below the summit there was still one more enormous high Lakeland view that I had yet to feast my eyes upon. However as with all summits that we plan and aim to reach, one moment it is but a plan, then in a moment, the blink of an eye, the summit becomes something that is done, achieved, past. But soon the cycle of plan, execution and achievement continues with another new summit and that perhaps defines the reason why people bag hills. Wainwright said that life without ambition is just aimless wandering and while there is joy to be had from re-climbing old favourites again and again, there is perhaps

At last, the author bags Scafell

nothing to compare with the thrill of reaching a grand high mountain summit for the first time.

I fully expected a fantastic far reaching view from Scafell and I was not disappointed. Because it is the last high mountain westwards before the Cumbrian plains and coast, the view is particularly sweeping and extensive in that direction, with the Isle of Man easily picked out on a clear day. Most of Wastwater is seen, although of course not as profoundly or dramatically as from Great Gable's Westmorland Cairn. For the lovers of tarn spotting Burnmoor Tarn, normally quite a shy thing in views, is clearly seen. I was surprised to see a decent chunk of Derwent Water in the north, as well as the familiar outlines of Skiddaw and Blencathra well displayed. Nowhere is the great Mosedale flank of Pillar better seen and even though Scafell is only 200 or so feet higher than Great Gable, Gable seems unusually small and subdued from the summit of Scafell. I hardly need say that Stan and I spent a good hour or so soaking in this scene, during which time I was surprised at how few people disturbed us. When we arrived at the summit we had a good twenty minutes or so to ourselves, something I never expected on the second highest mountain in England on a warm April day. Even when people did turn up it was only in ones and twos, rather than in great parties. Yet a short distance away, and separated only by the obstacle of Broad Stand, we could see the usual hordes and crowds surrounding the cairn on Scafell Pike, like bees around a honey pot.

Having spent 14 years recounting stories of the West Wall Traverse and Deep Gill to me, it was entirely natural that Stan should want to take me on to the opening of Deep Gill and the summit of Scafell Crag. Deep Gill looked steep and rocky, but after 14 years of hearing about it I, of course, had to remark to Stan that it did not look that difficult! Such a pity that boulder is, as far as I know, still hanging perilously over the entrance to Lords Rake, making it unsafe for walkers. The summit of Scafell Crag is yet another awesome vantage point on this walk and was not to be missed, even though it was further out on a limb from our finish point in Eskdale. It is always great fun to be a mere walker perched at the top of something as dramatic as Scafell Crag, with the terrain of the climber just inches away. In this situation only the fool ventures any further without ropes and an array of metal climbing things.

It was half past five by the time we left Scafell's summit for the big return to the car in Eskdale, but the late April evenings are long and the satisfaction of a red letter day in the fells kept us talking and reminiscing and planning all the way back to the starting point. There were now just four more Wainwrights to go.

The Final Four

And so in the summer of 2007, eighteen years after I had accidentally bagged my first Wainwright, High Tove, I contemplated the final four and completion. Of those four, which were Seathwaite Fell, Hen Comb, Lingmell and Mellbreak, only Mellbreak had been deliberately left so late in the exercise of completion. The others had for various reasons found themselves as part of this final mopping up exercise. On reflection, although my last four are perhaps not the most celebrated fells in the Lake District (with the possible exception of Mellbreak), I can honestly say that for different reasons each of the final four provided something special and each in its own way typified the reasons that had kept me feverishly fellwalking for nearly a generation of years.

However, with any agenda, even the most pleasurable such as fell bagging, there are certain constraints, pressures and stresses. Having done Scafell in the spring of 2007, the final four had to wait on the back burner until my next planned trip to the Lake District, which was a week in late October of 2007. Summer has never been my favourite time in the fells. Crowds, heat, hazy views and midges are the main reasons why I prefer cooler, more varied times of year. So the break that was to see Stan and I complete our round of Wainwrights was planned for the height of autumn, the week the clocks go back, when frosts and glorious autumn colours were hoped to be the order of the day.

While this was wonderful in prospect, anyone who has walked for a number of years on the fells knows that the weather is always a key factor in doing anything. While autumn and winter are perhaps my favourite seasons in the fells, they are also the least reliable weather wise. So given that Stan and I were desperate to complete our round in 2007, Wainwright's centenary year, we knew that as far as was humanly possible we had to leave nothing to chance. However, the trouble with rounding up the last few fells was that they were all separate walks. Long gone were the days of being able to string several new Wainwrights together in a day via high ridges. In theory Hen Comb and Mellbreak could be combined in one longish day, or even Seathwaite Fell and Mellbreak with a drive in between. But at the tail end of a round, reflection and nostalgia have a habit of creeping in and we found ourselves wanting to enjoy to the full these last four new peaks, rather than attempting some kind of logistical marathon that would have involved rushing them. Fells should, if at all possible, never be rushed.

Herein lay the conundrum. Given a week's holiday in late October/early November, could we rely upon at least three decent weather days and ideally also a glorious sunny day for our final Wainwright fell? The answer was a definite no. And so we knew that we had to try and bag at least two of the remaining four on a short, sharp bagging raid to the fells. Thankfully I have a very understanding wife, who even though she had only ten weeks before given birth to our third child, a baby girl, allowed me to slink of to the fells for one night only in early October. Thankfully the weather for that short break allowed Stan and I to bag what we wanted to bag.

Seathwaite Fell is a somewhat neglected entity. Many thousands of people head around its flanks every year, either via Grains Gill and Sprinkling Tarn, or via Styhead Gill and Styhead Tarn. For the fell's roots are home to two of the most trodden paths in the district, heading for a plethora of justly celebrated fells, such as Great Gable, Bowfell, Esk Pike and the most sought after peak of all, Scafell Pike. Almost everyone ignores Seathwaite Fell, heading for the higher and grander honeypots, including, up until this point, me. To be fair to myself, I did attempt Seathwaite Fell some years earlier on a day which started dry, but which by the time we got to Sprinkling Tarn had become a day of high wind and heavy rain. On reflection though, I am glad Seathwaite Fell was saved till near the end and for a better weather day, for its neglect is wholly unjustified. I am also glad I did not just do the baggers thing and knock Seathwaite Fell off from Sprinkling Tarn, as this route does not do the fell justice. For hidden amongst some of the least thumbed pages in the seven *Pictorial Guides*, is a gem of a route up this fell.

Even though it was early October and the height of the popular season was past, there were still a steady procession of people heading from Seathwaite Farm to Stockley Bridge, including for the second time in my walking career, someone without a map asking me the way to Scafell Pike! However, soon we had passed over Stockley Bridge and had left the crowds behind by heading up pathless through damp and boggy grass. We were making for a rather steep looking gully that is called simply 'Route A' in the Seathwaite Fell chapter of Wainwright's *Southern Fells Guide*. We stopped at a slanting boulder, which was marked in the guide by the ever meticulous AW. We were now ensconced in our own mini wilderness, but with the main path to Styhead Tarn still only about 400 yards from us. Some of the crowd of walkers on the main path probably wondered what the two figures heading over pathless bog were up to. Perhaps they even thought we were lost. But when we looked towards the main path from our remote vantage we realised that we had made the right choice for us. For in all my days in the fells, I don't think I have ever seen such a procession of people as I saw on the path to Sty Head that day. They might as well have been holding hands in some giant party conga for all the space there was between them. Great parties of walkers, merged with couples and quartets of people and probably buried in this seething mass was the odd poor sod of a solitary walker. It reminded me of the kind of crowds I encounter walking to work through London's Docklands.

I find it hard to imagine how anyone can truly enjoy experiencing the hills in this way, with largely inane chatter and noise pervasive and the constant feeling that either someone close behind you is trying to hurry you up, or someone in front of you is not going fast enough. But then if all the walkers in the Lake District instead distributed themselves evenly over the 214 Wainwright fells, the lovers of solitude and space such as me would probably be even grumpier with the state of things than we already are.

However our thoughts of the crowds soon became replaced by the kind of all encompassing thought of 'how the hell am I going to get up there?', as we contemplated the steep grassy gully that is the focal point of Wainwright's Route A. In dry weather this gully would be nothing more than the easiest of scrambles, but that day the ground was at its wettest and most slippery, with patches of black ice and about half way up the gully there was a moment where we were presented with three awkward choices, one of which had to be surmounted. One was a slippery mossy haul up of five feet or so. The second and third choices were a grassy shelf to the left, or a slippery icy rock shelf on the right. It was only a short problem, but for a few seconds hands and knees were used and a slip here, while not disastrous, could have caused some personal damage. However on reflection this was not only a highly entertaining gem of a route, but also a wonderful hidden sanctuary in these popular fells. I remember commenting to Stan that even so near to completion and with so many experiences now behind us, the Lake District could still throw up drama and surprise.

Where the steepness of the gully levels, a short two minute detour leads to the top of a rock tower to the left of the gully, from where an impressive drop down to Grains Gill and the crowds of people heading up to Esk Hause, can be appreciated. This is a truly lonely and marvellous place for a stop. From here it is only a short ascent to what Wainwright regarded as the summit of Seathwaite Fell. I say this because the lonely and rocky little top is actually only situated at approximately 1970 feet, whereas at least a couple of other tops, on the complicated summit plateau of the fell, are actually over the 2000 foot contour. It is therefore one of the very rare examples of a Wainwright where the official top, as designated by AW, is not actually the highest point of the fell. As a bagger of course this presents another of those annoying little conundrums. Is it acceptable to just visit the top AW stated was his 'accepted top', or does one need to visit the other slightly higher tops as well? For the record I did visit the other higher summits, but I am inclined to agree with Wainwright that the 1970 feet summit, with its birds eye view of the Seathwaite valley, is worthy of being the true summit.

However Seathwaite Fell is about so much more than the highest point, the tick, or even the views. A study of the quite extensive summit area on the map will reveal some tarns and rocky outcrops, but this is one of those occasions where the bare facts of the map do not tell the whole

One of the many tarns on Seathwaithe Fell

story. For Seathwaite Fell is a delightful place to explore, a place of numerous rocky tops and outcrops, as well as many jewel like tarns. A good half day could be spent in fascinating exploration of this fell. On our visit we indulged in the simple pleasure of tarn counting. We counted at least ten tarns of varying shapes and sizes and characteristics, from rocky tarns hidden in steep hollows, to more open tarns with great high mountain backdrops. Tarn counting may sound a simple childlike game, but then the pleasures of hill walking should be simple and complex matters should be left as far behind as possible.

I would go as far as to say that I found something kindred on Seathwaite Fell that day to the kind of thoughts and feelings that Wainwright had about Haystacks. Indeed in its exploratory nature, complex twisting and turning landscape and secluded tarns, there are I consider parallels with AW's beloved Haystacks. I have only been on Seathwaite Fell once, but already I can see myself returning to its lonely summit and quiet rocky pools again and again. I can see it becoming for me what Haystacks was for Wainwright. Seathwaite Fell is a place to lose oneself in quiet simple contemplation. It is a refuge in a crowded, popular part of the Lake District. So if you go there, please don't go in a party but go in as small numbers as you can, or better still go alone.

Having extolled the virtues of Seathwaite Fell and perhaps risked increasing its popularity, I very much doubt that anything that I am going to say about Hen Comb is likely to increase the traffic on that fell. This solitary and slightly bleak fell does have certain redeeming qualities and although these qualities don't leap out at you, they are nonetheless still there to be found. Hen Comb had for years been a fell that I kept meaning to climb but somehow never got around to. It just never seemed to fit in to a plan, being isolated from other fells. So I ended up with Hen Comb and neighbouring Mellbreak as two of my final three Wainwrights. As it had been decided by Stan and I some years before, that Mellbreak would be a worthy final Wainwright, we knew that we wanted to bag Hen Comb on the break before completion, rather than leaving two neighbouring hills as the last two fells in the round.

It was rather peculiar as we began the walk, to see the path up our final Wainwright, Mellbreak, heading up into the conifer trees, while our route to Hen Comb headed round the base of the trees. It was like a view into our own near future. A future that would encompass the very moment of completion and the end of 17 years of fell bagging. It was a future that lay only a few weeks away. I suppose true freedom in the hills would mean the ability to decide just to have done Mellbreak then and there, but sometimes a free approach does not always give the best overall experience and Mellbreak, having been chosen as the final fell for good reasons, had to remain the final fell, even if it was at that moment tantalisingly within our grasp.

Wainwright's guide to the Western Fells describes Hen Comb as being surrounded by water, like a moat round a castle. Vast areas of bog around Floutern Pass extend north from the summit, while Mosedale Beck and Whiteoak Beck effectively cut the fell off to the east and west. Wainwright states that this 'is the only fell that can be put out of bounds by excessive rain', although these days some convenient stepping stones have been placed over the crossing point of Mosedale Beck and in early October it was no worse to cross than many a Lakeland stream.

Hen Comb is generally a rounded and grassy fell, but there is a little drama to be had by visiting the subsidiary summit of Little Dodd, where some narrow tracks skirt the edge of a flaky cliff. It is about as much drama or excitement as is to be had on Hen Comb and in truth this fell is more about solitude, silence and easy restful walking. It is probably a contender for least visited Wainwright and we met no-one on our visit. However one great thing about the Wainwright guides is that on such bland fells Wainwright appears to take great delight in documenting seemingly innocuous or mundane features. The guide told us that there was something labelled a 'fenced boghole' on the ridge between Little Dodd and Hen Comb's summit and there was a simple pleasure to be had in locating this (it's not difficult). Sometimes delight can be found in the small features of a fell. The boghole was duly located, replete with four wooden fence posts. Whether the posts were designed to warn sheep or humans about the bog I am not sure, but in their current state, as four unattached posts, there is nothing preventing a sheep falling in, although they might make a human stop and think. A test with my walking pole revealed that the boghole indeed merited some warning posts, as it nearly consumed the entire three foot pole, which came out covered in a green slimy coating. There are many grander places I have visited in Lakeland but whose names I will forget over the years, but I doubt I will ever forget the fenced boghole.

Unfortunately Hen Comb, being surrounded by water, is liable to attract any midges that are about and as this particular day was humid and wind free, the summit of the fell had become a kind of midge convention. At such times I admit that I can be a bit of a summit bore. There was Stan frantically dancing around trying to avoid midges and wanting to just bag the fell and leave. Then there was typical me having to plonk myself down, soak in the view, play a few tracks of Sibelius on my MP3 and be generally cussed and dogged about having my moment of reflection on the summit. Such summit rituals are only good to a point and when the midges appeared to be forming a kind of midge balaclava over my entire head, even I had to admit that this was not the place for contemplation and it was time to get the hell out. Stan, I apologise!

So it appeared that we now had only two Wainwrights to bag in order to complete our round. However I found as completion drew ever nearer, that I began to check my list of completed Wainwrights, to make absolutely sure that I had actually reached the true summit of all the fells that I thought I had completed. It would after all be awful to think I had done all the 214 fells, only to find that I had failed to reach the true summit of some fell or other. Upon checking the 212 that I thought I had completed so far, there was just one fell that gnawed at my conscience. This fell was Helm Crag and it presented a definite conundrum to any would be completer of the Wainwright fells. For the true summit of the fell, known variously as The Lion Couchant, The Howitzer and The Lion and the Lamb (although not the more popular Lion and the Lamb as seen from Grasmere), is an awkward slopping rock tower, which can only be surmounted by a little bit of rock climbing. Now had Alfred Wainwright climbed this rock tower, there would be absolutely no doubt in a baggers mind that completion of the 214 fells could not occur unless the true summit of Helm Crag was reached. However although Wainwright left a space in the Helm Crag chapter in the *Central Fells Guide*, to announce that he had reached the highest point, and although he set out to climb it on several occasions, a lack of resolve meant that Alfred Wainwright himself never actually got to the highest inches of Helm Crag.

So a potential completer of the Wainwright fells is left with a dilemma to which there could be in theory three answers. It could be argued that as Wainwright did not get to the top of Helm Crag and as any Wainwright bagger is following in Wainwright's footsteps, that there is no need to actually climb to the top of The Howitzer to bag Helm Crag and the cairn on the main body of the fell nearby is sufficient. In the agonising time spent mulling over this problem I had some sympathy for this argument. Wainwright after all must surely be regarded as the authority on the fells of Lakeland and surely must also be regarded as the first known completer of the Wainwrights. To argue that Wainwright, who spent fourteen years, climbing, writing about and drawing every fell from every angle and every route, did not in fact complete all his 214 fells would seem to be churlish. This argument also had some merit for a non rock climber like me, who on two previous visits to the summit ridge of Helm Crag had, like Wainwright, tried and failed to climb the Howitzer (Stan being more capable on rocks had managed to get to the true top already and had no such dilemmas as I now did).

Then there was a second school of thought which was rather more free spirited and which this non rock climber again had some sympathy with. This argument says that each fell represents a unique experience and as long as one has truly experienced the fell, it does not matter whether the highest point or the highest stone on the highest cairn has been touched. Having already climbed Helm Crag twice and taken in its views and the delights of its chaotic rock strewn summit ridge, I felt I could say that I had experienced Helm Crag. It was not as if I had climbed half way up and headed back again. I had been on the summit ridge twice and touched the cairn twice. So from a more relaxed perspective did it matter that I had not touched the utmost inches?

Then there was the third argument and this was the one that really nagged at me just prior to completing my round. This argument says that the utmost top of each fell and nothing but the utmost top has to be physically attained in order to claim the tick. This argument would therefore also and very wrongly in my view, say that just as Sir Hugh Munro listed all the Scottish Munros, but failed to climb all of them and is therefore not regarded as the first Munroist, so Alfred Wainwright who catalogued and detailed all 214 Wainwrights, by failing to reach the utmost inches of Helm Crag, was not in fact the first to climb them all. I tried to rail against this argument and champion the other two arguments in my mind, but I knew deep inside that I had to have another go at attaining those utmost inches on Helm Crag. I had spent seventeen years bagging the Wainwrights and I did not want any doubt in my mind.

So in truly ungainly fashion and with the help of a leg up from Stan, I wriggled my way awkwardly and nervously to the top of the Howitzer. I can honestly say that I won't be going back. If I ever get to within one of completing the 214 Wainwrights for a second time, I will say to hell with the Howitzer!

Now both Stan and I were happy in our minds that we had both done 212 fells, there remained just two. Unfortunately though we each had a different two left to bag. Mellbreak was to be the final fell, but there still remained Rosthwaite Fell, which I had done in 2000 on my own and Lingmell, which Stan had done before on his own, but which I had ignored on my two previous climbs of Scafell Pike. However this combination of luck, fate and poor judgement in fact led to two of my finest experiences on the Lakeland hills.

Rosthwaite Fell although part of the Southern Fells and technically the northern terminus of Scafell Pike, is seldom given much attention by walkers. Like nearby Seathwaite Fell it is overlooked as people are bound for higher and greater things. Yet I was indeed to be glad of the fact that although I had once climbed this fell, Stan had not. For it allowed me to experience a different and altogether more exciting route to the summit. One of the greatest delights of fell bagging and indeed mountain walking in general is that a hill can seem totally different when approached via a different route. This difference can be so marked that apart from the actual summit itself, the rest of the walk might as well have been on a different mountain altogether.

My previous ascent of Rosthwaite Fell had been a quick bagging exercise from Coomb Gill and up steep grassy slopes to Tarn at Leaves and then on to Bessyboot (the summit of the fell, although Rosthwaite Cam is higher and before you ask I have also visited it!). No climb is dull, but certainly up until Tarn at Leaves this route is not the most exciting. However, now a quick study of the Wainwright guide told me that there was no need to ascend via this route again, for Wainwright describes a totally different and altogether more exciting route, via Big Stanger Gill. By taking this new route both Stan and I had a new experience that day. In fact the steep stony cut steps of this route, which headed dramatically up through a natural shelter of autumn gold trees, were a direct contrast to the route I had previously taken. Rosthwaite Fell presented an altogether different and more adventurous side to me that day. At the top of Big Stanger Gill, there is one of Lakeland's hidden gems of drama. It is a place where the path suddenly narrows into a little shelf, while to one side slippery rocks ascend vertically above and to the other side rocks plunge vertically down to the gill below. It is a safe place, if you keep your wits about you, but also a place where it is difficult to not feel overawed and humbled by the chaos of nature hemming you in on all sides.

For most of the ascent the weather had been decent enough, with just the odd shower, but as we reached the boggy terminus of the gill and emerged into confusing upland terrain, a heavy curtain of mist and rain came over the fell. Whereas I had luxuriated on Rosthwaite Fell on my first climb, Stan had to content himself with a wind and rain strewn thirty seconds on the summit, before we took the route down to Coomb Gill as our descent route. The wind really picked up in descent and Stan had his camera case and the plastic bag that he kept it in ripped out of his hands. We have never been walkers who litter the fells and I regard litter on the fells as a kind of crime. So even though this littering was an accident, we were both determined to locate both camera case and gaudy orange plastic bag, even if it meant going out of our way over rough ground. And we duly located both, much to our relief. It may sound odd but I hate litter on the fells so much that I often take a plastic bag in my rucksack when I go walking on the fells, and pick up bottles or wrappers or cans that I find left by others, so that I can place them in a bin in Keswick where they belong. How people can just scatter litter on the fells is beyond me. Anything you carry up the fells should be carried back with you and it is pure laziness and selfishness to do otherwise. Walkers who litter the fells don't love or appreciate them.

Stan could now say that he only had one fell left to complete the 214 Wainwright fells, while I still had two to go. However it was only to be another 24 hours before we both stood on the very brink of completion. My previous two climbs of Scafell Pike, the first of which was the one described previously where my boot soles came off and my trousers ripped, were back in the early and mid 1990's. In truth Scafell Pike, due to its sheer popularity, is not one of my favourite high fells. However because on my previous visits I had been intent on just getting to the highest point in England, I had both times neglected to take the short detour from Lingmell Col to the summit of Lingmell. This seeming error on my part was now to provide a great joy in my hills career. For rather than throw in Lingmell, as I expect many do, as an appendage to a day on Scafell Pike, Stan and I decided to give this grand little peak its due and make it the sole objective for an outing from Wasdale Head.

Accompanying Stan and I for the direct climb up Lingmell we had the revised second edition of *Wainwright's Southern Fells*, with amendments by Chris Jesty, which had only recently appeared in the bookshops. Now Now I have to confess that when I first heard that someone was revising the Wainwright guides and amending all the details that had changed on the fells, in the forty odd years since the guides were written, I had feelings something akin to those experienced by certain religious people when a new version of the Bible comes out. This was the word of Wainwright and from a devoted rambler's point of view it was sacred scroll. However I must also admit that having now purchased the five revised guides that have been done to date and used them on walks, I do find them very useful and cannot but admire Chris Jesty's tenacity and his labour of passion in treading every inch of terrain in all seven guidebooks, or eight when he has also revised the *Outlying Fells*. He will have gone where few men have gone before.

Wainwright never revised the books himself. Nor was he keen to have them revised by anyone else in his lifetime. But he did say that if anyone should revise the guides, he would like it to be Chris Jesty. For a keen and meticulous lover of Lakeland, which I count myself to be, it is a joy to compare the old editions with the new revised ones and seek out every major and also the obscure and minor amendments. I can also have that same sense of excitement that I had when I purchased my original set of guides 16 years ago. The recently published revised edition of the *Northern Fells Guide* shows perhaps more than any other guide the need for this revision. Think of the recent shaving of Dodd, which now has a bald pate for a summit, as opposed to the thick sward of trees that crowded the summit when Wainwright wrote his guide. I think the job of revision had to be done, and Chris Jesty has done it as faithfully and unobtrusively as it could have been. It is good to see however, in a world that seems to change so quickly these days, that the vast majority of details that Wainwright described from roughly 50 years ago, remain accurate to this day.

The direct route up Lingmell leaves behind the more popular route to Hollow Stones and Mickledore. Instead it makes a direct approach to Lingmell, up a slope on which the uniformly scattered trees seem almost landscaped to either side of the path, giving the early stage of the climb something of the feel of a stroll through a park! As you climb the somewhat unremitting slope and pass over a stile in a wall, there are rewarding views down to Wastwater and out towards the Cumbrian coast, to compensate for the slog. Eventually the path becomes rockier, before levelling out onto a curious grassy plateau. Here it is as if a few acres from the rolling Northern Fells have been transplanted into the high drama of Wasdale. All the way up the views towards Scafell Crag and Pikes Crag are stunning and on the day we climbed Lingmell, these great crags were rendered doubly dramatic by a constantly shifting and glowering mist, which sometimes hung like a curtain over England's highest mountains and at other times parted for a few minutes, to reveal the summit ridges.

The top of Lingmell itself is not revealed until after another wall is crossed on the rocky top of Goat Crags. The mist had descended by this stage in our walk, although we could still just about make out the summit cairn ahead, seeming ghostly and shadowy. I am sure that other experienced walkers will agree with me that once you have experienced the whims of mist and low cloud on the fells a number of times, you develop a kind of instinctive knack for when the mist is likely to suddenly part and when it is unlikely to. This day on Lingmell seemed to be one of those days where a clearance seemed more likely than not and just as we reached the broad and squat summit cairn, a great hole tore into the mist and stunning plunging drops down to the great rift of Piers Gill and out to Sty Head Tarn and Borrowdale were revealed. Lingmell, in a few short minutes of spectacular drama, became embedded in my mind as one of the finest of my Lakeland summit experiences, a truly worthy second to last Wainwright. It had everything a summit should have, a rocky top, a dramatic plunge and sense of depth and a fine if slightly restricted view. As we revelled in the moment, the mist continued to shift about the summit, sometimes revealing far reaching views out to the Helvellyn range and sometimes lowering to plunge us back into a half world of grey. All this time the highest summits of the Scafells, Great Gable and Pillar, remained under a stubbornly grim cap of cloud.

On Lingmell we also noted the changed summit cairn described in the revised second edition of *Wainwright's Southern Fells Guide*. A squat cairn,

An aerial view of Wastwater from Lingmell's flanks

rather than a pillar, now crowns the summit. We were able to make the quick detour to the shapelier column like cairn on the precipitous north face of Lingmell, which affords startling views across to Great Gable and down to Lingmell Beck. Then the cloud lowered and descended in a way that spoke of permanence for the day and by the time we reached valley level and the car, it was raining. Lingmell at 2649 feet is a very high mountain in Lakeland terms and deserves to be regarded as one of the Wasdale giants. It is a worthy mountain in itself, rather than just an add on to the highest mountain in England.

While baggers may all seem to be similar in type they are in fact often entirely at odds in outlook and approach to the task of bagging. So when it comes to choosing the last fell, the fell of completion, there are different ways to arrive there. The ultimate planner might decide his or her completion fell right at the beginning of his or her journey through the 214 fells. A more laid back bagger might not know which was going to be the last fell until he had done all the 213 others. So how did Mellbreak become my completion fell? It was certainly not decided at the beginning, as it was not until I had done over 60 Wainwrights that I even knew I was a Wainwright bagger and certainly not till I had done over 100 that I started to think about completing them all. However it was also certainly not an accident that Mellbreak became the last fell for both Stan and I. Dredging back through the years of hills memories, I think it was in April 2002, while sitting with Stan on the humble, but lonely, Wainwright of Graystones and looking towards the great craggy northern end of Mellbreak, that it occurred to both of us that this was the perfect fell to chose to complete on. It encapsulated all that a Lakeland fell walking experience had come to mean to us. It had a rocky ascent amidst high drama. It was not a showpiece mountain or even that popular. It had grand views. Its highest point when approached from Loweswater is teased out thus giving a perfect sense of build up to the final summit and there also was the prospect of a grand low level tour along its base, by Crummock Water, to end the day.

Once Mellbreak had been chosen as the last Wainwright it was surprising how often it popped up in views from other fells, or how often we found ourselves staring up at its seemingly sheer northern end while heading through Loweswater bound for another fell. When we did Hen Comb we passed the start of the climb to Mellbreak and just over three weeks later, we found ourselves heading up the path through a small pine wood to the base of the dramatic north end of Mellbreak. The tongue of scree shown in Wainwright's guide book is conspicuous from the start of the walk, but now there is also a bypass route which zig zags its way up, hugging to the precipitous Crummock Water edge of Mellbreak. The first promontory marked in the guidebook is a fabulous place, with a fearsome gully splitting the crags in two. All the way up little detours along some mildly exposed paths can be made, to view the plunge down to Crummock Water. The climb is not long but the drama is high and all too soon it ends, as the path levels and Mellbreak North Top is reached. The North Top is a mere eight feet lower than the main summit of Mellbreak, but has a finer view than the main summit, especially towards Loweswater and the Solway Firth. We were bathed in a temporary patch of sunlight on North Top. At this point a part of us wanted to hang around on North Top, tease out the experience of completion, try and hang on to the fact

Mellbreak on the morning of completion

that there was still one last summit to bag. An equal part wanted to move on, to have that moment of completion, to experience one of the highpoints of our lives. It was eagerness that won the day.

The two thirds of a mile that lies between North Top and the higher South Top of Mellbreak is hardly riveting walking. It is a bit of a squelchy trudge to be honest. But when it is the day of your completion, such a squelchy trudge becomes a thing of joy and every metre travelled is savoured. After a small depression we began climbing for the last time to a new Wainwright summit. Perhaps now the import of the moment began to hit us. After this short and easy pull there would be no more new Wainwrights and a large chapter of our fellwalking lives, that had dominated 17 years, would be over. But if there was any sense of sadness I don't recall it, as the overriding emotions were ones of joy and togetherness. It meant a lot to be completing with a great friend who had shared the journey with me.

Eventually the moment came when we saw the summit cairn. Nothing grand, just a small and neat pile of stones a hundred or so yards away. But it meant the world to us. We slowed down slightly, trying to eek out the final moments, and then came the moment when the summit was touched and in that moment the 214 Wainwright fells were done and an exhilarating and absorbing journey of freedom was completed.

Now I am not one to make noise on the fells, but we were all alone on Mellbreak and this was a special occasion. So suffice it to say that a few whoops of joy were emitted. Stan surprised me by opening his rucksack and revealing a small bottle of champagne. The cork was popped (and retrieved I hasten to add) and we literally drank in the moment. It was a moment of happiness, untainted by regret or sadness.

Is there Life after Completion?

In the immediate aftermath of our completion celebration, we found ourselves sitting a few hundred yards away from the summit cairn on Mellbreak, where the ground slopped away sufficiently to reveal truly awesome views of Crummock Water and Buttermere below and the craggy face of Grasmoor opposite. Despite having just completed the round of 214 Wainwright fells there was no sense of our Lakeland exploration being over. There may be some extreme baggers in this world that having done all 214 summits, move on to some other bagging challenge, never to climb a Lakeland fell again. I imagine however that this breed of bagger is few and far between. I expect the vast majority of people completing the Wainwrights will realise, as we did, that although all the summits have been done, there is far more to a love of Lakeland than merely having a new summit to climb each day, or a list to tick off.

Grasmoor from Mellbreak's summit edge

In truth some of the answers to what lay ahead for this bagger had been revealing themselves for some years prior to completion. Favourite mountains had sprung up that provided no new ticks but which had been climbed again and again for their own sake. I had for a little while taken to the idea of combining a low level walk with a high level walk in the same day. Just prior to completion I had walked down the west side of Derwent Water, before heading up onto Maiden Moor, where it rained heavily, thus continuing my unlucky relationship with the Newlands round fells. In addition, experiences, such as doing Rosthwaite Fell and other fells by different routes, had taught me that merely standing on all the 214 Wainwrights summits was just the beginning of a true and deep knowledge of Lakeland.

At the same time I could not deny that especially when it came down to the last 20 or so, there was a feeling that it would be quite nice to have them all completed and have no sense of having to climb a particular new fell on any given day. So a sense of total freedom is one of the delights that await the bagger upon completion. But while I wanted to glorify in this new found freedom there was also a part of me that could not totally suppress the bagger's urge. Fundamentally bagging for me has been about exploration, the desire to see and explore as much of Lakeland as I can in a lifetime. Despite the new found freedom that urge still remained.

And so, while reclining on the Crummock edge of Mellbreak, the conversation was not of regret or sadness or even nostalgia, but of what lay ahead. And within a few minutes of completion we had already decided that we had enjoyed the experience so much that we wanted to do a second round of the Wainwrights. This may sound like ultimate baggers speak, but I have always believed that if a thing is worth doing once it is worth doing again and there were still over 120 Wainwright fells that I had only ever been on once and some of them many years before.

However we both decided that there would be a difference this time. The second round would not be something we would make plans for, it would be something that would creep up upon us; something to perhaps occupy another 20 years. The second round would be subservient to our new found sense of freedom in the Lakeland fells.

Those beautifully crafted guides of Alfred Wainwright were also part of the key to the future of our Lakeland exploration. Nearing completion, on one quiet evening when my three children were asleep, I had found myself making a list, using the guide books, of different routes of ascent up fells that I would like to do as a priority. Some fells, such as Bannerdale Crags, I had already gone back to and explored a different ascent route, the fantastic East Ridge in this case. But there were a whole host of ascent routes that I had yet to do. The Tongue ridge of Dollywagon Pike, Kirk Fell direct from Wasdale, the long and lonely routes through upper Eskdale to Esk Pike and the Crinkles. Having done the 214 Wainwright fells, there is perhaps an even greater challenge, the ultimate treading where Wainwright has trod experience and that is to do all the routes of ascent catalogued in the seven guides. I intend to add this into the melting pot of plans for my middle age and later years of life. Anyone who undertakes all the ascent routes will not only gain a knowledge of Lakeland like few others have had, except perhaps AW himself, but will also find many of Lakeland's hidden sanctuaries of loneliness, peace and sometimes high drama.

Appealing more perhaps to the new found sense of freedom, I have in recent years found myself heading more and more off the beaten track, away from the paths and into nooks and crannies where few people go. I have written about a few of these places here, but there are many more to be found and savoured in a lifetime. So if you see a walker heading away from the path seemingly lost, it may well be me.

And for those who have completed all the fells in the seven guides, but simply cannot resist having the odd new summit to tick off, Wainwright also wrote a guide to the Outlying Fells. Although he wrote it for older fellwalkers, it has to some extent in recent years almost become regarded in the same light as the seven main guides and rightly so. Having done a number of the Outliers I can only say that they are a joy and delight and often have views and scenery that are comparable with many a true Wainwright. Black Coombe for instance is not only quite a bit higher than some of the 'true' Wainwrights, at nearly 2000 feet, but also boasts one of the finest views in Lakeland and perhaps the finest prospect of the sea from any fell in Lakeland. No fell walker's education of Lakeland would be complete without an ascent of Orrest Head (where Wainwright began his love of Lakeland) and the same applies to the likes of Gummers How, Caw, Stickle Pike and a host of other outliers. The fells of Shap will appeal to the lovers of wild walking, while the likes of Burney and Beacon Fell are short climbs where you can rest, relax and enjoy wonderful views, without having the usual requisite amount of slog. There are some dull outliers. Dunmallet is in my view merely a wooded hill and not a proper fell. However, often you will visit corners of Lakeland far removed from the popular areas and again this will add to a comprehensive knowledge of Lakeland. So, I also intend to at some stage stumble upon completion of the Outlying Fells and yes, before you ask, I have already planned a final outlier. This will be Hesk Fell, which although condemned by Wainwright for being as dull as ditchwater, has always appealed to me as a climb, partly because it has little in the way of redeeming features, although I do feel it has a certain wild appeal about it. Stan has often derided my love of Hesk Fell and so I now intend to make it special by honouring it as my last Outlying fell.

One other thing that struck both Stan and I in the aftermath of completion, was how much we both owed to Wainwright and to those wonderful and unique guidebooks. Before we had discovered the guidebooks we had been drawn only to the high and popular places. Wainwright showed us everything else, from those peaks which are fantastic but unjustifiably neglected, to those which are genuinely rather worthy of neglect. So it seemed rather fitting the day after completion and with I must confess a slight hangover, to be heading in a kind of pilgrimage to the place that meant more than any other to AW. This is of course Haystacks.

These days Haystacks is a justifiably popular fell, but on a rather misty moody day, we still managed to pass a few lonely minutes of reflection by Innominate Tarn, a place that perhaps epitomises what is so special about the high Lakeland landscape. Here I was reminded of a passage from the end of the final guide, *The Western Fells*, where Wainwright says that 'the fleeting hour of life of those who love the hills is quickly spent, but the hills are eternal'. Perhaps the greatest legacy for anyone who completes all 214 Wainwright fells, is to have truly lived that fleeting hour of life and enjoyed those rare times when we manage to find ourselves removed from the stresses and strains of mortality and for a few moments connect with the eternal spirit of the fells. Enjoy your personal journey. It will be quite unlike mine or Wainwright's or anyone else's. It will be your own unique experience to be treasured. And if you, like me, have completed the 214 fells, or are nearing completion, remember this is not the end, it is merely the beginning.

Also from Sigma Leisure:

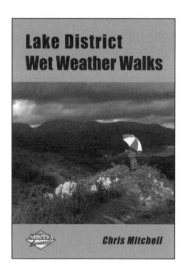

Lake District Wet Weather Walks
Chris Mitchell
There are hundreds of guide books on the Lake District but none of them deals specifically with the problem of where to walk and what to see in wet weather. After some of the wettest summers on record, 20 walks have been chosen to cover all regions of the Lake District so that you will be able to try them out wherever you happen to be when the weather closes in.
£7.99

Walks in Ancient Lakeland
Robert Harris
Discover stone circles, standing stones and burial cairns. Follow ancient trackways and explore largely unknown areas to uncover the mysteries of the lives of our ancestors. Accurate sketch maps guide you to sites in valleys or the wild and remote fells.
£6.95

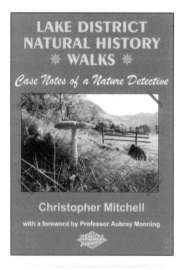

Lake District Natural History Walks
Case Notes of a Nature Detective
Christopher Mitchell
18 walks suitable for all ages and abilities Fascinating facts help you interpret the country- side by looking at the effects of geology and plant life on the animal population of the area.
£8.95

Lakeland Hikes
Off the Beaten Track
Doug Brown
This is for walkers who enjoy a challenge, like to test their navigational skills, want to use their GPS and locate interesting landscape features. Doug Brown has found many remote and unusual routes, with optional exciting scrambles.
£7.95

Best Pub Walks in the Lake District
Neil Coates
This, the longest-established (and best-researched) pub walks book for the Lakes, is amazingly wide-ranging, with an emphasis on quality of walks and the Real Ale rewards that follow!
£7.95

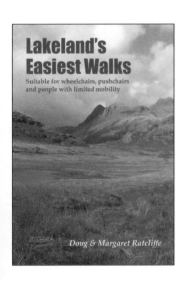

Lakeland's Easiest Walks
Suitable for wheelchairs, pushchairs and people with limited mobility
Doug & Margaret Ratcliffe
These 38 specially selected short walks are all equally suitable for people with limited mobility and for very young children.
£7.99

Walking the Wainwrights
Stuart Marshall

This book links all 214 peaks in the late Alfred Wainwright's seven-volume Pictorial Guide to The Lakeland Fells. Clear route descriptions are presented with two-colour sketch maps.

"An excellent, concise manual on how to tackle the 'Wainwrights' in an intelligent way." – A. Harry Griffin MBE

£8.95

Waterside Walks in the Lake District
Colin Shelbourn

25 stunning walks along the shores of some of the most beautiful lakes to strolls beside rushing rivers and wild water- falls. Whatever the length or location you choose you'll meet with stunning scenery, a richness of wildlife, and many interesting places to visit.

£7.95

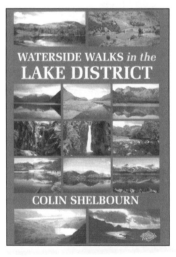

Walking In Eden 2nd Ed.
Ron Scholes

A book to guide you through this forgotten wilderness in 30 circular and direct walks which illustrate the rich variety of walking in Eden. The text includes outline route maps, attractive photos and line draw- ings to convey the feeling of this remote and attractive area.

£8.95

All-Terrain Pushchair Walks
North Lakeland
Ruth and Richard Irons

30 walks from Ennerdale Water to Lowther Park and from Haweswater to Bassenthwaite. There's something for every type of walker. Ruth and Richard Irons are experienced parents and qualified outdoor pursuits instructors.
£6.95

All-Terrain Pushchair Walks
South Lakeland
Norman Buckley

30 graded walks from level routes around pretty Lakeland villages to the more advent- urous (but safe) hikes across the windswept hills. Whatever the age of the family here is the ideal opportunity to escape into the wide-open spaces.
£7.95

Lakeland Walking on the level
Norman Buckley

Walk among the highest mountains of Lakeland and avoid the steep ascents – with no compromises on the views! *"A good spread of walks"* – Rambling Today.
£8.95

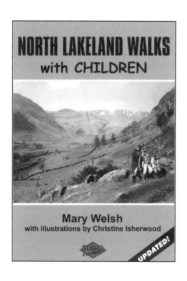

North Lakeland Walks with Children
Mary Welsh; illustrations by Christine Isherwood

"It has been great fun speaking to children I have met on the walks and listening to what they have to say," says Mary Welsh. Written specifically for parents of reluctant walkers.

£8.95

South Lakeland Walks with Children
Nick Lambert

"With Nick Lambert's lively commentary, there seems little likelihood that recalcitrant children will be bored or fratchy."
– The Keswick Reminder

£8.95

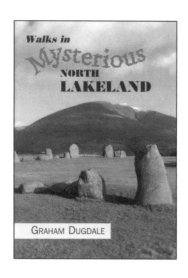

Walks in Mysterious North Lakeland
Graham Dugdale

30 walks to places with a strange and mythical history. "Each walk features remarkable hand-drawn maps and stylish, entertaining writing that is almost as good to read before a roaring open fire as on the open fells." – Lakeland Walker

£6.95

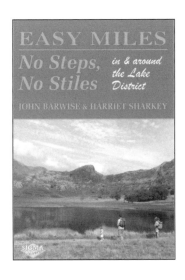

Easy Miles, No Steps No Stiles
In & around the Lake District
Harriet Sharkey & John Barwise
Easy Miles features 30 walks ideal for pushchairs, wheel- chairs and anyone who just wants an easy stroll. Each route has clear numbered maps, helpful information and photos.
£7.95

In search of Swallows & Amazons
Arthur Ransome's Lakeland
Roger Wardale
An extensively revised edition of a popular book originally published in 1986. Enjoy the original stories and discover the farms, rivers, islands, towns and hills that formed their backdrop. *'Recommended reading'* – The Daily Telegraph
£8.95

All of our books are all available on-line at **www.sigmapress.co.uk** or through booksellers. For a free catalogue, please contact:

Sigma Leisure, Stobart House, Pontyclerc, Penybanc Road, Ammanford, Carmarthenshire SA18 3HP
Tel: 01269 593100   Fax: 01269 596116
info@sigmapress.co.uk   www.sigmapress.co.uk